The New Manhood

The Handbook for a New Kind of Man

Steve Biddulph

EasyRead Large

Copyright Page from the Original Book

The New Manhood: The handbook for a new kind of man
First published in 2010 in Australia and New Zealand by Finch Publishing Pty Limited, ABN 49 057 285 248, Suite 2207, 4 Daydream Street, Warriewood, NSW, 2102, Australia.

12 11 10   8 7 6 5 4 3 2 1

Copyright © 2010 Stephen Biddulph and Shaaron Biddulph

The author asserts his moral rights in this work throughout the world without waiver. All rights reserved. No part of this publication may be reproduced, stored in a retrieval system or transmitted in any form or by any means (electronic or mechanical, through reprography, digital transmission, recording or otherwise) without the prior written permission of the publisher.

The National Library of Australia Cataloguing-in-Publication entry:

Biddulph, Steve.
The new manhood : the handbook for a new kind of man / Steve Biddulph.
9781876451882 (pbk.)
Includes index.
Men--Conduct of life.
Men--Identity. Men--Psychology. Men--Family relationships. Man-woman relationships.
Masculinity. Fathers and sons. Sex role.
305.32

Edited by Sean Doyle
Editorial assistance by Catherine Page
Text designed and typeset in Minion Pro by Meg Dunworth
Cover design by Creation Graphics
Index by Madeleine Davis
Printed by BPA
Cover photograph by David Hancock

Reproduction and Communication for educational purposes
The *Australian Copyright Act 1968* (the Act) allows a maximum of one chapter or 10% of the pages of this work, whichever is the greater, to be reproduced and/or communicated by any educational institution for its educational purposes provided that the educational institution (or the body that administers it) has given a remuneration notice to Copyright Agency Limited (CAL) under the Act. For details of the CAL licence for educational institutions contact: info@copyright.com.au

The 'Author notes' section at the back of this book contains useful additional information and references to quoted material in the text. Each reference is linked to the text by its relevant page number and an identifying line entry.

Finch titles can be viewed and purchased at **www.finch.com.au**

This book has been printed on Australian offset paper certified by the Programme for the Endorsement of Forest Certification (PEFC). PEFC is committed to sustainable forest management through third party forest certification of responsibly managed forests.

TABLE OF CONTENTS

INTRODUCTION: A message of hope and change	iii
ONE: The problem	1
TWO: You and your father	32
THREE: Men and women	71
FOUR: Real sex	121
FIVE: From boy to man	171
SIX: The five truths of manhood	201
SEVEN: Being a real father	241
EIGHT: Meaning	295
NINE: Real male friends	323
TEN: Finding a job with heart	367
ELEVEN: The journey down	403
TWELVE: Spirit	437
Epilogue	459
Author's notes	461
Acknowledgements	482
Contacts	484
Permissions	485
Index	487

There are men who wake up in the morning energised and happy.
Whose partners and children love and trust them.
Who do work they believe in and enjoy.
Have loyal and interesting friends.
And are deeply involved in the wider world.
They may not be famous or wealthy.
They value something quite different.
They are learning how to be real.

This book is dedicated to my son and daughter

INTRODUCTION

A message of hope and change

I'm standing backstage at Melbourne's Dallas Brooks Hall, and my heart is threatening to beat right out of my chest. I'm sweating, my vision is blurred, and I can't catch my breath. This is a perfectly natural response, for out there in the summer evening, 800 people are making their way to hear me speak, for 90 minutes, on a spotlit stage. I don't often get stage fright, but when I do it hits hard. So I use a trusted remedy – I slip out into the lobby, where the early arrivers are gathering, and quietly chat to people, reassuring myself that these are good folk who mean me no harm.

I've been out there about five minutes when, from the corner of my eye, I see a man staring at me. You can't miss him: he's big and muscular, with a blue singlet, tattooed arms and a beard. He sees me notice him, and turns and speaks to two other men beside him. They stride across the lobby, and in seconds he is inches from my face, head tilted back and frowning.

'You been following me around?'

My mouth does a goldfish imitation; the ability to speak completely leaves me. But he doesn't let me suffer long – his face breaks into a wide grin.

'That bloody book of yours – that's the story of my bloody life, mate.'

I grin too, as I slowly work it out, and soon he is introducing his father and brother. He explains, while they both nod in agreement, that the three of them had barely spoken for years – had been basically estranged – until he read my book, *Manhood,* and then sent it to the other two, and they had 'sorted things out'. They have come along to say 'thanks' and to hear what else I might have to say. As we break off to enter the theatre, their eyes are shining, and I think mine might be, too...

For a family psychologist, job satisfaction doesn't come much better than this, and yet, by the late 1990s, I had heard such stories of reconciliation hundreds of times. Making peace between fathers and sons was a wonderful thing, but it was only part of a bigger picture: all across the globe there was a rising tide of masculine change. Young men were becoming better fathers. Thirty-year-olds were helping at-risk teenagers. Couples were forging happier marriages. Middle-aged men were quitting corporate jobs to find more fulfilling lives. Old men were seeking help for grief and depression, which they had always struggled with alone. Something was happening, a shift away from the idea of a man as a buttoned-up, lonely work machine. The wall that isolated us from our loved ones and from other men was being torn down. *Manhood* was one of the tools helping do the job.

Released worldwide in 1994, the book sparked hundreds of press articles, TV features, radio debates and conversations about the idea of men changing, not because they *should* (a famously unsuccessful formula for change) but because they wanted to. Advertising and other media reflected the theme of men opening up, breaking the mould. Even the TV series *Seachange* had a men's group.

The message of *Manhood* was simple: *there is so much more to a man's life than we have settled for.* More than just being a walking wallet. More than endless hurry, kids who don't like you and a marriage on life-support. More than pretending to be fine while feeling angry, hopeless and depressed. When we were young we dreamed of adventures and great deeds. Of a creative and energised life. That was our birthright and we needed to recapture it.

This message was much needed. There was a masculinity crisis worldwide, showing up in depression, violence, divorce, alcoholism, road deaths, and destructive behaviour on a planetary and personal scale. (There were, at the time, shallow and dishonest men in the White House, the Lodge and 10 Downing Street, and a sense of deep disillusionment towards our leaders, too.) One book couldn't change the world, but it could offer a map for those who wanted to, starting with themselves. The premise was at least a plausible one – damaged and unhappy men were the heart of the human problem. In creating more good men, could we tilt the balance of the future?

Where did we go wrong?

This is a book about the personal, about starting with yourself. But to navigate the 'voyage' that is your life, you have to understand the currents that you sail across. If your life appears to be impossibly hard, it's not all your fault. We are all products of the past, and the last century has been a cyclone of change. These are not normal times; no-one alive today has even known normal times. Without realising it, every one of us stands gasping for breath at the sheer pace of history. For 100 years the hammer-blows of war, economic depression, more war, relocation and emigration have rained down upon us. Every family and every person took damage; intergenerational wounds sprang up and were not addressed.

Somehow, through all of this, women coped better: they supported each other more, hung onto their humanity. Men were at the bruising end of things – we were the soldiers, the miners, the factory fodder, the corporate drones. In the onslaught of all this change, we suffered a legacy of severe emotional wounding that had no time to heal before the next blow fell. With so much damage done to our hearts, we were less able to nurture our children, love our wives, or teach our adolescents. We lost the linkages by which healthy manhood is shaped and passed along.

Your life, and your everyday difficulties with your family, job and world are closely linked to this. The changes your parents, grandparents and great grandparents lived through had no precedent in history. It was a heroic story – we weren't conquered by fascists, or destroyed in a nuclear war. We survived the bombed cities, the bloody jungle wars, the food queues, the factory shutdowns, the voyages to an unknown fate. We made it, but it took its toll. We lost connection with our own hearts.

That's what this book sets out to fix: to regain our humanity as men, all that we lost in the long nightmare of history. Men are meant to be free, and we can be again. If this book is successful, it will reconnect you with a wellbeing and purpose that you didn't even know you had lost. Your life can be so much more than you have dreamed.

Can men really change?

Everyone can see the problem. Mothers hear on the daily news of stabbings and road deaths, and pray their sons will come home safe at night. Wives see the confusion and unhappiness in their husbands, and wish they could find their direction. Young women search for a good man to love, and find only shambling boys. And millions of men sit hunched at computer screens and wonder – is this all there is to life?

> There is so much more to a man's life than we have settled for.

To most people, though, the idea of large-scale masculine change seems an impossible dream. Yet even the most cynical must admit that something is happening with the male of the species. (Just think of the world of difference between George Bush and Barack Obama, and tell me there is not a generational change in men.)

There is one outstanding piece of evidence for a massive change being possible – women have already done it. In just four decades from the early 1970s to the present, and against fierce opposition, an entire gender has redefined itself. The Women's Movement overturned thousands of years of oppression and restriction, an unprecedented and historic shift. When the human race *needs* to change, it can do so very fast.

Women are still not where they want to be, and that may be for one important reason – men have not changed too. Wherever men and women mix, you will notice a very odd thing: men and women seem unevenly matched. You see it everywhere, from bedroom to boardroom – the vibrant and articulate woman with the self-conscious, stiff and angry man. The men seem unequal, struggling, and it makes everyone unhappy. To transform our society into a truly free one, we need *both* genders to be fully alive. The world is waiting for men – it needs the activated and fully awakened male to confront everything from the fossil-fuel industry that is baking our planet to our children's needs to play happily with Dad in the backyard after work.

So, it's time to get started. A lot has happened since the first release of *Manhood:* the shift in men's lives has gathered speed, just as it did for women 40 years sooner. But it's early days. Perhaps, for you, 'male liberation' is a new idea, and perhaps you will be part of the generation that makes it all come true. I hope you will.

Please be warned (and this is written with a smile) that reading this book has consequences. Men reading it are prone to spontaneous weeping. They may drop everything to go and seek out estranged parents or siblings. They may walk away from soul-destroying jobs, even well-paid ones. They start taking their wives gently by the hand.

They begin to sing in the shower. Their kids start to like them.

On a larger scale, who can say it isn't time for a new kind of man? That with the planet in ecological collapse, greed and rapaciousness everywhere, it isn't time for good men to find their feet? To stand at their full height and do what's needed to put the world to rights?

The premise of this book is that we are made to be unified and whole, happy and full of life. What is good for your soul is also what is best for your loved ones, and your world. So let's begin.

Steve Biddulph
Tamar Valley
2010

xiii

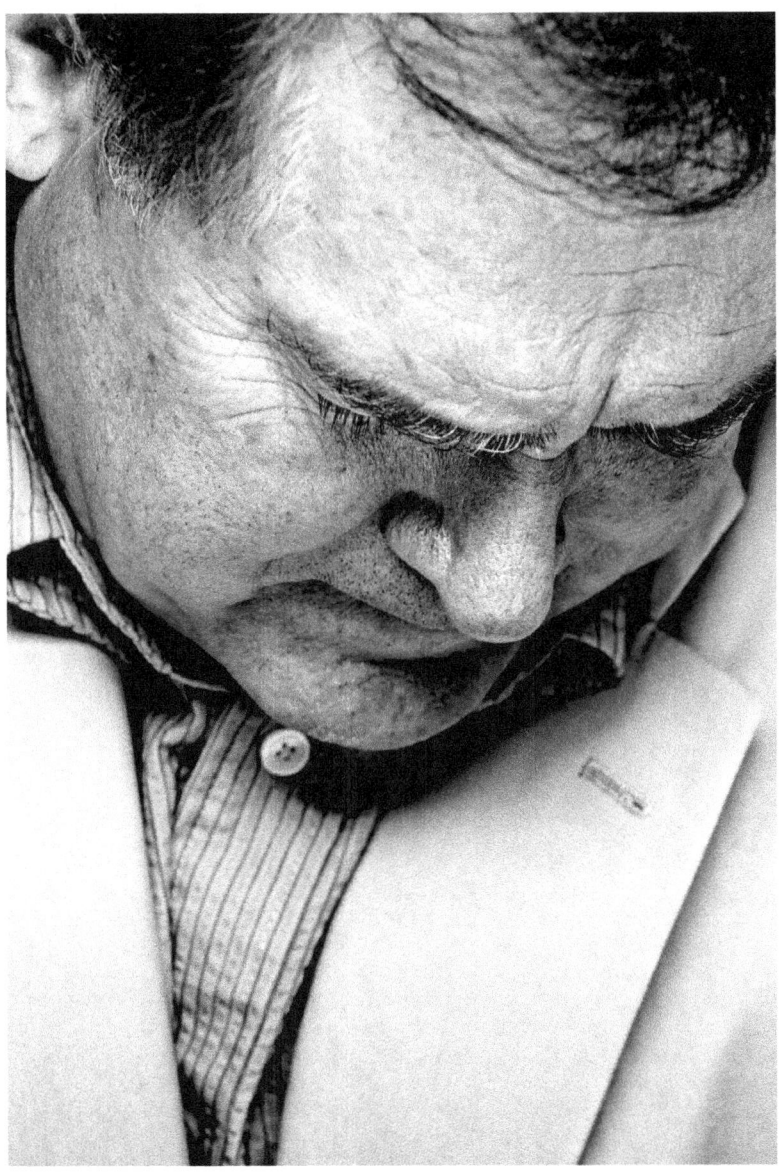

Image 1

ONE

The problem

'Have you seen the look in the eye of a 35-year-old man?'

Robert Bly

The problem can be put very simply. Most men don't have a life. What we call our life is mostly just a big act, a mask that we clamp onto our faces each morning and and don't take off until we fall asleep at night. Most men are flat out every day living a lie. We've all grown so used to this, we don't even notice it any more.

It wasn't always like this. Throughout history, men have needed to 'act tough' at times, but they could also drop the act, so as to love, laugh and be close; feel grief and build friendship. Today the mask stays put, and behind it is often a confused, scared figure. Most men spend their whole lives pretending that they're fine when they're not. Pretending, and having a life, are very different things.

The problem starts early. Usually in his mid-teens, confronted with the problem of 'becoming a man', a boy tries on several of the stock male masks on offer – cool dude, hard worker, good bloke, tough guy, or 'sensitive new man'. He decides which one will work best in his social world of family, school and street. The mask usually has a fixed, wooden smile. 'It's cool.' 'I'm fine.' The process is mostly unconscious; a boy may have only the vaguest idea that he is doing it. And since every other boy around him is doing it too, it feels totally normal.

Masks have a purpose: they prevent vulnerability and exposure – important if you are not sure who you are or what you are allowed to feel. Nobody can hurt you in there. If they can't see the real you, they can't laugh at you, reject you or judge you. You can 'play the game'. But this pretending has a cost: hidden away, not really showing anyone our real self, it gets very lonely. Parents sense with sadness the boy shutting himself away. Friends, potential girlfriends, older adults who might have been of help sense a brick wall going up, and pull back. But the one who suffers most is the boy-becoming-man himself. The mask becomes a lifelong obstacle to healing and love.

Image 2

Most women are not like this. Spend just a few hours in the company of women (especially women who have lived a little) and you will find that they are more real and more alive than men. There is a sense of inner feeling and spirit that bubbles out in the way they talk, move and laugh. Women have their problems, but most women at least act from a clear sense of self. Women generally know who they are and what they want.

How did this difference come about? Little kids of both sexes start out well enough: it's a child's nature to be open-hearted, expecting to be happy, expecting life to be an adventure. That's why small children are so delightful to be around. But early on, a young boy's spirit begins to shrivel. By school age he is already becoming stiff and ill at ease; by the teen years, unhappiness is mapped into every muscle of his body. By the time he is a grown man, he is like a tiger raised in a zoo – prowling about, confused and numb, with huge energies untapped. He feels that there must be more, but he does not know what that 'more' is. So he spends his life pretending – to his friends, his family, and himself – that everything is fine.

The cracks appear

Round-the-clock pretending is hard work, so it's not surprising that, sooner or later, cracks start to appear in a man's façade. Sometimes they arise through getting a glimpse of what could be; a man finds himself alone in nature, in the surf or the landscape at sunset, and he feels a blissful connection with the ocean, trees and sky. Or he experiences a certain kind of moment with a woman, of passionate intensity or tender closeness. Or playing with his children, he suddenly feels like a child himself, tingling with life. He glimpses something, unsettling but beautiful ... and then it's gone. He cannot get that feeling back. He goes back to business as usual, but it has shaken him. He knows that something is missing from his life.

> Not showing anyone our real self gets very lonely.

Sometimes the cracks are more sudden. If a man is very good at denying his true feelings, the tensions may build up unseen over many years. Then one day, like pressure that has built up deep in the earth, the fault-line suddenly gives way. Then the damage is rapid and severe – a sudden health breakdown, a humiliating career failure that shows all the signs of self-sabotage, a shocking car accident for which he is clearly to blame...

More often, though, there is not even the buzz of drama, but merely a creeping despair. A man begins to suspect (often wrongly) that he is not loved by those around him; to realise (often rightly) that he is not even known by them. His connection to his own life suddenly hangs by the thinnest of threads.

- I am addressing a room full of school principals, 30 or 40 of them, at the beginning of a seminar. Something feels wrong in the room; so wrong that I actually ask – what is going on? They blurt it out: *one of their colleagues took his life* the night before, and the news has just reached them. Spurned by his wife for another man, he jumped into a river and drowned. Everyone in the

room looks hollow-eyed. How could he do it?
- At my high school, in Year 12, a boy I have known for years gets the top marks for the school. He is set for success, a scholarship in Engineering. The day before university begins, he takes a rifle from his father's cupboard, hides it, then sneaks out just before dawn and fires it into the roof of his mouth. Years later, I track down the coroner's report. It simply states 'no suspicious circumstances'. As if that's all that needs to be said.
- In my home state, Tasmania, the truck drivers' union makes a plea in the newspapers. Their members are being traumatised and having their mental health damaged because a plague of suicidal men are driving their cars into trucks head-on. Suicidal, and selfish. They seem bound up together somehow.

Needed: liberation for the rest of us

For the 20 years from the 1970s until the 1990s, the focus of my profession, psychology, was on helping women. It was the same in teaching, social work, health. Women were breaking out of narrow, crippling roles and restrictions. Anyone with a sense of fair play got on board with this. The changes were historic – in sexuality, career, education, family roles – the whole shape of a woman's life was transformed. It was an exciting time. But gradually it dawned on some of us that this story was incomplete. That men too were often caught in traps not of their own making. That just because men were 'on top' in jobs, earnings, and many outward measures of power, this didn't necessarily make them winners in any sense of the word. So we began to look more closely at men.

What we found was startling. There was clear evidence that all through the twentieth century, and into the twenty-first, men had risk factors all their own. Suicide, premature death, accidents and addictions – the statistics were all dominated by men. And hurt men also tended to hurt others: physical violence against spouses, child sexual abuse, divorce and moral bankruptcy in business and politics all pointed to something badly wrong with large numbers of men. School shootings, serial killings: men, always men. As Robert Bly said at the start of his famous book, *Iron John,* 'Are you depressed enough already?'

The big question was, are malfunctioning men – from serial killers to prime ministers and presidents – just the exceptions? Or is there a flaw in the whole weave, causing *all* men to be so loosely connected to life that they risk floating off into oblivion? Do we need to start again, in the way we raise little boys, nurture teenagers, and support the lives of young men? Do we have to change men's lives as much as we had to change women's? The answer is yes, of course.

Facing the facts

Here are some of the facts about being a man today:
- Men, on average, live for six years less than women do. They also have higher death rates in every age category, 'from womb to tomb'.

- Men routinely fail at close relationships. (Just two indicators: over 40 percent of marriages break down, and divorces are initiated by the woman in four out of five cases.)
- Over 90 percent of acts of violence are carried out by men, and 70 percent of the victims are men.
- In school, around 90 percent of children with behaviour problems are boys, and over 85 percent of children with learning problems are also boys.
- Young men (aged from fifteen to 25) have three times the death rate of young women, and these deaths are all from preventable causes – motor-vehicle accidents being the greatest.
- Men make up 80 percent of the homeless.
- Men comprise over 90 percent of gaol populations.
- The leading cause of death among men between fifteen and 44 is self-inflicted death.

Mental health, physical health and mortality – men win the prize in every category. Just being male is the biggest risk factor of all.

How did men go astray?

How did we get to be this way? Why are men so unhappy? In the early 1990s, writers and commentators began pointing out something that should have been blindingly obvious – that compared with thousands of years of human history that had gone before, boys and young men in the modern world were horrendously underfathered. In other words, they were not given enough affection, teaching and example from either their dad or other male figures to help them grow into mature men.

Affection, teaching, and example are the three essential vitamins of human growth:
1. affection – to let them know they matter
2. teaching – to help them understand their lives, and
3. example – so they can learn by observation how a good man feels, thinks and acts.

A good dad and a few good uncles, teachers who are friendly and show you how a good man behaves – it doesn't seem too much to ask. But these ingredients almost disappeared from the lives of boys. Without this training, boys' bodies still grew into men's bodies, but they were not given the knowledge and skills to match. They didn't get the 'software' for how to be male.

> If you live in a male body, you need to learn how to 'drive' it...

Most rearing of boys and girls is carried out by women, and mostly this goes pretty well. After all, we are all 'human' and learn how to be and live from other 'humans'. But we are also neurologically wired-up, hormonally orchestrated, and behaviourally shaped by being the sex we are. So although boys can get a huge amount from women, and girls from men, we all need people of our own gender if we are to learn to deal with our unique biology, and to reach our full potential. If you live in a male body, you need to learn how to 'drive' it – preferably from someone who knows how to drive their own. Part of the reason for this is that you can't learn human qualities from a book – for a boy to become patient, he has to *see* patience. To be kind and generous, he has to *see* that, lived out, in someone who could be an older version of himself. To learn restraint, commitment, exuberance, humour and generosity may require spending hundreds of hours with men who demonstrate these traits and present them as desirable and admirable.

Older cultures provided this: there was long and intense training given to boys by men. But today men are just too busy to give it the time it needs, even if they knew how. The result is footballers who act like idiots, drunken yobs in the streets, young men who rape or kill ... but most often, just men who do not know where they are going in their lives. Encompassing billions of men, this adds up to a world in trouble.

The seeds of change are sprouting – young fathers of this generation are vastly more involved with their children (some studies report a trebling of father–child time) compared with the previous generation. But do those young dads know what to pass on? For those of us who are adult men today, the wounds remain. Our fathers were often remote, disturbed, emotionally awkward, or just plain absent for much of the time. This is the crux of the matter: whether we are mothers or fathers, we want to pass on to our sons the full, deep river of healthy masculinity, all that a fine man can be. Yet if all we received was a little trickle, this can be hard to do.

The rip in history

It's natural to ask, if the 'river of masculinity' flowed for thousands of years, how did it get blocked? Where did men start to go wrong? In fact, the disappearance of men from the lives of children arose from a specific historical event, which began about 200 years ago. The Industrial Revolution started in the English Midlands, but it rolled tsunami-like across the globe. Wherever it arrived, it took us in one generation from small, rural villages to huge, industrial towns, and from working together as men, women and children (there was as yet no school) into sharply divided lives. Suddenly everything changed – women were stuck at home, men went down coal mines, and boys began to fall through the cracks.

We are so used to the minor role that modern fathers play that it's hard to imagine it any other way. Yet in the pre-industrial world, the picture of childhood and parenthood was totally different; you can still see this if you visit Indigenous cultures in the Pacific, Asia, Latin America or Africa. The men are affectionate, skilful with kids, engaged and always teaching and supporting the young. (You still see these qualities in men like Nelson Mandela and the Dalai Lama – they light up those around them.) But for around six generations in the West, as men went off to work in foundries, mines and mills, no longer seeing much of their children, this pattern of male nurturing and teaching was ruptured and lost. To make matters worse, a succession of catastrophic events –

world wars, recessions, migrations – added to the damage. The returned soldier who brooded in silence, only to explode in fits of violence, or who used enormous amounts of alcohol to keep his nightmares at bay, was a standard male figure of the twentieth century; there was one in every street. The labourer in the factory or mine, crushed and powerless, drunkenly beating his wife on a Friday night, was another. With this kind of baggage, it's little wonder that late-twentieth-century fathers were struggling to know what a good man even looked like.

To make it worse, men in the neighbourhood and community, the uncles and mentors of an earlier age, pretty much disappeared from the scene. Today, unless a boy is very good at sport, joins the Scouts or encounters a really special schoolteacher, he may not know any men closely at all. This creates a huge vacuum in a growing boy. He does not have a model to base his own manhood on. This is why we have the phenomenon of men 'acting'. Not able to know the inner world of real men, each boy is forced to base his idea of self on a thinly-drawn image gleaned from externals – TV, movies, his peers – which he then acts out, hoping to 'prove' he is a man. Each boy does his best to live using this one-dimensional façade, which does not really work in any of life's more personal arenas – friendship, closeness to a woman, raising kids of his own. These intimate tasks require a sense of self, of a warm, beating heart that others can feel close to. So the young dad becomes like the old dad, and the damage continues into another generation.

By contrast, a girl's development is much more supported. Girls usually grow up with continuous exposure to competent and communicative women at home, at school and in friendship networks. From this they learn an open and sharing style of womanhood that enables them to befriend other women and give and receive support throughout their lives. By the time they reach young adulthood, most women have had thousands of hours of conversation, contact and encouragement from their own gender; they have role models 'hanging in the sky above them' like protective angels. Their peer friendships, while not perfect, carry some of these qualities of nurturing as well, and they will draw on these through all the major events of their lives. Men's and boys' friendship networks – if they have them at all – are rarely like this. They are awkward and oblique, lacking in intimacy and often short-term.

There were boys I was close to at school, spent thousands of hours with, whose inner lives I simply never knew. My mother, volunteering at the canteen, came home with stories that shocked me. One boy who often sat beside me had gone through the wrenching divorce of his parents. Another was beaten regularly by his father, and in the end was spirited away by the teachers to an agricultural college so he could finish his schooling in safety. But we boys never, ever, discussed these things.

When school ended, the friendships ended too.

It was the same at university. When classes ended, so did the contact. It wasn't for lack of feeling or closeness; when I visited my old high school decades later and wandered 'round the now-empty buildings, my heart ached with longing for the good times and the lost connections. But there was no language of closeness, no conversation to sustain it, so friendships simply stopped dead when the school bell rang for the last time.

When boys are not given affection, care and mentoring by dads and uncles and other men, they do not grow up very well. Mothers and women offer a great deal, and a loving and focused mother can get a boy 'almost to wholeness', but it never quite knits together, because how to be a man is the one thing she cannot teach. The lack of elder male connections during our childhood leaves us bereft and struggling. Whether we are attempting to be the 'Sensitive New Age Guy' or are clinging to the Clint Eastwood, tough-guy image, we keep finding that it just doesn't work.

> Denying your feelings is not always a bad thing...

By now you might be thinking – what a disaster! How can this ever be fixed? But as we stand here in the twenty-first century, there is hope of change. Before, all we saw were the symptoms. Now we can see the cause, and so the solution. And not all men have come through in bad shape. There were good fathers, who had good fathers, and there are men whose lives work very well who can show us the way. We 'have the DNA', and we can recreate what fully alive manhood looks and feels like. We can even create a newer, better kind of man than ever before.

Beginning to grieve

For a damaged and wounded man, getting well again, becoming whole, begins with a small step. It begins with admitting the sorrow of what has been lost. Let me tell a story to show what I mean.

In the early 1990s I began giving talks on raising boys for parents in many countries around the world. I began each talk by laying out this problem of father-hunger, and how it affects us as dads. I told stories of the rifts between fathers and sons, and how they could be mended. More than once during this part of the talk, there would be men who would get up and leave the theatre. I assumed they were answering their mobile phones, or needed the bathroom. At one event, three men left in the space of five minutes. I spoke to the ushers afterwards – they had actually been waiting to tell me. Those men had left in tears.

As a man starts to really feel what he has missed out on, the fathering and nurturing that was almost there but not quite, he replaces the dull sense of 'lostness' with a sharp and painful grief. This is a positive step, though it almost always feels worse. Change starts with acknowledging where you are – so important for us men – precisely because the denial of the pain is what holds us in our inner prison.

Denying your feelings is not always a bad thing: it serves an important evolutionary purpose. If you are a soldier pinned down by machine-gun fire on D-Day, with comrades dying all around you, then getting in touch with your feelings might not be a good idea. Likewise if you are unemployed in the Great Depression, with children hungry and depending on you. But denial is meant to be a short-term strategy, not a way of life. Older and wiser cultures knew this, and deliberately built in ways to help men let go of pain and move on.

Near Taupo in New Zealand, hidden away from the tourist traps and fancy hotels, a small Maori-owned hot spring lies at the head of a small valley. A creek runs over a scalding, bubbling area of volcanic mud and rocks, then re-enters the forest. There, in a leafy glade, a hot, steaming waterfall dives over a small cliff. This was a sacred place, where warriors, returning from battle, washed away the hate, fear, and bloodiness of war, and became human again. As they did so, they grieved for dead comrades, for the pain and awfulness of killing. They wept and cried out under the torrent of heated water. The women sang to them, and welcomed them back into the peaceful world of the community and the family. The gods had taken away their pain, rage, and grief.

Toughing things out, tightening your muscles, shutting out sensation or feeling does not work as a way of life because you become more and more deadened. The natural safety valves of sadness, being held, sobbing or letting go are not available, so a man becomes more and more pent-up. Grief is the body's answer to loss; crying and shaking or sobbing mean that a release is happening, we are facing what we have lost and the price we have paid. When a human being cries (and we are the only species on earth who does this) powerful morphine-like chemicals are released in our bloodstream, which help us to bear the pain. With the help of those chemicals, we can look at those parts of our own mind that are shut away, and begin to integrate them.

Scientists have found that trauma that has not been shared or properly processed is held in the primitive limbic system of our brain, and is frozen there for later processing. The problem with this part of the brain is that it has no sense of time: the traumatic memory feels as if it is still happening. Once it is talked about, and the feelings properly expressed, the trauma shifts across to the neocortex, where it becomes just memory, 'something that once happened', a story in our bigger life.

This is why, when we survive a near-miss in a car or have a horrible encounter with danger or death, the urge to tell someone about it is almost uncontainable. That's how humans disperse intense stress, and at the same time learn from it. We deal with a crisis first, and deal with the feelings later, when there's time.

Grief – the allowing of such feelings to flow – doesn't feel good at the time, but it feels better than being deadened and numb. Grief is a sign that we are becoming alive again. It serves as both a renewal and a compass, since it starts us yearning for what we have lost, so that we can begin the journey to recover it. It readies us to accept what we have tried to pretend we didn't need: closeness, trust, friendship, love. Much of the time, when men seem angry, they are actually hiding grief. Anger never resolves the grief, though, since it drives people further away – when we really need them to stay close.

The end result of doing this inner healing is that a man becomes calmer, steadier. He speaks comfortably about his emotions when they occur, so there is no drama, no backlog, no 'disproportionate response'. The nightmare for many families – the 'ticking time-bomb' father with his sudden eruptions – becomes a thing of the past. Grieving is often the pathway to family peace.

Out of isolation

There's one more thing to know about 'the problem'. That is, that men and women are on different paths to the same goal of liberation. Women in the twentieth century had to overcome the straightjacket of expectation and limitations on what a woman was supposed to be. So the 'busting-out' energy of anger was appropriate and helpful in forcing change. But men's difficulties are with isolation. The enemies, the prisons from which men have to escape, are:
- loneliness
- compulsive competition, and
- lifelong emotional timidity.

> Human beings go into competition when they do not feel loved.

These require a more careful, exploratory kind of change. Our loneliness is self-created. If we are always putting on a front, people sense this and never quite trust us. When other men around us are also acting, we and they can never really feel close.

Men can be around each other for years and never know the other man's true situation. Often when a man has committed suicide, his friends say they had no idea that he was unhappy. When a man has huge problems in his marriage, or has a child with cancer, a parent with dementia, or frightening health problems of his own, he may never speak of this to even his closest friends. If he does mention something so intensely personal, his friends may not know how to respond, and either ignore him or make a dumb joke that discounts his feelings, so that he does not try again.

Competition is linked with this loneliness – it's the natural consequence of treating others with constant mistrust. Human beings go into competition when they do not feel loved. If we never felt the love of our father penetrating through his mask, then we would never feel good enough or safe enough in his regard and affection. Faced with this, many young boys began a desperate lifelong effort to win approval. (Whole business empires have been built on this motivation – the Packer dynasty may be a classic case.) In this struggle, other men are competitors, not allies or friends. In a family without enough love to go around, brothers and sisters who could have become lifelong allies instead start to beat each other down to gain what little attention there is. By the way they give love, parents set up the architecture for their children to either love or hate each other.

Without some closeness to our father, it's hard to trust other men, since he is our first example of male friendship. When a dad snuggles his child up and reads to him, or laughs and tickles him, he is not just offering short-term comfort, he is also showing the child that love, relaxation, care and patience can all be male qualities. The ability to trust a man is learnt very young.

Finally, as a result of not seeing the emotions of older men expressed close up, twentieth-century men simply became emotionally timid, retarded in the language of 'feelings'. I've known tough-as-leather ex-soldiers, firemen and policemen who would face any physical danger but be terrified at the prospect of an honest conversation, or the idea of, say, giving a speech at their daughter's wedding. These men still have feelings, but they are buried deep. What their friends, wives and children experience is a kind of distant signal through ten layers of dark glass. They know there is someone inside there, but it's a guessing game, uneasy and unsatisfying for them. This is what we have to overcome.

Women's enemies were largely in the world around them. Men's enemies are often on the inside – in the walls we put up around our own hearts. As we begin to let ourselves feel, others can be close to us and care for us, and we can care for them. We can identify what it is we need to be happy and well. After that, it's easy!

IN A NUTSHELL

- Most men don't have a life.
- The reason is that we 'pretend' our manhood: in our teens we put on a mask, and we wear it for the rest of our lives.

- This pretence stops others from getting close to us.
- Sooner or later, cracks appear; our life begins to break down.
- The reason men wear masks is because nobody taught them how to be real men.
- There is a 'river' of healthy masculinity that used to be passed on to each new generation by the older one.
- The Industrial Revolution took men away from their childrearing role, so this river ran dry.
- Because of this nameless loss, there is a huge grief just below the surface in men today.
- Only when we come out of our isolation and emotional shutdown can we really be free.

Image 3

TWO

You and your father

*Oh will you never return to see
Your bruised and beaten sons?
Oh I would, I would, if welcome I were
For they loathe me everyone.*

Traditional folk song

About 100 fathers, aged from their mid-twenties to early fifties, are seated in a room for an all-day seminar. A room filled with this many men has a certain energy, calm and solid on the surface, but crackling with tension underneath. When the group has begun to settle in, around mid-morning, I ask the question that is the pivot of the whole day. 'You are here because you want to be a good father. But how about your own experience of being fathered? How well do you get along with your own dad?'

There is an uneasy silence. Some of the men don't even like the question — there are glares and frowns scattered around the room. Then I ask for a show of hands. Here is what we find:

About 30 men out of 100 are in the worst category of all. They barely speak to their father, rarely make the time to see him, and don't like it when they do. They are basically estranged from him. The anger and hurt in these men is palpable when they raise their hands.

About another 30 men fall into category two – they see their fathers at birthdays, holidays and family gatherings. They get along. But there is something wrong, a prickliness; the relationship seems to consist of the mutual exchange of disagreements, even if it's just about which brand of lawnmower is best. There's a connection, but it's 'cactus'; there is not much relaxation flowing between these men. They come away from their encounters bleeding from a thousand small cuts. Their women sigh in exasperation, not sure who to blame.

There is a third category, again about 30 in a hundred. These are the well-behaved men. They drive down to visit their parents in the retirement village once a month, or phone them at a regular time each week. And since we know that the human heart is never regular, that our feelings really come and go a lot, you can guess that the motivation for contact is not a yearning or spontaneous warmth. Rather, it's the d-word. Duty. Duty is better than nothing: if you are in an old people's home, staring at the door waiting for a visitor, duty may be all you can count on. A regular contact still has meaning. But it easily becomes rote, just ticking off another chore. Not exactly life-affirming for either party...

You will be getting the picture now, and it's not very good. So far, we have 90 percent of the men in poor relationship with their fathers. That's a shocking situation, yet one we have somehow come to accept as normal.

There is one more, smaller group of men. They wait calmly, until the other men have finished speaking, but I can pick them out clearly from the front of the room – their eyes and faces are alight. They finally speak up, clearly and gently. These men have wonderful fathers. Better than friends, these are fathers who act as an emotional backstop in their adult son's life, men who they admire, enjoy, and feel deep support from. Who will remain close to them until the day they die. This small group of men are living their lives blessed with the knowledge, in every cell of their body, that they are loved by, and a source of pride to, their fathers. These men, at most, are 10 percent of the men in the room. The lucky ones. What a terrible score that is! How different would the world be if we all, men and women, had this experience?

> If you are at war with your father in your head, you can be at war with masculinity itself.

How about you?

Where are you at with your father? And with older men in general? This is an important question – your happiness as a man is hugely impacted by the answer. Manhood isn't an age that you reach, it's more like a flow of knowledge and skill, like a river, which you receive and grow strong in, and then pass on downstream to others. Unless you can connect to the inherited masculinity of generations of older men, your manhood may never flourish or grow. Thousands of years of masculine learning will be missing for you.

For better or worse, your father is the first conduit of this learning. Of course, uncles and grandparents, teachers, books, movies, friends, your mother and other women all help to teach you about maleness, but your father takes a primary place. Your masculinity – consciously or unconsciously, whether you like it or not – is based on his. He was the first male you knew, who you took in deeply as an example. (If he was absent, or dead, or ignored you most of the time, then that is what you took in – a hole, waiting to be filled.)

For many of us, this is not good news. Most men realise (with alarm) that their father's mannerisms, attitudes and way of speaking are deeply a part of them and likely to emerge at any time. If you are at war with him in your head, you can unwittingly be at war with masculinity itself. If you didn't feel loved and respected by him, it will be hard to respect yourself. If you hated him, you may deep down hate yourself as well. These things can be healed, but first they have to be uprooted and looked at in clear light. They cannot be glossed over. It's very hard to become a whole and happy man with the father-wound still bleeding.

Breaking free, coming back

At certain stages of growing up, most fathers and sons experience some serious friction. All through history, and in every society, sons and fathers have always passed through a natural cycle. They move from the closeness of little boys and their dad, through a degree of crankiness in the mid-teens, to the son venturing away, determined to make his own course in life. Then, once he feels secure in himself, the young man returns to be truly close, on a friendly and more equal level, with his dad.

Mid-adolescence is the friction peak. Teenage hormones act as the 'second-stage rocket' that kicks this process along. At age fourteen, a boy's testosterone levels soar upwards, 800 percent higher than at age ten. A fourteen-year-old boy will argue with a road sign! That's why mentors and other men are essential for a teenage boy's safety and growth. They overcome the limitations of the dad, and free the boy from that too-intense attention that can so easily turn into arguments. Travelling away from Dad and Mum to return as an adult is a natural cycle. But in the twentieth century, this natural cycle worsened, and became a fatal rift. The small boy does not even get close to his dad, the teenage boy hates him, the adult man never comes back.

'Coming back' to your father and forgiving him for not being all that you wished or needed is a vital step in finally making it to happy adulthood. Today we find that many if not most men need to make this 'coming back' step. It's not a small or easy thing; it can be terrifying. It needs care and thought to get it right. In spite of these fears and dangers, though, it's essential at some stage of your life to have a profound conversation or series of conversations with your father, aimed at healing the almost inevitable rift that most of us have. Only by doing this can you get an understanding of his life, his reasons for behaving the way he did, his failures and his successes. Until you take this step, you will always be building your manhood on shifting sands – on guesswork and childhood impressions that were never the whole story. Other older men and women may supplement what you didn't get from your father, but his primary place in your life will still be there. Even if he was an alcoholic, a wife beater, a child abuser, or he abandoned you – even if you never met him – your biological father still matters. Until you come to terms with him, he will haunt you from the inside, where he symbolically lives forever.

One of the ways your father will 'hang around' is by colouring your attitude towards older men. Perhaps you don't trust older men because you couldn't trust your father. Perhaps you are rebellious to authority in general because your father was unloving and harsh towards you. Perhaps you try to impress older men because you couldn't impress him. Perhaps you have been feeling superior to older men, that you can do without them, or can outsmart them, because you were in competition with him.

The fact is, until you reach a place where you can feel love and respect for your father and/or receive the love and respect of older men, there is a danger that you will not fully mature. Think about this for a minute – living your life in reaction to your father is as unfree as obeying every word he says. A man whose father was oppressively religious might become an atheist. A man whose father drank might become a teetotaller. A man whose father was a farmer might choose to live in the densest city. A man whose father was a failure might become a compulsive success. Or vice versa. But this does not deal with the problem, it's just avoiding it. You still aren't free.

A wound that needs healing

At some stage in your boyhood, it's likely that your father did not meet your needs, to such an extent that your development was harmed. The danger is that your development will be frozen at that place, still waiting for those needs to be met so you can finally grow up. It's important to figure out if this is the case, so that at least you can make a choice: to pursue him or to seek help elsewhere.

There are many men whose father died or abandoned their mother and was never seen again. There are men whose father committed suicide, often when they were still just young boys. This leads to deeply buried hurt and confusion, since the message a little child always takes from abandonment is, 'What did I do to make him leave? What's wrong with me?' Men can suppress this pain by hard work and denial, but will still be prone to outbursts of deep distress, often masked by anger.

Some of these men decide to do something proactive about this. They make a deliberate journey into their father's past, which often means a real-life journey across the country or across the world. I've spoken to men who made the pilgrimage to POW camps in Europe, or who sought out the contemporaries of their father back in Asia or America to learn more about him, or who looked up long-lost relatives to find out more of their own roots. Barack Obama wrote a book, *Dreams of my Father,* about such a journey, and it clearly had a huge impact on him. By making this outward journey, these men were also making an inner personal journey to better understand the whole picture and let themselves and their fathers 'off the hook'. They were putting together the jigsaw of their own life, finding how all the pieces fitted together.

The journey might be physical, or it may simply be into your own memory banks, as long-forgotten incidents and experiences surface. Sometimes dreams bring memories back. Or listening to other men's stories helps to trigger memories that were long buried.

> I was sobbing with the memory of being tenderly loved.

As a young man, I was very focused on the deficiencies of my father, the things he didn't do or offer me, especially during my adolescence. Naturally my psychology training fed into this – parent-blaming being a major industry at the time! Then, one evening, I was watching a movie my wife had brought home, which she felt might interest me. It was a film about fathers and sons, and included a scene where a physical fight erupted between an adult son and his father. As the credits started to roll, the strangest thing happened. I began to cry – something I had scarcely ever done since childhood. It was not just quiet weeping, either, but huge, gulping sobs. I was suddenly remembering specific positive things my father had done when I was very young.

They all involved incidental or indirect forms of affection. Keeping me warm inside his coat at a soccer game. Bathing my sores with cool lotion when I awoke at night in pain and distress with chicken pox. Holding my hand as we walked out on snowy nights when I was about six. I had blocked out these memories because they didn't match the story in my head, that my dad was never close. Now they came flooding back, memories of gentleness and care from that often mute and awkward man. The real story was so much more complex, rich and valuable. I was sobbing with the memory of being tenderly loved.

For those of us whose fathers are still alive, the situation is easier – somewhat. We have a real person, and his mysteries are waiting to be revealed. Robert Bly tells the story of a man phoning his father, long distance. The younger man is making an attempt to bridge the gap that has grown between them. Father and son have had little contact in recent years, and the son has been doing some thinking. When the father answers the phone...

'Hi, Dad, it's me.'

'Oh! Hi, son! I'll go get your mother...'

'No, don't get Mum. It's you I want to talk to...'

There's a pause, then...

'Why? Do you need money?'

'No, I don't need money.'

And the younger man starts on his somewhat rehearsed, but still vulnerable speech...

'I've just been remembering a lot about you, Dad, and the things you did for me. Working all those years in a job you hated, to put me through university, supporting us. You provided the house, the clothes, the food. You told me I could choose what to study, what career to pursue. My life is going well now and it's because of what you did to get me started. I just thought about it and realised I'd never really said, "Thanks"...'

Silence on the other end of the line. The son continues. 'I want to tell you ... thanks. And that I love you.'

There's a long pause before the father answers.

'You been drinking????'

Whenever an audience hears this story, they laugh out loud, but many laugh with eyes wet and shining.

Respect is not what you think

Coming to terms with your father, having a rounded view of him, is especially important if you are a father yourself, and even more so if you are in any kind of leadership role. You will never have respect until you can give respect. Not blindly, but recognising leadership and experience when you see it.

Authority has a bad name these days, and for good reason: lying and cheating by our leaders in politics and business have become something we almost expect. But in personal life, for our own wellbeing, we need to find people to respect. Climbing the cliff face of becoming a good human being, it's more encouraging if you can see people up ahead, and routes they have taken to get there.

There is a huge misconception about respect, which has misled several generations and deprived their lives as a result. This is the mistaken idea that respect is given for the benefit of the receiver, as a kind of worship. In fact we do not respect people for *their* sake, but rather for *our* sake, because only when we respect can we let in the gifts they have to give us. Seen in this way, disrespect is a kind of blindness (the word 'respect' originally meant to look again, to look twice, and the second time see so much more). Not everyone deserves our respect, but in almost everyone there are things to respect – the good that is there in spite of the bad.

When we are children, we see people as either good or bad – a simple rule of thumb that protects us in that vulnerable time of life when we are weak and small. But a huge part of growing up is seeing that other people are both good and bad, or are good but with bad aspects or faults. We can respect them in part, and take responsibility for what we take in and what we set aside. Having no admiration for others, being totally cynical, is the refuge of a wounded person. As we heal from these wounds, we are more receptive to the nuggets of goodness around us. We aren't blinded to the dross and garbage of the world, but it's not all we see.

What fathers wait to hear

Every father, however much he puts on a critical or indifferent exterior, will spend his life waiting at some deep level to know that his sons (and daughters) love and respect him. Make sure you absorb this point. *He will spend his life waiting.* This is the huge power you hold in your hands, just by virtue of being a son. Everyone these days accepts that a parent has the power to crush a child's self-esteem. Few realise that a child, in time, holds the same power in reverse. Parents wait, however defensively, for their children to pass judgement. That's how life is.

A man I knew had a father who was so 'impossible' that he walked away or went out of the house whenever somebody tried to talk to him about matters of emotional importance. This old man developed cancer, and lay dying in hospital, with tubes in and out of him. My friend journeyed across the country to see him, stormed into the hospital, closed the door of his father's room and said, 'I've got you now, you bastard!' He began to tell him how angry he was, and also (after a time) what he appreciated about him. At the end they were holding hands.

There is a responsibility here that sons and daughters have towards their parents – to address the necessary damage of growing up, to be honest about the wrongs, and appreciative of the rights. To stop fudging it and pretending that all is fine, while inwardly skating away from any real contact.

Having these conversations may challenge you to the core. You may fear that you will make things worse. (In a few pages' time, we will look at how to make the process safer, although it is never completely safe.) For now, though, you need to know that if you are a man and you do not confront this dragon, then your father will die hurting, and a part of you will die as well. Robert Bly writes in *Iron John,* 'Many men go to their graves convinced that they have been an inadequate human being.' They do this because of the lack of respect that has developed with those they love – not the least of these being their sons, their primary connection with masculine life. The pain of this cannot be overstated.

> The words are not as important as the sense of having arrived at peaceful closeness.

It is possible that your father will seek you out one day to deal with this himself. It is possible, but unlikely. You are the one who has the benefit of the insights of our generation. You are the one reading this book. You are the one who has grown bigger by standing on his shoulders. It might be up to you to make the first move. The words 'I love you' are cheap and easily said, which is part of the reason we hesitate to speak them. It's all about arriving at the place where they can be honestly spoken. The words are not as important as the sense of having arrived, of peaceful, authentic companionable closeness. This feeling settles on you both as you sit there, with immense relief and a sense of great freedom. And you know you are there.

Your father is not who you think he is

You may have in-built prejudices against your father, for a surprising reason. Often, and sometimes with the best of intentions, a mother will turn her son against his father. Look closely at your view of your father – is this really just your mother's view? Is it just possible that this is not the whole story? This on its own is a huge reason to go and find out more.

If you're a father with an adult son, then why wait? If you're a son with a living father, the challenge is clear. Are you ready to make that journey? Often, to start with, you don't feel a lot of love for your father, much less respect him. Perhaps you hate him. If there are differences between you, these cannot be ignored. Don't pretend things are okay. It simply won't work and you will feel cheapened. Differences have to be dealt with (more on this later).

Lots of men I have worked with do eventually, when the trust between us has grown, admit to a secret despair. They feel that they must be defective, almost genetically so. Without really knowing the real story behind their father's choices and struggles, they see only the failures in his life. And they become convinced that they are made of the same stuff. They condemn their father, and they condemn themselves. Sometimes they condemn the whole male gender! To avoid this potentially crushing self-doubt, finding an understanding of their father's choices is necessary work for all sons. Respect – that is, love mixed with admiration – is the food of the male soul. Sons have to 'discover' respect for their fathers, which is not the same as pretending it. They also need to receive respect from their fathers.

Image 4

Remember – respect does not mean blind or uncritical admiration. We can and should see many faults in the older generation (and they in us). Nor does it mean agreement. It means looking again, looking deeper, seeing the wealth of experience, suffering and courage that makes up that person, and acknowledging that they will always have things to show and teach us.

The approval all sons crave

In a Christian book on men's development, *Healing the Masculine Soul,* Gordon Dalbey tells this story:

A young man, in his late twenties, writes to his father. The young man is a successful professional, but plagued with insecurities and hurt by the difficult times he had with his father through his teens. In his letter he is direct and to the point. He asks his father whether he loves him. It's a very brave, vulnerable thing to ask. A letter comes back in reply, courteous and formal in tone: 'I love all my kids – you should know that.' The young man is crushed: this is not an answer to the question, in fact it dishonours the question. A personal question deserves a personal answer, something the 'old bastard' must realise.

The feeling of being short-changed is so familiar – this was what always happened, throughout his childhood. 'I love all my kids...' Direct praise is avoided. Direct contact is never made. The father is unwilling to risk the emotional intensity, and vulnerability, of making a direct connection. Encouraged by Dalbey, the son does not give up. He writes again. He is frightened to do so, but he takes a chance. Here are the exact words of the father's reply:

'I have to thank you for pushing me with your question. I guess I hadn't really thought that deeply about it. But when I did think about it, I realised that I do love you, Peter, and I need to say that for myself probably as much as you may need to hear it.'

Nothing is more powerful in the psychology of childhood than the need for love and approval. Unless a child receives clear and tangible demonstrations of these, he or she will wither like a plant without water. It's as basic as that. Those of us who are of northern European descent are inheritors of a cold culture, though we don't like to admit it. I've watched tiny children in hovels in Calcutta dancing and singing for their family and friends, who respond with warm applause and hugs. I've also watched British and Australian children bring home their report cards from their expensive private schools, young faces eager for praise, only to receive cool, critical appraisals from their performance-oriented, uptight parents. A chance for love and simple joy is lost forever.

What is the result of a lack of closeness with your father? If love is what we hunger for and it is not forthcoming, then a warp in our life sets in. When our natural need for love is fulfilled, it settles into the background and we can get on with our life. Unfulfilled, the need drives us like an obsession. So many men become workaholics or burned-out failures, driven by this unfulfilled hunger.

'See, Dad? See what I can do?'

'But Son, can't you do better?'

There are other causes for a generational rift between fathers and sons. Consider the problems raised if there is a major difference of orientation – for instance, a gay son (or a gay father, for that matter). Still, at heart, the issue is really the same: do you love me, even though I differ from what you expect? Even though I am not the one you dreamed of? The movie *The Sum of Us,* with Jack Thompson and Russell Crowe, is valuable for any father to watch. *Untouchable Girls,* the hilarious and very moving documentary about New Zealand's Topp Twins, shows how the most conservative parents imaginable could still come to celebrate their children's identity. (Born on a dairy farm in New Zealand in the 1950s, both Topp Twins and their brother turned out to be homosexual. They often joke that it must have been something in the milk!)

Expectations and hopes are part of the psyche of every parent. It's equally important to let go of these should they not work out. Many terrible wounds arise at this time from fathers who wanted a son and got a daughter; wanted an athlete and got an artist; wanted a musician and got a labourer; wanted Olympic Gold and got cerebral palsy. The problem is not the different outcome, but the refusal to grieve and then move on – to love what you have got instead of what you wanted.

> *Nothing* is more powerful in the psychology of childhood than the need for love and approval.

It might be one of the biggest stretches imaginable for our hearts on this earth – to abandon our shallow, egotistical dreams and to realise how much better our real children are than any dream could be.

Fixing it with your father

Clearly, things are best worked out between living fathers and sons. Once you accept this as a necessary step in your own liberation, it comes down to practicalities. Men I talk with often say they avoid starting any real discussion with their father for fear of starting a huge fight – of making matters worse. 'He's too old to change now', they say. 'It's better to let things be.' Perhaps many fathers also live in fear that their sons will show up armed with sacks full of blame and criticism of their inadequacy. They are hardly likely to expect a good outcome.

Here are the instructions!

How to talk to your dad

1. *Always go in with an open mind.* Don't start with your fists up and an attitude of, 'Justify yourself, you bastard!'

2. *Talk to him alone.* You must talk to him when your mother is not present, or he will never be able to be completely truthful. Many men make compromises to make their marriage work. You need to be somewhere where he can be his complete self.

3. *Create the setting deliberately.* Don't just go out for coffee, at least for this critical stage – a cafe is too public a place for tears to flow, or voices to be raised. Arrange for some privacy.

4. *Give it some time.* There must be no hurry. If you sense it will be hard to get started, consider inviting him on a trip, or at least a drive. But if you really want to move things

along, spend a couple of nights away, camping or fishing, go interstate for a concert or a sports game, or whatever you both might enjoy.

5. *Start with a sense of inquiry.* Ask him for the real, true story about his life. Especially ask how it was for him when you were born, and during your childhood. Ask him about his work, his life and the decisions he made. Be non-judgemental. (If you find it hard to be this way, imagine that one day your son will weigh you on these same scales. That usually helps!) Try to have no agenda other than understanding. Your father may well be suspicious, waiting for you to spring the trap. Unless you can really be open, you may not get the real story.

6. *Be prepared to give your version.* Let him know how it was for you, but without being vengeful or attacking him. You may be angry and say so, but do not attack or impugn him. There needs to be to and fro. The truth – his truth – will often be quite different from your childhood

> impressions. You are humanising your father in your own mind by doing this, filling out the picture, letting him step out from the role all children cast their parents in.
>
> Some fathers will be totally evasive, leaving the room, refusing point blank to speak. I've known fist-fights to develop, but I don't recommend this! Remember the goal – you are breaking down the barriers, the pretences, not the man. Take it slowly.

A young friend in Germany had always known that his father had survived something terrible in World War Two. All he knew was that his father had been about eleven when Russian soldiers came to their village; he had never spoken of what happened. He had always been a remote, tense man, though deeply caring for his children.

My friend asked his father for help with redecorating his apartment, knowing the father would make the long journey to help. They painted and worked for five days. On the last day, the father finally began to talk about the war. What he recounted having witnessed was horrific (there is no need to detail it here). He wept, and the two men put down their brushes and held each other. The old man needed his son to understand what he had been through, what had made him so tense for all those years. He was finally ready to do this.

It happened because my friend created the time and the place, and was patient, so the two of them could find peace.

The problems between fathers and sons can sometimes be very simple, not traumatic at all. Trevor (now in his early fifties) gave this example.

When he was a boy, Trevor's father would take him on a paper round by car each morning. They spent about two hours together each day in a peaceful rhythm of teamwork, as the sun slowly came up and melted the frost. It was his favourite time of the day: he loved the closeness to his father and the feeling of being useful in a man's world. Then one day, his father was offered a chance to leave his day job (which he hated) and be a partner in the newsagency that owned the paper round. To his son's dismay, he turned it down. The newsagency business was sold and the paper round ended.

Trevor stayed angry about this for 30 years. 'He doesn't want to be with me!' When his dad got old and sick, Trevor asked him about it.

'How come you didn't buy into the newsagency and keep up the paper round?'

'Because the partner had a gambling problem, and we would have gone broke.'

Simple as that.

Children often do not know what is going on, and we as parents don't always make the right judgement about when to involve them and when not to. They may just come to the conclusion that we don't like them, and keep that conclusion for life.

These are important things to clear up. As you talk to your father, you may find that things fall into place. One of the biggest things is to simply say, 'Thanks'. There may be many specific memories or instances that you recall as a beautiful part of your growing up. Your father may have no idea that he ever 'got it right'.

Other families preserve a kind of mythical consensus that they were always happy and got on just fine. Which of course no family ever really is, or does. This can cause real problems, as the barrier to trust is the fact that the real picture is not being faced up to. It is okay to tell your father what you hated, what you found terrifying, or how lonely and sad you felt through his lack of appreciation and warmth. He may rail back at you. He may just criticise you all over again. Don't give up – you are not a child now. Stay clear-headed. Ask why. Ask to know everything. Eventually, some understanding – some forgiveness, perhaps an apology or some perspective – will enter the air between you.

No-one can predict how this will happen. Prepare to be surprised.

One of the few definites that emerged from twentieth-century psychology was that unfinished business has to be finished. It isn't enough to 'forgive and forget' – to say 'They had it tough' or 'They were only doing their best' or 'They're old now, so why make waves?' This doesn't address the truth, nor does it address the child in you who has real hurt that needs to be acknowledged. *It isn't possible to forgive what hasn't first been acknowledged.* Avoiding this work patronises your father and sells you short. Deep down you both know it's a lie, and you just become more distant. Forgiveness is the goal, but you have to make the journey to reach that goal, without short-cuts.

Remember that the aim is to get things right between you. You are not there to get even, to 'make him suffer like he made me suffer' or anything like that. That would just spin the wheels of pain around one more time. You are aiming for a resolution that is real and complete. Remember that old saying, 'the child is father to the man'? That means sometimes it's your role to help your parent grow up. It's natural and normal for offspring to bring growth and healing to a parent's life. The aim is a good one: to heal both of you, before it is too late.

At peace with yourself

Most men find talking about their father an uncomfortable subject, and men have succeeded in avoiding it for many generations. This is a pity, because in doing so they cut their own roots. Therapeutic lore tells us we have to make peace with our parents, but ancient tradition takes a less compromising approach. In a sense, you are your father. You are an individual only to the extent that you build your own structure on top of what he has given you. Deep down inside you stand on all kinds of foundations that you must get to know, allow for and understand. Most of us have discovered, uneasily, that we have gestures, mannerisms or ways of doing things that are exactly those of our father. The answer isn't to try to eradicate them. The psyche throws nothing away. You have to learn to love 'your father in you'. If you don't deal with this, then you will very often be at war with yourself.

How many men do you know who are like this? As they split the wood or fix the car, or write a letter, you can almost hear them muttering in argument with a long-dead ghost:

'You're making a mess of that, son!'

'Piss off, Dad!'

Forgiving your father – not just by an effort of will, but by actually understanding his life – will be one of the most freeing things you ever do.

Some men get very sad at this point because their father is already dead, and the conversations I am suggesting can never take place. It seems that an opportunity has been lost forever. Not true. He is in you, and you can begin the process. In imagination, in dreaming, by talking to his gravestone or writing him a letter, you can begin to shift the grief. It is awkward, but important. You can go on an actual, personal odyssey – finding out more information, travelling to his place of birth and locations of significant events in his life, talking to his contemporaries, starting to fill in the missing details. Very often, it helps you to discuss this quest with other men on similar journeys. We all have so much in common – we can help to release each other's grief, finding support and clarification at the same time. A surprising amount of feeling flows out with this process, and much health and strength flow in to take its place.

Don't run from the past; it is always, eventually, a treasure trove.

IN A NUTSHELL

- Out of 100 men, usually only ten are close to their father.
- There is a natural cycle of boys being close to their dad, then being more prickly in their mid-teens, finding independence, then coming back and being very close as adults.
- Today most men are estranged or distant from their dad, so this cycle is not completed.
- The 'father wound' really harms men in their growth and happiness.

- Healing things with your father is often the key to feeling good as a man, to unblocking the river of your masculinity.
- Many men are making this journey and, though difficult, it can be very liberating.

Image 5

THREE

Men and women

'Anyone who is afraid to break, within and without, is in the wrong marriage.'

Michael Ventura

Unless you are Canadian, you have probably never heard of Alden Nowlan. He was a newspaperman and poet, probably Canada's most famous poet of the twentieth century. Photos of him show a big-bodied, whiskery man, with thoughtful eyes behind thick glasses.

Nowlan was not your typical poet. Born in the Great Depression to a fifteen-year-old unmarried mother who soon abandoned him, he had a tough life even for those tough times. Leaving school at the age of twelve to work in logging camps, he eventually made his way into journalism. Somehow, along the road, he acquired an extraordinary perceptiveness about male feelings, and the struggle to be ethical and good. He died a wise and much-loved man.

One night, travelling home after midnight from his job at a city newspaper, Nowlan glimpsed a scene in a side street that inspired one of his best-known poems. Through the fast-falling snow, he saw a sailor arguing with a young woman in thin party clothes, who was lying on the ground, unable or unwilling to get to her feet. The traffic lights changed, and he had to drive on, but couldn't shake the scene from his mind.

He surmised, rightly or wrongly, the story. A group of young sailors out on the town met up with some girls, also looking for a 'good time'. They all drank way too much. The young couple were somehow separated from the group. Now, with her too inebriated even to stand up, he is responsible – not something he had bargained on. If he is late back to his ship, he is AWOL ('absent without leave'), a serious offence. If he just leaves her, she might well freeze to death. It's 20 degrees below, there is no-one about. The poem ends with a trenchant line: 'He's finding out *what it means to be a man,* and how different it is from the way that only hours ago he imagined it.'

The poem is titled 'Rites of Manhood', giving a clue that it is more than a cautionary tale about dating. It is about being adult, and the very surprising depths of that journey.

As the young man in the tale began his night on the town, he had what almost all young men have: an idea about women based on their obvious delights. Soft flesh, laughter, beguiling eyes, the promise of exciting encounters ... gifts to be gained. We all come to women with the idea of *what they can give us.* We think we are so manly in this sexual intent, and yet it's infantile, too. We are looking for candy; someone to make us feel better. Someone to mother us, if we are honest.

Then, for the young man in the poem, this girl does something very challenging, which all women sooner or later do (to our great benefit, though it never feels that way). She turns out to be human; all too much so. In this case, drunk almost to the point of coma. Not only will she not be his lover, she won't even cooperate in being rescued! Even in a one-night stand, but more importantly in a lifelong relationship, things always turn out to be more complex than we planned.

Nature is bountiful, and young love gives us a free ride on the energies of natural attraction. But sooner or later, every partner, woman or man, turns out to not always be interested in *being the mirror reflection of our want*s. This comes as a shock, because it isn't part of the fantasy. Sooner or later, a young man has to wake up to the fact that women are real people. Neither angels nor devils, but just like us, fallible and difficult, sometimes giving, sometimes needing. Love is a flesh-and-blood thing, and it asks a lot of us. At this stage, it's important not to panic, not to think you have fallen out of love because you are in a rough patch. Relationships deepen by going through storms every now and then. They get better and better, and you become stronger and more loving, if you know how to navigate through these times. This chapter is all about how you do that.

> Sooner or later, a young man has to wake up to the fact that women are real people.

Deciding to commit

We spend twenty-plus years of our lives, and a lot of effort, becoming independent – emotionally, practically and financially. Then partnering puts this into reverse. It means giving away some control over your life, making joint decisions and sometimes compromises. It also means becoming vulnerable. If we give our heart to someone, will they betray us? If we give our body to someone, will they be faithful? My favourite Steve Martin film, *The Jerk,* has this beautiful line:

> *'She made love with me! She's had my name tattooed on her butt! It's right there in the D's.'*

If we live together, will they do their share of the cleaning up? If we lend them money, will they pay it back? (Watch a week of *Judge Judy* episodes and see how many 'emotional two-year-olds' are forming adult relationships these days.)

The word 'interdependence' is a good one for what we are seeking as mature adults. We know we can make it on our own, but we choose to interweave our life with another person. The big steps in life – marrying, deciding to have children – require depending on each other to a degree that is breathtaking. It takes a lot of courage to say, 'I will need you to be there for about thirty years. How about it?' Deciding to have children really seals the deal: you will need each other utterly from that moment on.

Why would anyone take such a gamble? Firstly, it should not be a total gamble, if you take the time and go through a few testing experiences to see who this person really is, in good times and bad. The real reason for taking the next step is that *a couple is an amazing thing to be part of.* It's much more than just an escape from loneliness; in fact that's a poor reason to start with. (You have friends for that.) In a loving partnership you can be braver and truer to your dreams and ideals; your partner encourages and supports the best in you. Together you can attempt goals that would never have been possible on your own. Life is more fun. You have someone looking out for you, you learn each other's strengths, and cover each other's weaknesses. A partner who loves you is an incredible gift. The question is – do you have what it takes? We'll look at that next.

Being able to nurture and care

The young woman in the Alden Nowlan poem was foolish to drink so much. But nerves and inexperience catch all of us sometimes. Will she be able to count on this young stranger to get her to safety? We go out on dates to have a good time, but underneath is the search – will we find someone with those qualities that *would make us want to stay?*

Women, perhaps more than men, are conscious of what is at stake in life. They come to a potential mate with important questions. Is this person kind?

Will he run away if things get tough? Is he strong in a crisis? Does he have himself sorted out? Or is he just interested in *what he can take?*

Some men are eternal babies: they look at women as a series of mothers to take care of them. It's clearly not a two-way thing. There are usually enough gullible women for these man-babies to be able to move from one to another, gradually wearing out their welcome on planet earth!

If, as a young man, you don't feel ready for interdependence, then don't start. It's better to spend a few years growing up, fending for yourself, travelling unaccompanied; being really, really lonely – and discovering that you don't die from it. All of these experiences work to grow you up and give you inner strength. Then you can decide whether you want to go to the next level. *Only when you have mastered independence can you step safely into closeness.*

The heart of the matter is this: a boy approaches a woman wanting to take; a man approaches a woman willing to give. He brings reserves of kindness and nurturing, knowing that greater rewards come when rewards are not all that you seek.

Choosing commitment, couplehood and family is like choosing to go for Olympic Gold. You only have one life, and while there can be new starts, time is precious. Deciding that with this woman, at this time in my life, I want to start to create a family is an enormous thing. It will take everything you've got, and – hopefully – give you everything back. There is nothing in life that beats the feeling of seeing your kids grown up, their kids running about, everyone safe and happy, and your wife slipping a tender arm around your waist. But it's a big mountain: the climb is dangerous and hard. Zorba the Greek called it 'the full catastrophe'. It's not for the faint-hearted or the unsure.

Your needs matter, too

While love is built on willingness to give, that doesn't mean being a martyr. It takes balance – we have to respect our own needs and values while also caring about someone else. It's a kind of dance, and everyone stumbles a little while learning it.

Young men in love tend to take extreme positions. They are either totally besotted – 'I would do anything for her' – or totally selfish – 'I have to possess her as my own.' Neither is a recipe for a long and happy relationship.

Human beings have needs (beyond food and shelter) that are necessary to our wellbeing. Here is a rough list:

- To be loved
- To be appreciated
- To have time to oneself
- To socialise with friends
- To exercise
- To be creative
- To do useful work
- To have a sexual life, and
- To have a spiritual life.

Each is an 'essential vitamin'; leaving even one of these out will bring you unstuck in time. If you are interested, go back over the list and choose which is missing for you at the moment. Can you feel how that may be harming you? How could you do something about that?

Denying one's own needs works only in the short term. A relationship is never static; it's a lot like a dance – a bit this way, a bit that way, first you lean on me, then I lean on you! Long-term, it has to make everyone happy at least some of the time. A family or couple is dysfunctional when they cannot find a way to balance the needs of all. A functional family is a *happiness-generating system:* people thrive, nobody misses out. In a dysfunctional family, *someone always gets harmed.*

> A functional family is a *happiness-generating system:* people thrive, nobody misses out.

A mature man, then, is *not* one who has swung right across from being selfish and pleasure-driven to being a martyr. Rather, he stands in the middle place. He cares about the other person. He cares about himself. He gives out of his fullness, which is a deeper well than he might realise. He is flexible, generous and nurturing. He also asks for what he would like to have happen.

He is careful not to demand or intimidate; but he puts his needs out there with dignity and self-respect.

What he wants might be that they both take a trip to the beach, or that he spends a week away with friends, or that they buy a sailing boat with the money they saved for furniture! Often what men mean, when they think about wants, is, of course, sex. (So often is this the case that we have a whole chapter on it, coming up next.) But for now, let's stay with the bigger picture.

Standing together, alone

Love is a journey. It's also a kind of classroom. The way we do it at the start is very different from how we end up.

Young and newly formed couples get close by almost melting into each other. They are a tangle of arms and legs, breathing each other's breath. Refugees from loneliness, they cling together in relief at having found someone who cares. The odd thing is that, at this stage, they don't really know each other at all, *but they make up for that with imagination.* It's as if each provides a blank screen onto which the other projects all their hopes and dreams. The problem is that, being so linked, their happiness totally depends on the other. Deeply insecure, they watch intently for any sign of diminished love.

Then, as the hours and days together start to add up, the real relationship begins, the long struggle *to birth the real person* behind the fantasy. Gradually, each partner becomes more real and more delineated – they act more like themselves. Over time, if they don't panic, but allow the relationship to contain differences of preference and direction – if they respect the other person's separateness – then something good happens. They both strengthen as people; they become more whole. People in healthy relationships will notice this and comment on it – 'I am a better person around her', 'He makes me feel more able to be myself.'

It's not only in couplehood, but also in life overall, that you gradually become more yourself, strengthened by the push and pull of relating to other people.

Zen teachers tell the story of a man who lived in a cave for 40 years and achieved profound peace. When he finally emerged back into the world, walking back among the crowded marketplace, a clumsy young man tripped and bumped him into a barrow full of fruit. The enlightened monk was so startled that he swore, turned in a rage, and punched the poor boy in the face! So much for the cave! It didn't teach him to be peaceful *amidst people.*

Living in a relationship helps you develop a clear sense of your boundaries, define your values and limits, and acquire a healthy self-protectiveness that prevents you melting like a mush into each other's emotional troubles. You can care for the other person without having your emotions tied up in theirs. It's not helpful if 'he is down when she is down', or if 'she is angry with him for being angry with her'. It takes time to learn this. If you get to a point of real conflict and leave the relationship, you do not learn. A new relationship will have to get to that same place all over again, and still you might or might not break through.

As we grow, we strengthen. So even though our love deepens, our dependency gets less. It's a paradox that takes a bit of grasping. People can hate each other and be very enmeshed; usually they are. And people can love each other and stand separate and apart. You sometimes meet old couples who have cracked this secret: you will see them holding hands and laughing as they walk. Their eyes sparkle, and they can sum you up in a glance. They are feisty and cranky with the world and with each other, but it's a tender crankiness.

When your partner is difficult, or draws boundaries, and does not always want what you want, welcome this – it is helping you both along to this goal. Only when you are fully individuated, clearly your own person, can you really be close. You are no longer role-playing: it's the real you and the real her. It's a remarkable feeling.

The two deadly myths

Today we think we are modern and hard-nosed about relationships, but some of our expectations are straight out of a fairytale. Two common 'Hallmark' myths that need to be booted out are:

1. That people who love each other do not argue. *If you argue, it means you have problems.*
2. That the key to happiness is finding a compatible partner. *If you find someone who likes what you like, then everything will be fine.*

I may as well 'give it to you straight': both of these beliefs are untrue. Healthy and happy couples argue, too, especially in the early years, as well as at certain key times of growth and improvement. And compatibility is no guarantee of success. You can be very different, with different interests, and still get along very well. Sometimes better.

Remember when you were a little child, and sometimes you made a friend whom you thought was just the best friend ever? You played the same games, liked the same things, laughed and had fun. Then something went wrong: they wouldn't do what you wanted, said something mean, or wouldn't share. Then you hated them – they were the worst person. It was all very immediate and very intense. But you got over it, and gradually learnt that friends don't always agree. As a Russian proverb puts it, you are not really friends until you have had a fight.

Not arguing can in fact be a very bad sign. (One typical pattern in a failed marriage is many years of not arguing, followed by a huge bust-up.) Differences are like garbage, something that just has to be dealt with. Some people take out the garbage every week. Others let it pile up for ten years, then *send for a skip!*

The trick lies in *how* you argue, and in this respect happy and unhappy couples differ a great deal. If you are at a tough place in your marriage (and all growing marriages have these), you need to learn how to argue *better* – to disagree without causing hurt or harm, and hopefully sort out the differences. For we men, who are not always as quick or as good with words, this can be hard. As with so many aspects of a man's life, we haven't been taught this very well.

How to argue well

'I've been married for fifty years. And I'm winning!'

This is a joke because it defines marriage as a contest; and for some sad folks, it is. So here's the secret of a dynamic and positive marriage – don't argue to win. Argue to find a better way forward, using both your and her ideas. One old man told me, 'It's taken me forty years to learn that two heads are better than one. You can nut out something that's different from what you went in thinking, and you don't mind a bit.' Often, better ideas come from the heat of disagreement if you can just stay flexible. Don't fold for the sake of peace, but don't be dogmatic, either.

If you are not sure how to do this, here are the steps.

Image 6

Arguing well

1. *Think before you speak.* Something the other person says, does, or asks of you does not seem right. It's wrong for you, or unfair, or doesn't match your values or ideas about what should happen. Before you open your mouth, go inside yourself and check out your thinking. Check that you are not just being mean-spirited, or taking revenge for something else (e.g. 'You were grumpy with me when I walked in the

door. I won't agree to those new curtains. That'll teach you.').

If you *are* being grumpy about something else, do not proceed with this argument. You will be arguing about the wrong thing.

2. *Speak out, gently and respectfully.* 'That doesn't feel right to me.' 'Can I tell you my point of view?' (Don't start unless you get a 'yes'.)

3. *Ask to hear more of her side of the story.* 'Tell me why you think that.' 'Can you say some more about why you want to do that?'

4. *Consider their side of it.* Looked at from her point of view, does her argument make sense? Would you think that way if you were her?

This step is so important that I want to spell it out more. Neuroscientists believe that the hardest thing for the human mind is not astrophysics or brain surgery, it is *being able to step inside the point of view of another person, without letting go of your own.* Being able to put yourself into someone else's skin is a big leap, and yet once you can do it, you live life on a whole different plane. Keep trying and it will come. Try asking yourself, *'If I were her, how would I feel about me?'* There is hope for you if ever, in the heat of an intense argument, you suddenly have the thought, 'Perhaps she has a point!' But at the same time, don't abandon your own point of view just for the sake of peace (or because you want to maximise your chances of a good time in bed that night).

5. *Re-evaluate.* Does her point of view, when you really try it on for size, impact on your own views at all? A lot? Not at all?

6. *Keep talking.* Refine the argument to its essential point. Pinpoint where you disagree, but also say where you *do* agree. Be willing to shift, and let her know this. At least *let her know that you can see her point of view,* even if you don't see it the same.

Continue doing these steps: listen, think, speak. Listen, think, speak – and notice how it goes. You might find that you can compromise, or in fact that you are persuaded to her point of view. Or it might be that you just have to go on disagreeing. It's not a drama to have some parts of your marriage or relationship that are differed on, so long as they are not core values (more on this shortly). Some things in life might take 30 years to get sorted out – 'Oh, NOW I see what you mean!'

Sometimes, of course, you do 'win', in that your point of view is the one decided on. But it's because your partner has understood and appreciated your thinking. And when you 'lose', it's not losing, because you have seen that she's right. You will know the difference because you will feel light and uplifted on the inside. *You will feel closer to her.*

Women want men who are real

While you shouldn't aim to win, you shouldn't aim to lose either. Many men are surprised to realise that being a wuss, agreeing with their partner for the sake of peace, does not make her happy or lead to a peaceful life.

Women are only human. This means they are sometimes right and sometimes completely wrong. Not only can your partner at times be immature, perverse, prejudiced, competitive or bloody-minded, sometimes you and she just will see things differently. Women *often* don't understand men. How can they unless we explain ourselves to them? That doesn't mean you can't get along, just that you have to keep negotiating!

I have heard hundreds of women say in frustration, 'My husband won't fight with me, he won't even argue. He just walks away.' Perhaps the husband walks away because he doesn't want to get violent, like his father used to do. Or perhaps he had a pushy mother and a weak father, and thinks that's just what men do. Retreating is all he knows how to do. To have a happy marriage, a man has to be able to state his point of view, to debate, to leave aside hysteria, and push on with an argument until something is resolved.

Gordon Dalbey tells of a woman who phoned him after he had counselled her husband.

'It's obvious Sam's getting stronger, speaking up for himself and letting me know how he feels,' she said, hesitating. *'I know I've always wanted him to be that way ... but ... I guess there's a part of me that kind of enjoyed having the upper hand and being able to manipulate him into doing what I wanted. I want to be strong enough myself so that I don't do that any more.'*

It's a great tribute to this woman that she is willing to give up some power in order to experience a really equal relationship, based on intimacy and negotiation, not on emotional dominance.

The Warrior

There is a part of every healthy man or woman's inner being which we could call 'the Warrior'. The Warrior guards the walls of your emotional castle and protects you from mistreatment or abuse.

When I work with sexually abused clients, a final step in the healing is to help them become so angry and experience such burning rage that they mobilise all their physical and mental energy. They have never breathed so deeply, yelled so loud, focused so clearly. Once this energy has started to flow, I have no fear that they will ever be abused again. People who have access to their inner rage are awe-inspiring. When the Warrior is mobilised, the child within can finally feel safe. A woman who does this work can now begin to be close to a man. She will feel able and willing to bear a child. I have known fertility problems to disappear through this work – as if a woman's body would not bear a child until her mind knew she could and would protect that child.

> We all want to be close, but no-one likes the feeling of being swamped or taken over.

For a marriage to thrive, both partners need to bring their Warriors along. It's not that the other person wishes them harm, just that people getting close will inevitably overstep the other's boundaries, and need to be reminded. Often it's enough to say, 'Hey, you are crowding me', 'Please don't make my mind up for me' or 'Let me choose my own clothes.'

'Will you leave my desk as it is – I know where to find things!'

'But I was just tidying it up.'

'Well, please don't.'

We all want to be close, but *no-one likes the feeling of being swamped or taken over.*

Both partners can learn more respect for the other's need for selfhood. Sometimes you just need some space and time to yourself. At other times, there will be a real clash of realities, and more exploration will be needed. Couples fight in order to root out fixed attitudes or longer-term misunderstandings, and pull them into the light of day. *Sometimes, it gets down to the wire.* John Lee, in his book *At My Father's Wedding,* wrote about confronting a wife's drinking and abusive behaviour.

After decades of constant compromise of my essential self, I will not do so to be loved by you. I'll compromise on where we live, where we eat, how many children we have, what movie we see, where our children will go to school, but not on matters that jeopardise my soul – I need you to stop drinking in this house. I need the abuse to stop. I demand safety. I need mutual respect and equality. I will not settle for less than what I know I deserve, which is health. I will not compromise my recovery to be in a relationship.

There are bottom lines to what we can accept in another person's behaviour – care with money, relating to others, keeping promises, being trustworthy, how time is allocated, sharing the work. In most strong relationships, these issues have at some time to be confronted. Don't duck away from them; they will not go away of their own accord.

Safe fighting

It's paradoxical that we can only let our feelings flow freely, and only be truly passionate, when we have certain boundaries laid down. Trust has to be there. To fight safely means:

- never being physical or threatening
- not storming out of the room or out of the house mid-fight, or slamming down the phone
- not using abusive or put-down language, sarcasm or scorn
- staying on the point and not bringing in other material
- talking in specific terms about here and now – not 'You always...' or 'You never...'
- listening to the other's point of view while honouring your own, and
- taking time out, by agreement, if it becomes too heated – to think it over and return later with a fresh point of view.

These rules allow you to debate cleanly and respectfully, until understanding is reached.

None of this talk of being reasonable and careful should be taken to mean that sometimes a flaming row isn't what's needed, or that if you occasionally become passionate in disagreement that isn't a good thing. While hysterical escalation and the playing of 'uproar', with its walkouts and poisoned exchanges, is to be avoided, sometimes a calm and uptight couple need to explode a little. *Sometimes until you start shouting, you might not know what it is that you need to shout.* Jungian analyst Marie-Louise von Franz tells a story about a woman friend who had a series of disastrous marriages. They always started well, but each time the arguing eventually led to physical fighting and divorce.

The friend's fourth husband was different. The very first time the wife 'threw a fit' (her words) and began to be wildly abusive, the man simply walked quietly to his room and began packing his things. He refused to fight 'dirty' as was being expected. His words are beautiful: 'I know I am supposed to act like a man now and shout and hit you, but I am not that sort of man. I will not allow anyone to talk to me in the way you have, and I am leaving.' The woman was so shocked, she apologised. They are still together.

There is a capacity in all of us for blind rage. If you feel this rising in you, better to make your excuses, politely, and negotiate a breather. Sometimes all we really need is some time to be with ourselves.

There is something to add here that is a little mystical and dark, but that many readers will appreciate. We have a long history of gender-inflicted pain in our civilisation, thousands of years of mistreatment. If we are not careful, we can catch this dark energy and pass it on. A personal argument can turn into all-out gender hatred, summoning all the frustration of womanhood towards all men, and of all men towards women. No individual can bear to carry the intensity of all this suffering. And no-one deserves to.

Ending domestic violence

***Stuart Anderson** is in his mid-fifties but has the energy of a much younger man. He has that rare quality of being both humble and at the same time very clear and grounded in what he is on about. In short, you feel you can trust him. I have known him for 20 years; he does the best work in Australia on helping men to stop hitting their wives. Stuart works in the Lismore region with rural men, including Aboriginal men, on the problem of domestic violence, and his approach and training of domestic-violence workers takes him all over the country.*

Domestic violence is a pervasive and often intractable problem that causes misery in families, and may recur down the generations. It's a problem that men themselves increasingly wish to overcome, so that they can both show and receive respect from their partners and families. Early programs, such as the US-based Duluth approach, took a controlling and judgmental attitude:

they were based in ideas of generic male badness and, not surprisingly, showed very poor results.

There are some key understandings needed to deal with men caught in a pattern of violent anger. The first is that anger itself is not the problem. Safe and responsible people get angry, too, but they do it in a different way. (Schools in the Lismore region now offer programs for both boys and girls called Keeping Kool, which specifically teach anger management.)

Becoming safe to others involves first of all recognising your own body's early warning signals. Many violent men have very poor self-awareness, and simply do not recognise that they are getting worked up. A twitching stomach, shallow, fast breathing, tense shoulders and a racing heart can, if noticed and responded to with a positive strategy, help you avoid a blow-up. Taking a breather, going and sitting in the car (but probably not driving away!), going to another room, taking a walk ... To sidestep the *potential violence,* you have to first notice that the *build-up* is happening. This skill can be learnt.

For men to change requires the help of other men. To admit to the fear and confusion (most anger is a cover for fear, insecurity and and inability to know what else to do) means that you have to feel emotionally safe yourself. The worker has to create a bond with the man who is caught in violence. This means that a non-judgemental attitude is essential. Being non-judgemental is not the same as condoning violence. Judgement comes from feeling superior. It automatically breaks the connection, and no useful work can then be done. It's possible to show great concern for the consequences of a man hitting his wife, and a clear message that this is wrong, without judging or rejecting the man as a human being.

Knowing that he will not be attacked, or have his emotions rejected, creates a context for a man to change. The leaders of the program are clear that they too make mistakes and own them, have emotions and own them. Since they are not different from the man caught in violence, it is plausible that that man can also change and become mature and safe. In this way, the man's sense of aloneness is lifted. (When others around us always wear masks of competence and toughness, we may be fooled into thinking we alone are defective, that we are beyond help.)

The programs then begin to help men dismantle the unhealthy patterns, and strengthen the side of them that is caring, respectful and strong. This strengths-based approach builds on the wish to be an even better father, husband and friend.

Time is spent bringing to the surface the unhealthy self-talk, which Stuart calls 'Stinking Thinking'. *'She's out to get me', 'Here we go again', 'I need her to feel the pain I'm in', 'They deserve everything they get'* ... Everyone who harms others seems to have a grab-bag of self-justifying and escalating statements that really don't stand up, and need to be challenged.

Many men live in an emotional desert, deprived of masculine support. There are few situations where boys and young men can learn from older men how to go about being a man, let alone how to go about being a good, principled man, and the rewards that this brings in terms of the respect, love and trust of those around us.

Treating and changing human beings is not something you can learn out of a manual. I am convinced that the healing of domestic violence depends on the heart and the maturity of the man or woman delivering the program. When frightened, out-of-control men or women sense the solidity and acceptance of another person, who will spend as much time as necessary helping them, they can begin to re-program their whole idea of themselves and their choices about how to act.

Violence to women does not exist in isolation. All men and women have their own power tactics, and most use them. In his training program, Stuart elicits from professional workers a very long list of ways that they use to control others in intimate relationships. These can range from raised eyebrows, silence, grunting, being distant or unfriendly, sulking, keeping secrets or not saying where one is going, to angry words or storming off to the pub, right through to threats of leaving, taking one's own life, taking the children, hurting or killing. *All* classes and genders of people use power tactics *whenever* they do not know how to do otherwise. Moving towards relationships based on the honest sharing of feelings, the respectful sorting-out of differences, and a deep-down commitment to respect and equality is a journey we are all on.

Loving incompatibility

Once you can disagree constructively and know how to work things out, compatibility of interests is not such an issue. The heart of the compatibility myth is: if I find someone who likes what I like, *then we will always get along!* Just find someone who loves bushwalking, the beach, war movies, frequent sex, and sport – we can be happily married. (Don't laugh – almost everyone tries.)

I have photographs of my wife in the first year we were going out, on a range of mountaintops around Australia. Closer examination of these pictures reveals that she is laughing, heartbreakingly beautiful, and deeply exhausted. There are no more mountaintop photographs from the subsequent 31 years of our marriage.

Back in my late teens, I dated a warm and outgoing girl whose main interest was the grooming and care of her miniature poodle. I spent many Saturday afternoons amidst the doggy paraphernalia – the combs, the bows, the conditioning shampoo. I don't know what I must have been thinking...

The idea of compatibility is that if we have the same interests, we will have a fun time and, most importantly, *we will not need to fight.* But the truth is, even if you agree on most things, sooner or later conflict has to arise. Let's say you marry someone who does like climbing mountains: you agree to climb Mount Bangahoola. You agree on everything – the route up the mountain, which gear to take, what to eat for dinner each night – and you wear matching shorts. But on the fifth night, she wants to keep going by moonlight, and you have stomach cramps.

There is always something that will cause disagreement. It's how you manage the disagreement that makes the difference. If it's noisy, hysterical, manipulative and wildly escalating across a range of topics, you may as well call the lawyers. But if it's calm, amicable, focused carefully on the issue, and open to the other person's point of view, a remarkable thing becomes possible: you might be able to be blisteringly happy with someone who is almost totally different to you!

One of the happiest couples I know are as different as could be: she a classical musician and lover of croissants, he an environmentalist rancher in the Santa Fe mountains. Their marriage vows included their own special clause – that he never had to go to an opera, and she never had to sleep on the ground!

Values – what are they?

Compatibility of interests is good, but not essential. Compatibility of *values* is a different story. *A partner with shared values is worth searching the world for.*

Values are the principles you run your life by, things you believe in and stick to – such as not hurting people, putting people before possessions, valuing adventure over security (or the other way around). They underlie the choices you make. Values are the core of your self; they are hard-won through painful experience and, in a relationship, have to be shared for things to work out.

Peter was totally smitten with Shanelle. She was affectionate, bubbly and curvaceous. To an IT expert who spent Saturdays polishing his Saab, she was a breath of fresh air. But he began noticing little things. She stole an apple as they walked past a city fruit stall, winking at him as she did so. One day she told him about finding a wallet in the street. *And keeping the cash from it.* Five hundred dollars. He suddenly realised: this is not my way.

Try this little (semi-serious) values quiz.

I believe that it's important in a relationship:
1. to be honest
2. to be reasonably honest, or
3. to be very careful not to be found out.

We are in this world to:
1. make it a better place
2. have fun, or
3. amass a wonderful collection of furniture.

Couples should have children because:
1. it moves you beyond your own importance and into a place of giving and caring that brings lifelong satisfaction and joy
2. ah, well, that's just what you do, or
3. they are *so cute!*

Would your partner give different answers to yours? That might be a problem. Values are what matter to you most deeply. If you have incompatible values, you might as well drill holes in your own kneecaps – it will be less painful in the long run. You might marry a girl because of the curve of her upper lip (there are worse reasons). But whether you are still married 40 years later *will depend on her values.* Values determine how your life will work out. Get the values right, and you will die happy. You need a partner whose life is going in the same direction.

Image 7

The science of happy couples

Psychologist John Gottman is world famous for helping couples. His approach to understanding love and marriage is rather like that of an accountant. His research team uses video sampling of a couple's interactions to predict whether they will divorce or stay together. Astoundingly, they can do so with a 95-percent reliability rate *after watching the couple for just one hour.* Here's an example:

Drew and Claudine walk into the room. Both are in their early thirties. The interviewer says, 'Thanks for coming. What we want you to do is choose something from your life that is a small area of disagreement or contention. And then just go ahead and discuss it.' The interviewer then leaves the room, and a video camera begins to roll.

They discuss getting a dog. Drew doesn't want a dog – their apartment is small, he doesn't think a dog will work very well. Claudine talks about how much she wants one. She definitely wants one, and is going to get one. The shape of the conversation becomes clearly evident: Claudine doesn't listen. They will get a new dog and that's that.

The couple watch the video afterwards, and joke about it, but the interviewer isn't so sure. 'They are newlyweds, still in the glowy phase. But the fact is that she's completely inflexible. They are arguing about dogs, but it's really about how they handle a disagreement. She simply takes no account of his feelings. What Claudine wants, she gets.' The conclusion of the researchers is clear: this pattern of interaction will probably end the marriage, though it may take years. *One day, Drew will have had enough.*

Studying patterns in a couple's conversation style has led to some powerful behavioural options that can help couples shift to a happier way. The key is flexibility. When a person shows flexibility and *willingness to listen* early on, it creates a bond of understanding that, together, you can get through differences.

Gottman found that couples in trouble show four distinct danger signs, which he calls 'The Four Horsemen of the Apocalypse'. These are defensiveness, stonewalling, criticism and contempt.

Defensiveness essentially means going on the counterattack whenever there is implied criticism. Instead of saying, 'Please tell me more', and having a willingness to improve, the partner counterattacks: 'How dare you criticise me.'

Stonewalling is slamming the communication door, refusing to talk about it. The cumulative effect of this is that problems simply pile up and the relationship ices over. You can't feel warm towards someone who won't listen to you.

Criticism seems obvious, but can be hard to acknowledge if you are the critic. You probably think you are just being 'helpful'. The solution lies in the way we speak. If we say, 'I really feel depressed when the kitchen is messy when I get home from work. Please wash the dishes you use', that isn't a criticism, it's a statement of feeling. 'You are such a lazy, thoughtless slob' is a criticism. In case you didn't know!

Contempt is the big one, the atomic bomb of marital destruction. Gottman believes that when one of a couple *habitually shows contempt for the other,* the marriage is essentially doomed. A partner who rolls her eyes, sighs, turns away, sends a very toxic message. Marriage has to have respect. The presence of contempt doesn't mean that a marriage can't be saved. But for it to have a chance, this behaviour has to stop dead in its tracks.

What happy couples do

What is most helpful in Gottman's work is his study of what happy couples do. He believes that deep analysis is not as important as just doing more of the things that work. *If you do more of what happy couples do, then you become happier.*

In happy couples, it's the affectionate, good-humoured and warm exchanges, the soothing contact through touch or smiles that dissolves tensions. All human beings are naturally anxious; we are a deeply social animal. We need small signs of warmth and being valued, even when, and perhaps particularly when, we are sorting out conflict. Even the biggest, toughest man hates feeling that he is not appreciated or liked. Positive messages can signal to a spouse that this is just a passing concern, that nothing is fundamentally wrong. The ratio of positive messages to negatives should be high – around five to one.

The deep-down heart of Gottman's work is that there are not happy and unhappy couples intrinsically, but that if you do the right things you will be happier more of the time. Happy couples still have negatives, but *they don't let them set the tone.*

Your partner's world

Most couples today spend a lot of time apart, and even when together, we are often rushed and busy with our kids' needs. A single strategy may be Gottman's greatest discovery – that happy couples keep a 'database' of their partner's world, a kind of mental map of their challenges, concerns, interests and values. They keep this up to date and they are concerned and interested in how things are going. It might be the last thing they talk about in bed at night, or they might take time once a week to go out for a long lunch, or every night they turn off the TV and just allow some cool-down time after the kids are in bed, to ask, 'How is your life?' This is different to discussing shared problems – the credit-card balance or which school to send the kids to. This is, 'I want to hear about you.' It's a very sweet thing to be able to unburden oneself or to dream and share successes with someone else, knowing they really care and are our support person in life.

> It's a very sweet thing to be able to unburden oneself or to dream and share successes with someone else...

Happy couples have a lot going for them: they live longer, laugh more, and achieve more of their life goals. Best of all, they are just the same as you and me, but they practise these positive aspects. Like most things in life, the more you put into love, the more it gives you back.

IN A NUTSHELL

- A young man rescues a girl from freezing to death, and discovers manhood is quite complex.
- Deciding to commit is a big thing. It brings great gifts, and asks everything in return.
- Being loving and kind is important in relating to women, and so is honouring your own needs. This takes balance and grace.
- As couples grow and mature, they actually become more separate and stronger.
- Arguing well does not mean aiming to win. It means aiming to find a good solution.
- Women like men who stand up to them, in a safe and constructive way.
- Being trustworthy is a huge positive. No self-respecting woman settles for less.
- You don't have to be compatible in everything, but you do have to be compatible in values, because those set the direction of your whole life.
- A good partnership makes life fun and exciting, and gives you courage

and passion for living. It enables you to do and be more in the world.

Image 8

FOUR

Real sex

'Slowly, slowly in bed with a woman, I am learning to be human.'

Jesse Kornbluth

The heart-melting, pulse-pounding joy of making love, with someone you deeply care about and trust, is one of the most intense experiences that human life can give. It makes the whole world seem beautiful, every brick, lamp-post, bird and tree. Even when you are shabby and dishevelled, your surroundings ordinary and your life a struggle, good sex can make it all worthwhile. When you get it right, it can be a glimpse of the sacred – your boundaries dissolve and you are lost among the stars.

Sex can be such a gift. But for many men and women it is nothing of the sort, just an endless source of conflict and pain. For all our knowledge, the millions of words written and spoken about it, sexual joy is still a rare thing, and sexual contentment rarer still. Whereas sexual misery is all around.

Sex really matters to men. The physiological drive in us is huge, and closely tied to it are our feelings of being loved and worthwhile. The result can be a lot of tension loaded onto what is meant to be a flowing and generous experience. We can drive our partner away with our neediness. Being a good lover and partner is actually a difficult skill, because it's a 'people skill', not just about where you put your hands. The ingredients of good loving – kindness, humour, playfulness and passionate connectedness – are all qualities that take time to acquire. These skills are rarely taught to us. This chapter is aimed at remedying that.

Sex is a kind of love

The key to a happier love life lies in understanding our human makeup. While sex is basic and animal on one level, we are not just animals – our hearts and minds have evolved to quite a different plane. Sex is more complicated for us, but it's also much more full of meaning and potential. A wolf or a bear mates and moves on. A human being may intend to do this, but something makes him or her turn back. 'What was that all about? Something shifted inside me. A gateway opened. Where does it lead?'

Knowing about this 'heart connection', that sex is a mind journey as well, changes how we go about it. Sex becomes more than just a hunger to be satisfied. Sex-with-love is one of those combinations in nature that is more than the sum of its parts. You don't just do sex to have it over with; your love life is a story that is going somewhere. Sex is a transformative force, intended to push us deeper into our relationships. Problems with sex are not due to nature being cruel. It's simply that if we are not living up to our potential for love and closeness, our heart will always protest. Sex will go wrong. But it will go wrong in a way that is meant to teach you something.

Whether you are a lonely teenager full of yearnings, or a man in mid-life desperately frustrated by your wife's lack of interest, it's important that you know you are not alone, nor are you lost, but rather that this is a starting point from which all good relationships can grow. Almost all men experience sexual despair and a deep loneliness at some times in their lives. We all yearn to experience deep physical love. But to earn real love, we have to grow up, and grow strong.

The splitting of sex from love

Ours is a bizarre society. Sex is 'in our face' every time we turn on a TV or walk down the street. But at the same time, we seem almost totally ignorant of sex's true meaning and purpose. We don't even have a good language to describe it. Even the word 'sex' itself is too naked, too brightly lit. Something magical and powerful has gone missing.

What a consumer culture often tries to do is isolate us – to make us think sex is just a commodity, like ice cream or beer. Luckily, we are not easily split: human beings are whole and powerfully made. Inside us, everything connects to everything else. Hormones send excitement singing through our brain. A touch on the skin can soften our heart muscles. Our spirit soars when we feel respected, and is crushed when we betray ourselves. Because of this inner unity, what we do with our bodies has to have the consent of all our other parts, or a terrible inner tearing takes place. (That's why prostitutes often turn to drugs – for the numbing required to live such a deception. To be so intimate with strangers requires all kinds of internal conflict and pain.) Try, as so many do, to separate sex from heart and soul – it simply can't be done.

> To earn real love, we have to grow up and grow strong.

Young couples soon discover the 'erk' moment when love-making just doesn't work because they are simply not right with each other. Love can be forgiving: sometimes we can make love when we are furious with each other, and find that it burns the anger away. 'Sexual healing' is a real and tangible thing. But sometimes we have to spend weeks sorting out some comment about curtains and her mother, and something we don't even remember saying, before sex can feel right. (It's not that she is 'holding out', though of course she may be. It's that we can't act close when we are not; it doesn't feel right.) In fact, an 'erk' moment can become an 'erk' month, or year. A relationship barrier needs to be overcome – we need to grow up to the next stage. Men who understand this don't panic, they don't sulk, they grin and get to figuring it out. We want real connection, and this is worth a little pain.

Sex in committed couples is a kind of fiery furnace. Marriage manuals talk about 'working on your relationship', but it's more that your relationship works on you. It melts our egos, and re-forges our relationship into better shapes, over and over again. Our yearning for love drags us yelling and screaming, against our will, to become all that we can be as a man.

A whirlwind of change

Times sure have changed. A man in his sixties has lived through a time when nobody talked about sex, when women were often deeply unfulfilled, and there was a pervasive shame, coming partly from religion and partly from the smutty schoolboy way it was dealt with during one's growing up. The adults who should have passed on the sexual flame to us did not themselves understand or deal with it, so it came laden with fear, guilt, and frustration.

My grandfather, a corporal in the Battle of the Somme by the age of nineteen, came home and married a housekeeper five years his senior. Her generation of women was short of men, over 4 million of whom had perished in the trenches. The pair had three children in rapid succession, then she refused any further sex. He drank, raged, possibly abused at least one of his daughters. Then he took a mistress in a nearby street, diverting much of his money to

her support. It was a disaster. I am sure there were people who forged happy marriages in the first half of the twentieth century, and raised children in laughter-filled and secure homes, but they must have been extraordinary people.

Then, in the late 1960s and 1970s, came the 'sexual revolution'. Suddenly there was openness and discussion about female orgasm, masturbation and 'foreplay'. Unless you lived through this time, it's impossible to convey the sense of relief that sprang up, let alone the excitement and liberation. The contraceptive pill removed, almost in an instant, the eternal fear of pregnancy and disgrace, especially for the unmarried. Homosexuality, once a dark and dangerous world, began its journey towards acceptance. Men and women could access help and information, talk about needs and feelings with partner and friends and, above all, feel normal: that one wasn't a pervert, or insane, for having sexual feelings.

Then, somehow, it all went off the rails. In Gore Vidal's words, we went from a sexual revolution to a sexual circus. We hadn't understood the needs for boundaries, especially to protect the vulnerable and the young. The corporate hyenas moved in, advertising and TV teaching kids that sex was a fashion accessory or a passport to popularity. Today, fourteen-year-old girls photograph their genitals or breasts with their mobile phones, and email the pictures to the boys. Eight-year-olds make themselves vomit to keep slim. Parents dress their babies in t-shirts that read, 'Daddy only wanted a blowjob.' Sexual assaults happen in primary schools. Rape and torture are described on the six-o'clock news. There is a feeling, even among those who campaigned long and hard for the sexual revolution, that things have gone, if not too far, at least in quite a wrong direction.

Where once the church made us miserable by condemning sex as sinful, the new religion of consumption promotes it as a must-do. Sexualised billboards and department-store ads assault us everywhere we look. The sexually posed teenage girl is the most common image in the world, visible everywhere, 20 metres high. Men notice them in a frustrated, resentful way; women feel insecure because they don't look like them. It's not clear that such public erotica makes anyone happier.

Junk sex and real sex

Sex is disruptive, wild and intense. Every ancient culture realised this, and surrounded it with taboos, initiations, secret teachings. It was rarely a free-for-all. Like precious metal or explosives, its magic had – and has – to be carefully handled. A craft like this takes time to master. Once we accept, even at the age of 40 or 50, that we are still learning the craft, we can let go of our panic and begin to apply ourselves. So what do we need to know?

The first, most fundamental thing to learn is that there are two completely different kinds of sexual experience. Let's call them 'junk sex', and 'real sex'. Junk sex – shallow, brief sexual experiences with partners with whom you have little emotional connection –

can be exciting and confidence-boosting. Junk sex can be addictive, and for many men and women it is the only kind of sex they know. However, 'a penis and a vagina going out on a date together' (as family therapist Carl Whittaker so pithily expressed it) is very soon a trip to boredom. Without their humanness, their hearts and minds coming along on the journey, it's going nowhere, and the first time is the best it's going to get. Junk sex, like junk food, leaves a nasty taste, doesn't nourish you, and slowly begins to poison your soul.

Real sex is nothing like junk sex. Your heart, mind and soul are all put on the line, transformed in the fire. That's why it's called 'making love'. Once you have made love, then just having sex is never enough.

There is a trap here for young men caught in the 'singles scene'. In pursuing junk sex, you may never experience the real thing, as it's reached by a very different route. You won't meet the right kind of person, in the right kind of circumstances for conversation and exploring common ground or values, in the kind of places people go for quick and easy mating. Someone who will have junk sex with you is 'likely to be as big a loser as you are' (as a shocked young man once told me). The recommendation on junk sex, the one-night stand – 'she's not Miss Right but she's Miss Right Now' – is to avoid it where possible. Hold out for the real thing (even with your existing partner), and you will invite the possibility that your life may take a completely different direction.

> Once you have made love, then just having sex is never enough.

Good things take time. (While it's possible to have a profound, life-changing relationship that lasts only for a day, it's a rare thing.) If you want to be still in love and excited at 40 and 60, be prepared for a substantial and careful search. Aim high. A woman worth winning will not be a pushover; she will need to see that you have got grit, humour and endurance. The old mythologies were right: finding the right woman – and, more difficult still, persuading her to like you – is a quest.

Differing appetites

Seeing sex as just a physical drive leads to many problems, both in beginning and long-established relationships. Most men desperately struggle, at some stage, with 'getting enough' sex. If a man stays stuck in this viewpoint, it actually leads to more sexual frustration. (A woman worth her salt will quickly sense that she is just a means to an end.) Your partner is not likely to find this an inviting prospect; neither would you, in her shoes. Sometimes a woman will be generous and accommodating, just to make her partner happy, but over time this feeling wears out. When sex isn't going well, the answer is not to examine the sex, but to examine the relationship – 'fix the love, and the sex will take care of itself'.

Deep down, a man wants more from love-making than simply to release sexual tension. You could pay a woman to have sex with you, but no amount of money would make her *want* you. Yet being wanted is what makes sex truly satisfying. A relationship is something that is meant to grow. A warm and feisty woman offers the chance of closeness, excitement and trust. However, she needs to be won, not once, but over and over. She too shares your wish for passionate, intense sex, but she needs a strong partner to have it with. How then can you win her; how can you find your way to real human connection? The first step is realising there is more to sex than you thought. It's about being the best person you can be, someone this woman would be excited and proud to love. It's not that men have made sex too important, but that we have not made it important enough.

Image 9

Three stages of love

The idea that love-making comes naturally is a common misconception, so it's little wonder that couples feel terrible if it goes badly. 'What's wrong with us?' It's an immediate relief to know that no couple who ever lived in this world had exactly equal levels of desire. The most outstanding thinker in this field, Dr David Schnarch, has worked with hundreds of couples with differences in desire, and he believes that such couples are totally normal. His work has revolutionised couples therapy by pointing out that it's only by growing through sexual difficulties that we progress out of adolescent infatuation into mature adult passion. His message, in a nutshell, is: don't panic.

In his book *Intimacy and Desire,* Schnarch describes how every relationship passes through three stages. The first is the free ride – exuberant early sex. Second, for all couples, come difficulties in communication and understanding, with what looks like a chronic problem of differing desires.

Then finally, if the couple hang in through this, keep talking, and develop emotional independence, there comes a strengthening and emergence of real sex.

Real sex is:
- adult
- independent
- mature
- generous
- non-manipulative
- freely-chosen
- desire-based, and
- loving.

You can't have good sex when your relationship is manipulative, codependent, abusive, mean, sulky, withdrawn, threatening, anxious or shallow (which covers just about all of us!). A process of cleaning out these immaturities, confronting the bad things in your marriage, is part of the return of desire.

Good sex celebrates all that you have shared and won, risked and accomplished. The love-making of a couple whose child has just been cured of cancer, or who have got their last child through Year 12, or who have lost everything in a bushfire and are starting again, or who have just spent a year as international volunteers, has a different quality to it. So does the sex of a couple who have faced their marriage demons and won.

Old wine

We men are slow growers: like a Huon pine, we reach full maturity only after many decades. In our twenties, most of us are a bundle of insecurities, emotional games, weaknesses and untried strengths. From 30 to 50 is often when we do our growing up. It's also when we raise our children, forge our careers, and get most involved in the world. It's a full-on time! Sexual tensions run through all of this, keeping us growing and seeking the depths of what closeness can mean.

Nobody tells us this – most people assume that great sex is the domain of the young, and disappears with age in favour of eating, knitting and going to bingo. And this is the big secret (or what would happen to cosmetic sales?): it's completely the reverse. For couples who know what's what, the older you are, the better it gets.

Teen sex today is often rather sad, with kids who haven't had time to get to know each other, pumped up on Internet porn and MTV, acting out the tricks as they plunge towards disillusionment. The barrage of explicit and empty sex on television, the pornography and sexual exploitation that washes over us all today, does terrible harm to the young: it robs them of their one chance for innocent and un-selfconscious exploration. It's a kind of rape. Sexuality needs to be unwrapped slowly for it to be real and empowering.

None of this is to disparage the young, or the depths of their feelings. There is a grace on all young lovers who open their hearts to each other along with their bodies, a glimpse of joy that is life-changing, glorious and never forgotten. As Theresa of Avila wrote centuries ago, 'all the way to heaven is heaven'. But this glimpse of the divine always disappears from view. We have to earn it back. It may take 20 to 30 years of growth to experience heart-stopping, soul-shaking sexual connection. Real sex involves a degree of trust and affinity which two people must often have gone through hell and high water to achieve. Only the deeply mature can deeply love.

> Good sex celebrates all that you have shared and won, risked and accomplished.

Getting sex right

So, how do we get there from here? The rest of this chapter is a guide for a man wanting to experience real sexual happiness, and have it last throughout his life.

The first and most important advice to any lover is: slow down. The sexually-unawakened man is easy to spot – he is always in a rush. Male sexual hunger is so single-minded, it runs like a six-lane freeway straight to the end of the ride. And as a freeway bypasses the scenery in its rush to the destination, we can arrive and yet still be nowhere. In our hurry to really be with a woman, we can pass right through her. (If we are honest with ourselves, it's as if she was not a person at all, just a well-made inflatable doll.) We have not connected. Sexual desire can prevent us from communicating as much as help us communicate.

Yet it's hard to slow down – perhaps she will change her mind, perhaps you will explode if you don't have sex right now! But in the long unfolding of a sexual relationship, things go best if you allow the inner journey to happen.

Good lovers pay attention; they are fully present. Next time you are lying with your lover, as you touch and are touched by her, focus on your inner sensations. Deliberately allow your body to soften and your heart to calm. You will discover that as you pay more attention to the tingling, rippling sensations of pleasure, all over your body, then that pleasure intensifies. Now pay attention to her inner experience. From the outer signs, her movements, breathing, facial expression, is she happy and relaxed? Is she feeling safe enough to really let you love her?

A young woman sexualised early by too much media input may be fearfully 'acting' her love-making, anxious about what she does or how she looks. She might be too insecure to relax. It's okay to talk, to reassure, or ask what is happening for her. Good sex is often awkward to begin with. It may even be that this is not the time or the place for it; maybe you just lie together this time. The vulnerability of going slowly builds trust. If you are too greedy to care, then you will go through, but not into each other, and end up nowhere.

By attending to what makes her relax, what makes her feel pleasure, you begin to really drink deeply of the experience. By shuttling between your own and her inner state, you can together build the energy slowly and powerfully, to an explosive meltdown of your separateness into fusion. Loving sex is something that happens to you, that you are swept along by, as much as something you do. It's not about 'achieving simultaneous orgasm' or any kind of performance goal; every time will be different and special in its own way. But you will feel you have connected, known and been known, and you will be changed by it.

A group of men in a men's gathering were talking about their early sexual experiences. Some of the more outspoken men espoused the benefits of a knowledgeable lover, an experienced partner who could tutor a young man in love-making. Then, gradually, some of the older men spoke up, men who had lived before the great tidal wave of sexual explicitness swept the culture. They talked about a different kind of initiation – with a young woman as naive and inexperienced as they were, and with extraordinary tenderness, vulnerability and eye-gazing slowness, finding their way to a place that left them deeply bonded and safe.

Sex is sacred. It is outside the ordinary, and requires ritual and care, and time to arrive. When men talk in men's groups about their sexual journey, it's clear that many of us are involved in a repair job on our souls, and that sex was one of the places we most wounded ourselves and others. Hardly anyone got here without much confusion and pain. By returning our souls to the activity of our bodies, we can begin all over again. We can start to re-enter the creative mystery that erotic contact with another person, or even with oneself, can bring into a human life. Sex is a holy place that's available to anyone – giggling, messy, un-photogenic, fallible and real. All the way to heaven is heaven.

Rediscovering 'whole-person sex'

Nature, even human nature, is tough, and it keeps fighting back against the shallow and artificial. Teenage boys who have been well loved (whose mothers talk to them, hug them, and affirm them as worthwhile; whose fathers are kind and interested) bring to their teenage sexuality an open heart, and a longing for soul connection. Even a boy from a damaged background still has a deep-down wish for closeness and commitment.

Our biology is designed to help this along. When we make love, our bloodstream floods with oxytocin, the hormone that melts hearts and makes us feel tender and trusting towards the person we have shared our body with. Having this act take place in a rushed, shallow way, without first building emotional safety, violates this connection. Our heart opens, is hurt, and closes down, hardening and shrinking. Will it open again?

I first learnt about this through treating people who had been sexually harmed. Young women or men who are raped, sexually abused, or forced into sex for money through severe circumstances experience a deep splitting in their being. They vacate their own bodies, deaden their feelings, go somewhere else. One young woman in recovery from childhood sexual abuse told me of being able to place her whole being into a hole in her bedroom wall; while things were done to her body, she simply went away to a safe place. The problem, though, was getting back again. That took years.

The problem is greater when ordinary, mainstream boys and girls in early or mid-teens are rushed and scripted – by the culture of TV soaps and ads, and the abandonment of adult care and supervision to a confused peer culture – into thinking that their body is just a tool for brief pleasure, or something to be traded for attention, or reassurance of worth.

Does this mean we should 'do' sex with a kind of soulful, pure-minded abstraction? That we should always feel loving and kind? No. Does lust have a place in the scheme of happy sex? Absolutely. It just isn't the only thing going on.

Are most men non-orgasmic?

Male sexuality, especially the nature of the male climax, is grossly misunderstood by men – and women. Columnist Michael Ventura put it this way:

> Does lust have a place in the scheme of happy sex? Absolutely. It just isn't the only thing going on.

...certainly the weakest, silliest aspect of feminism – which for the most part has been a beneficial movement – has been its description of male sexuality. It was a description that assumed a monolithic mono-intentional erection; that equated the ejaculation of sperm with coming. But ... to ejaculate is not necessarily to come. Coming involves a constellation of sensations, physical, psychic, emotional, of virtually infinite shadings. Coming may sometimes or often occur at the moment of ejaculation, when it occurs at all. But many ejaculations for many men happen without any sensation of coming.

Until a woman understands this she doesn't know the first thing about male sexuality. Nor do many men. (Just) as there are women who have never come, so there are men who have often ejaculated but never come. And they likely don't know it, as many women never knew it until a few began to be vocal about such things. These men live in terrifying and baffling sexual numbness in which every climax is, literally, an anticlimax. It is no wonder that in time they have less and less connection with their own bodies, and are increasingly distant from the women they want to love.

The popular term for sexual climax, 'coming', is such an interesting choice of word. Who is it that is arriving? Clearly it's a godlike feeling (even if it's a slightly overweight minor god hoofing through a woodland glade). The everyday sense of self is awed and overtaken by this feeling of being something bigger and better – by the truth, really, since our everyday sense of self is not the whole story of who we are.

John O'Hara, in *Appointment in Samarra*, has one of his characters express it this way:

> *I never made love before, I just screwed. But when it happened, it*

was like nothing I'd ever experienced before. I think I must have blacked out for a second and all I was aware of was some kind of incredible warmth, my whole body was filled with it ... I wanted to get closer to her, very close. I could feel the warmth of her body against mine, soft and gentle and for the first time in my life I stayed in a woman's arms and fell asleep.

Paul Olson, in *Wingspan,* comments on this passage: 'What he does with that experience only time will tell. He can deny it in the morning. Or he can enter it fully and never again feel the need to run away.'

Clearly, for us to experience this kind of union (what some might call 'sacred sex') requires all kinds of readiness, timing, openness and communication – as well as just good luck! A lot of other things have to be right. An important ingredient for total love-making is the inclusion of nature – of letting in the signals and rhythms that the natural world sends to our cells to tune them in. That's what romance means – it's not artificial. Nature tunes us in, makes us more open and alive. Standing on an ocean beach and watching the moon rise, in a lakeside cabin with rain on the roof, or impulsively tumbling to the ground together in the long grass of the dunes: sex is about going back to nature, giving way to wildness – something you should never get too old for! Romance means bringing a wild heart to an erotic body.

We have come a long way. When the first brave researchers began to document human sexual behaviour in the 1940s, they discovered that fewer than 20 percent of women were orgasmic and that many did not know such a thing existed. Some women enjoyed sex, but many endured it. As women became informed and empowered, their bodies responded with pleasure and joy.

Many men, too, need to become orgasmic – as opposed to just ejaculatory. One way to start is by placing less emphasis on the mechanical outer performance or actions, and more on the inner qualities of sensory and emotional experience. We men feel pretty lucky if our partner asks what we would like to do in bed. But the most magical woman is the one who asks what we would like to *feel.* If your sex life is lacking, consider the possibility that you do not really know what an orgasm really feels like. That there are levels of relaxation, openness, trust and energy that you have never felt before. Then begin to seek them out.

Sometimes being a good lover, and a happy one, comes down to a simple matter of focus. If we make love with our whole body, enjoying head-to-toe touch, caressing, holding, stroking feet and nibbling ears (if that's what your partner likes!), sliding bodies together, massaging backs and necks, relaxing, giggling, looking into each other's eyes, then sex is a whole-body pleasure that just grows and grows.

Self-love

It's 1966. I am a thirteen-year-old boy on a mission. In the school library, on its own special table, sits a dictionary the size of a doorstep. I wait until the place is deserted, sprint across to the huge book, open its heavy cover. I turn through to the M's with trembling hands. There it is! 'Masturbation, n., self-abuse'. That's all it says. I am not sure what abuse is, but there isn't time to check. I hear voices in the corridor, and make myself scarce. Later, as a teacher's voice drones on through a summer afternoon, I think about it some more. Then it comes to me – abuse is calling someone names. I am hugely, vastly relieved. The act that I have discovered for myself, full of beautiful images, a warm sense of closeness and explosions of starry wonder, is something quite different from that.

For centuries, masturbation was given a bad name; in fact it *was* a bad name. What tragedies of guilt and suffering must that have unleashed, since the action is almost a physical necessity, designed to freshen sperm supply and keep the 'pipelines' healthy and open. If you don't do it, your dreams will.

Today, sex therapists encourage masturbation as an important part of learning healthy sexuality. In a man's life, self-pleasuring usually begins in the early teens, long before we are emotionally equipped to establish relationships with real girls. Most men continue to masturbate during marriage, when it isn't right or possible to make love with their partners, and many healthy men will continue on and off well into old age. It's a long-term hobby that no-one ever lists on an application form!

Self-pleasuring is an exercise in sexual independence and in the development of sensuousness. By experimenting and finding what we like, we become more skilful and alive as lovers. A young man may find that he is imagining not just the physical aspects of sex, but also the relationship, the conversation, the mood and context, and so prepares himself for relating to a real woman. But there are dangers too: if masturbation is furtive and shameful, or distorted by the use of too much low-grade pornography, it can be a training in mechanical and tense sex, which conditions you to poor-quality love-making in adult life. The lack of human connection can lead to more extreme and perverse sexual tastes. Parents of teen boys need to minimise porn exposure (not having computers in bedrooms is a good start), to discuss the issues if they can, and help their boys meet and mix with real girls in the happier, if more demanding, real world.

> Sometimes being a good lover, and a happy one, comes down to a simple matter of focus.

The 'creepification' of men's sexuality

Cheapening of their sexuality isn't the only risk for boys and men. If the power of sexual longing doesn't flow in a good direction, it can sometimes go in a very bad one. This isn't a small matter. Child sexual abuse, to choose just one example, is horrifically widespread and does inestimable harm. We urgently need to get to the roots of how sex goes so wrong.

Jai Noa is a physically disabled man who, in his 'crippled condition' (his words), feared that he was turning into a creep. He then had a sudden insight that, in our society, this process perhaps affects all men. Almost all of us feel romantically 'crippled' at some time. In such a sexualised world, surrounded by women or pictures of women showing extraordinary amounts of sexual display, we can easily feel excluded and unwanted, and so begin to incubate a desire to make women suffer in 'revenge'. In Noa's own words:

I use the word 'creep' in a very special sense. 'Creep' refers to the ashamed sexuality of most men, which is an inescapable fact of our social life which each of us must confront sooner or later. It is ironic that if there is an almost universal manner in which men share a common crippledness, it is in the realm of sexual expression...

A creature of low self-esteem, the creep feels he cannot develop sustained intimate friendships with others. Despairing of intersubjective happiness, he takes the other [the woman] as an object to exploit as best he can. To validate himself through domination. The delightful joys of erotic pleasure are turned into their opposite by a guilt-ridden quest for power. The creep then is a voyeur, a pornophile and an exhibitionist. He enjoys not only invading the sexual space of others, but also a feeling that his penis has the power to cause a reaction, even if only one of discomfort or disgust.

The creep is a man who fails to live up to the romantic ideal and who feels crushed, bitter and resigned to this failure. And since most men suffer defeat in the romantic meritocracy at one time or another, the cripple can find his identity partially located in the world of men. Increasingly, during his teenage years and ... thereafter, the cripple can find a bond with any men who indulge in misogyny.

It's possible that Noa has explained one of the great social problems of our time. Let's pull out a key sentence: 'Despairing of intersubjective happiness, he takes the other as an object to exploit as best he can.' In other words, despairing of ever winning anyone's love, the man who becomes a creep prefers to have the upper hand. Here we can understand the rapist, the child molester, the pornography addict, the serial killer and the wife beater. The small boy who is always on the outer at kindy, the boy growing up in a dysfunctional or violent family, with no tenderness or comfort coming his way, needs our care if he not to turn into one of these men.

All human beings need to feel loved. But some men come to women with such a deep lack of inner worth, they will be tempted – instead of risking rejection – to use their strength, their sneakiness, their money and other power plays to impose their needs. This is a pretty sad state of affairs – from men who use tiny cameras to film up women's skirts, to violent abusers. Throughout history, millions of women have suffered and died because of this attitude.

For ordinary men, the danger is still there, and in a media-driven world that objectifies women on a daily basis, the drift is insidious if we are not awake to it. Football culture – or any group of boys or men who don't have good leadership or internalised values and the courage to stand up for them – readily slips into this. This harms the man himself – exploitative men attract exploitative women, and repel the self-valuing, equal kind of partner. Your partner will sense it the moment she becomes an object to you, and will start to pull away.

There is an important distinction that men should know about. Being attracted to children, or drawn to any kind of cruel, exploitive or harmful sexuality (and sex involving children is always harmful) is not rare. There are many men who have those feelings at times but would never ever act them out, because to do so would be a terrible betrayal of trust. It's *acting on* those feelings that is evil, and in fact requires a heartlessness and arrogance that is chilling to think of. At the same time, photographs, movies and magazines that encourage paedophilic or any other kind of abusive sex should never be produced or sold. Their inherent conditioning and implied consent will end up harming someone innocent in terrible ways.

Preventing rape

Andrew Renard is the Head of English in St Andrew's College, Grahamstown, a large boys' school in South Africa. He became convinced that through the study of literature and drama that dealt with rape, boys could begin to choose and strengthen their own values and behavioural choices. For many situations we find ourselves in, having a clear idea of what you stand for and what is the right thing to do before the event can make all the difference.

The existence of rape, and its terrible frequency in many parts of the world, is one of the horrors of human existence. Yet in male culture, there is often an unwillingness to acknowledge the pain, degradation and long-term effects that victims suffer. Addressing this problem headon, in a way that actually produces deep change in young men so that they choose to act protectively and respectfully around women, is a huge challenge.

Renard carried out his study for the International Boys' Schools Coalition, using action research methods, and his report is available to interested educators.

As part of an extra-curricular course, which ran once a week over eleven weeks, a group of seventeen Grade 10 boys were exposed to various types of literature which dealt with rape. They recorded their feelings in writing, anonymously, and also discussed them as a group. The findings suggest that the course was successful in encouraging them to be more empathetic and more likely to act against rape.

Renard made it safe for boys to develop empathy and to be honest by creating confidential and anonymous online journals. This led to a far greater degree of honesty, and his report is very poignant to read as the boys struggle with their feelings and distress about the realities of rape.

In the third session of the program, Renard read from the book *I Have Life* (1998) by 'Alison', as told to Marianne Thamm.

I read a few passages which described her rape and the vicious attack she was subjected to. I wanted to focus on one of the men who had saved her. Tiaan Eilerd had been on his way home when the group he was in found Alison on the side of the road. I wanted to focus on Tiaan as a male role model. This session proved to be a turning point in the research, and made a huge impact on the boys. There was a definite sense of anger directed towards her attackers and the boys were desperate to know what had happened to them. Suddenly rape was not just 'something that happened to other people out there'.

The boys in the study had much discussion about what constituted a 'real man' and how such a man would behave, and they examined and evaluated different ideas of manhood in South Africa. Here are some of the boys' comments.

Before, I thought rape was just a common thing that happened every day. I blamed no-one, cared little and overall did not take much notice. After this project I view it in a totally different way. I see the real inhumanity in it.

It made me realise that rape is not just a quick physical discomfort, but a sick act performed by men who have no respect for themselves or others ... Rape is a psychological dilemma that you have to live with your whole life.

...my only idea of rape was men desperate for sex, but now I know it is a power-hungry ... act.

I used to think rape was obviously pretty bad, but watching movies, listening to poems and reading articles ... has made me look at it in a ...

more serious way. It now seems more personal and I feel greater sympathy for anyone who has been through it.

The topic was not an easy one for either the boys or Renard to deal with; initially it was hard going. The turning point was reading the passages from *I Have Life*.

After that, everything seemed more important to them. Many of the boys ... hung around at the end of sessions and wanted to discuss issues. They also wanted to know more about the opinions of the class and how my research was going. In the final reflection, one of the boys whose written responses certainly suggested he was not interested in the project, suggested 'we should do it again'.

The seventeen boys who attended the course were sensitised in two ways:

1. Their attitudes towards rape, especially at the end of the course, suggest a repugnance of the act.

2. I hope, also, that should they ever be in a position to prevent, hinder or discourage rape, they would

not stand back, but that they would stand up as men and act.

If viewed in its entirety, the program proved more successful than I had expected. It would be fair to say that nearly all the literature was useful, and the combined impact influenced the boys' attitudes. They thought about what it means to be a man.

The small size of the group was also helpful. I have been asked by my headmaster to design a program for all the boys in the school, based on the findings of my research. An immediate concern was whether it would be possible to do it in groups of a similar size. Working with, at the most, seventeen boys provided a safe and intimate environment. In a larger group, this safe environment would be lost.

Owning your sexual charge

Okay, we're out of the dark side now, so (with a shudder) let's return to healthy and happy sex.

There remains one last monster to wrestle: the taking of responsibility for your own desire. Women hold such visual and tactile magic for men that it is easy to make the serious mistake of handing one's power over to them. They become the golden woman, the goddess. In seeing women as the holders of sexual attraction – as having power over men's desire – men actually give away their own sexual energy.

The so-called Playboy philosophy ... focuses on the enticing Playmate. The ... Playboy gospel is that the woman confers masculinity on the reader by sexually arousing him with her 'come-on' posture. In reality, however, the reader has simply yielded his manly initiative to the woman ... He has given his masculine spirit over to the goddess and, thus, lost it.

We put women on a pedestal, and then resent them for being there. We have to become aware that sexual attraction lies not in the way a woman looks, but *in the way we choose to look at a woman.*

No one arouses us. We arouse ourselves, no matter how convincingly we project such a capacity onto another. Men are not bewitched by women, but are bewitched by their own hoping-to-be engorged appetites, or more precisely, by their unwitting animation of and submission to such appetites.

Men say their penises have minds of their own, but men are geniuses at avoiding responsibility.

Image 10

Sometimes a woman is less than innocent, but this does not alter the man's accountability for his own choices.

Gordon Dalbey tells a striking tale about this.

A young married man sought his advice. An older and very attractive woman at work has been seeking him out with tales of her husband's cruelty. They were spending more time together and she was becoming increasingly seductive (or he was becoming attracted to her – depending where you locate the responsibility).

Dalbey explored the man's childhood, and found a pattern common to men in this situation. His father had been a remote man, who died while the young man was still in his early teens. The boy had always been his mother's comforter and confidant, more so after his father's death. By the time he entered adulthood, he had already learnt that comforting women – with subtle, sexual overtones – was his role in life. His father's abandonment and his mother's 'psychological incest' had set him up for just such a role.

The man owned horses (fortunately for the story). One morning a neighbour's stallion broke through the fence and was about to start mating with his mares. He found himself face to face with the highly excited, large black horse, armed only with a fence picket. He held his ground and herded the stallion back. Talking about this with Dalbey, the metaphor was so striking that he realised he could also face down his own desire, and draw a boundary with the woman at work. She was furious and hurt, but in the end she sought help from a woman counsellor instead. She later thanked him for not playing a game that would have harmed them both.

There will always be flirtation, temptation and the potential for life-affirming as well as life-harming exchanges between men and women. Good men are as alive to this as are other men. But they know they are in charge of their own sexuality. They have 'corralled the stallion'. Not castrated, just corralled, so you can take it where you want it to go. Men who have learnt this bring a kind of inner calmness to their encounters with women which confounds needy or controlling women and attracts those who are themselves mature and healthy. Women are looking for this very capacity in a man: someone who is emotionally independent and who has harnessed his energies, even though those energies are very much in evidence. But that's enough horsing around!

IN A NUTSHELL

- In human beings, sex is a heart-and-mind thing, as well as a body thing.
- The first lesson we need to learn is the difference between junk sex and real sex.
- Once you have made love, then just having sex will never do.
- Most couples have an exuberant sex phase, and then run into differences of desire. This is normal, and is the beginning of discovering real love.

- Real love takes a lot of practice and emotional risk, and involves becoming a better man.
- Relationships are a kind of furnace to bring out the best in us. We should neither panic, run away, nor get angry or manipulative. This is the time of fire.
- Most men mistake ejaculation for orgasm. Far greater joy and depths of feeling are possible as we learn to be more open.
- Creepification is a danger if men are not helped to get sex right.
- We are in charge of our own desire: like a powerful horse, we either ride it or it smashes us around.

Image 11

FIVE

From boy to man

> *'Between childhood, boyhood, adolescence and manhood there should be sharp lines drawn with tests, feats, rites, stories, songs and judgements.'*
>
> *Jim Morrison*

In the early 1990s I received a package in my mailbox with a US postage stamp on it, sent by my friend Robin Maslen. Since Rob lived in South Australia, I was naturally intrigued. Rob was one of my psychotherapy mentors, a remarkable man who had smashed himself up in his late teens on a motorcycle, abandoned plumbing as a trade, become a well-known social worker, the Commissioner of Scouts for South Australia, and one of the country's best-known teachers of therapists. When Rob sent you something, it was worth reading.

I walked up the half-kilometre driveway of my small farm in the hills behind Hobart, reading carefully as I went. The article was an interview with a 70-year-old American poet called Robert Bly, whom I had never heard of. Bly was pointing out something that should have been blindingly obvious, but that I had never thought about before: for hundreds of thousands of years of prehistory, men always helped boys into manhood with concerted and focused attention, processes and specific teaching. The whole community helped to do this (in those days, men and women actually lived in a connected community). For 95 percent of human history, boys weren't launched out into adulthood, they were *welcomed into it,* into a lifelong support network that would work to ensure their contribution would be a good one. Their wellbeing would be a priority to everyone around them. Today we give our son the keys to the car, then go inside and pray he will be okay. In ancient times, they were more proactive than that.

For most of human history, the most important task facing the whole community was turning each generation of boys into capable men (and girls into capable women). They could not afford to leave this to chance: by the age of fourteen, every young man needed to be safe, skilful, integrated and responsible. Everyone's life depended on it; there was no place for hoons in a Neolithic clan.

I talked widely with friends and colleagues about this, and soon began writing about how we had to raise boys with more direct and clear involvement from good men. Men shouldn't stand at a distance, but should team up with women, and with each other, to do this. We had to increase the male role model component in schools, homes and families, and tackle boy energy in a way that embraced it but also directed it firmly in good ways.

For the next 20 years I toured the world, talking passionately about this to parents and schoolteachers. I was sowing these seeds – boys need men, and boys need help to become good men; it can't be left to chance. And gradually, smarter people than me, who knew the teaching of boys inside out, began to put this into practice. For most of us, schools are our closest thing to community, where we have a sense of belonging, through our kids, and where they meet other adults of good calibre and shared goals. Schools are places that set out to make adults, but that have rarely taken up this challenge beyond the merely academic sense, and a few platitudes at Assembly. This is beginning to change. This chapter tells the delightful and moving story of some of the programs at the forefront of this change. I hope you will want these kinds of programs to be there for your children, too. May they spread wider and wider into education and the community.

> It's 5a.m. Looking down from the rim of the Adelaide Hills, the whole of the city is sleeping, peaceful in the pre-dawn light. Out beyond, the waters of St Vincent Gulf catch the moonlight, filtered through wispy clouds. It's an awesome sight, and it casts a silence over the families as they stumble from cars and gather at the lookout. A marquee is set up, lit with a single lantern; one of the teachers welcomes each family as

they arrive. Then, from each family, a boy separates out and moves into their position. Forty or so Year 9 boys assemble in a line on the escarpment, each about a metre apart, dark shadows against the sky. Their parents gather in a knot at one side, rubbing arms and shivering a little in the chill.

> Your boyhood is ending. Soon you will start to become a man.

The chaplain of the school the boys attend, a solidly-built man with a deep, calm voice, begins to speak. He walks slowly along the line of boys, and his voice carries in the still air.

'Look below you at this beautiful place, and this beautiful city. Down there in that city, or beyond, across the country, or for some of you across the globe – down there, out there – you have spent your boyhood. Fourteen or fifteen years ago, you were born, your parents excited and amazed, doctors and nurses helping you make a start.

Down there you were a baby, a little toddler, loved and cared for, going to the park and the beach. You played with friends, perhaps had brothers or sisters who were your companions. You got older, went to kindergarten and school. You had relatives and family, friends, mates you played with. What you needed was provided. You had a place to live, clothes and a bed. You were taken care of. Down there you swam at the beach, had holidays, perhaps travelled to other places and returned. You played and learnt, and laughed and cried, you grew up, grew stronger and smarter.

'You lived your boyhood. *Down there, out there, is your boyhood.* Think now of all the people who helped you. Who fed you and healed you and taught you and cared for you. The homes that sheltered you, the family that loved you. The enemies and the friends you made. The sun that warmed you, the cold that you shivered in, the rain that came down.

'Think of your boyhood, and all that went into it.

'Think of your parents, who may be here right now, or wherever they might be, and all their dreams and hopes for you.'

A teacher now steps from the shadows. His words ring out from a different direction, jolting the boys in the line a little; then they relax as they recognise his voice.

'Your boyhood is ending. Soon you will start to become a man. The journey to manhood is more than just Year 9, it's a long road, but you will begin that road today. Right now, you begin turning from boyhood to manhood. But first, this is a chance to say goodbye. Goodbye to being a boy. And goodbye begins with saying thank you. So just in your mind, send a thank-you for the people who down there in that city, or far away across the earth, wherever you lived and grew, who loved you, and cared for you, in small ways and large, the places, the experiences, the films, books, games, music, all that the human tradition gave you, that made your boyhood rich and good. Even the painful times – the hurts, the betrayals, the disappointments that made you who you are.

'Begin to say goodbye to boyhood. Say thank you for your boyhood. Breathe deeply, and carry with you all these gifts into the next, new stage of life, a man's life. Welcome to the journey of becoming a man.'

There are more than a few tears among the listening parents, mothers and fathers who are realising that, for them too, a stage of life is ending. A simple ceremony has burned itself into the hearts of the families, marking a stage, imbuing the year to come with purpose and expectation. There will be more ceremonies, but there will also be an impressive learning and growing process in between. The Year 9 program that this school has developed is called The Rite Journey, and it's a deliberate and intensive way of using a year of school to help boys turn into fine young men.

'The Rite Journey'

Schoolteachers Graham Gallasch and Andrew Lines have taught children and young men for a total of 40 years, specialising in physical education and sport. They combine the Lutheran tradition – a hard-nosed Christianity with its roots in the Reformation – with Waldorf education – the more subtle and creative schooling based on Rudolph Steiner's work, which emphasises myth and ritual as part of children's needs.

Andrew told me, when we met for breakfast in an Adelaide cafe, that he had grown concerned about the boys he was teaching, noticing their behaviour in the school and in the streets, and the attitudes in their written work. Their heroes were rock stars, sportsmen and others who showed poor treatment of women and girls, excessive drug and alcohol use, and self-destructive and stupid behaviour. The boys' attitudes, at least the ones they projected, were often racist, sexist, violent and stereotyped. Andrew suspected a root cause behind these boys' poor idea of manhood: *in most cases there was simply no respected male figure in their lives who could teach them to be fine men.* How could they be expected to turn out well?

He also noted another trend in the boys' lives: that much of their waking time was spent looking at screens. They were being educated about life by sources that *had no interest in their welfare.* Andrew was well aware of the research that showed today's young people to be the most troubled, anxious, lonely and disturbed of any generation of adolescents in history. He began to put two and two together.

As experienced teachers, Andrew and Graham had listened to many parents and fellow teachers who expressed total despair at how to help their boys and girls make it through adolescence. Then, in 2004, they attended a seminar run by the renowned futurist, Peter Ellyard. Ellyard pointed out that the whole of Year 9 in secondary school is traditionally a wasted year, when kids just do not want to learn. He suggested a radical idea: Year 9 should be turned from a problem into a solution. It should be a year focused on 'the mysteries of adulthood', specifically teaching how to function as a successful grown-up. To study the very thing these young men were most concerned about – how to become a man.

Image 12

The Rite Journey is overlaid onto Year 9 or 10 of secondary school. It is substantial and long term – the research indicates that programs for changing kids have little effect unless they create longterm relationships over a year or two, and are woven into the whole of their school experience.

The Rite Journey features ceremonies and retreat experiences, but at its core, for three lessons a week of around an hour each, *the boys study how to be a man.* Five C's – consciousness, communication, celebration, connection and challenge – form the framework of this. The boys develop and strengthen relationships with the special teachers who spend this year with them. They are helped to connect more deeply to parents, mentors, their own spirit, and the outside world. They listen and learn about life as an adult. They use innovative and potent ways of learning, such as the use of drumming as a metaphor for managing anger. They pass through the seven steps of 'the hero's journey' from boyhood to the start of manhood, facing tests and challenges, culminating in a solitary experience in the wild.

> Year 9 should be turned from a problem into a solution.

The first year-long Rite Journey programs were conducted in 2005. (A parallel program was also offered for girls.) Many students expressed profound gratitude for the experiences the course gave them. Parents, too, were deeply thankful for a program that helped their children grow, not just as academic learners, but towards becoming fine young men and women. Here are some of their comments.

I've noticed a lot of change in my sons. At the beginning they were still a bit immature, at that age of fourteen. By the end of the year I really noticed a new sense of self-confidence; they knew who they were and where they wanted to go in life.

The parent of a girl in the girls' program wrote:

She developed an honesty and earnestness that made her a human being to be reckoned with. The silence and inner anxieties which often accompany this age were left in the dust.

'Rock and Water'

When I first released *Raising Boys* in 1997 and began travelling the world speaking to teachers and parents about boys' needs, there was a considerable sense of excitement and relief from parents and teachers that boys' problems had a cause, and a remedy. Many teachers were inspired to develop their own programs that used the three key elements the book identified – that boys need *to know good men,* that boys need *initiatory journeys,* and that boys need to think, plan and train for *what kind of man they want to be,* in concrete and specific ways.

One outstanding program, Rock and Water, was developed in Holland after several boys were killed in acts of random violence. Holland is normally a very safe place, and there was an outcry from parents to do something to restore this safety. Educator Freerk Yrkema set about developing a program he called Rock and Water, which in the years since has become popular in schools worldwide. Rock and Water shows boys (and girls) how to actively prevent violence, to deal with conflict, and to intervene if harm is taking place. While it has a martial-arts philosophy (and boys love its physicality), Rock and

Water is as much about attitude, and its strategies apply to everyday conversation and self-awareness as much as to physical dangers. Supported by the University of Newcastle, the program has found wide acceptance in Australian schools. (Over 5,000 teachers are now trained in the method just in Australia.) Its name conveys its main message: *sometimes one has to be hard like rock, sometimes soft like water.* But it's the combination, knowing when to yield and when to push, that solves most of life's problems. Wherever it's taught, boys become more confident, protective, and able to express themselves in a crisis, and bullying or assault are reduced.

'NITOR'

The most exciting program I have come across in recent years is NITOR – a Year 10 program that teaches *a selected group of boys separately within a co-ed school.* This is a program that I can envisage being valuable in almost any school.

NITOR is targeted at *those most disengaged.* As every teacher knows, many boys tune out at this stage of schooling, whether through too much ability, or too little, or because of difficult family situations or other individual challenges. NITOR tackles this disengagement – which is really a hunger to get more out of school – with direct and positive action, and wonderful results.

NITOR is a Latin word meaning 'retreat in order to grow'. The program was developed at the Catholic Regional College, North Keilor, a small, friendly school in Melbourne's northern suburbs. After considerable reflection and planning, teachers Brian Horan and Eamonn Buckley introduced the program with the support of the principal and deputy principal in 2009.

Here's how it works. Towards the end of Year 9, staff nominate *which boys they feel are most disengaged and at risk of failure.* (This can be a large group, often a third to a quarter of all boys.) These boys are then invited, with their parents, to attend a special evening presentation. They are offered a chance to apply for inclusion in NITOR, a boys-only group who complete Year 10 together, studying the same curriculum as the rest of the school, but with a much more active, experience-based and intensive style of learning.

Unlike the regular timetable, where many different teachers teach a boy each day, in NITOR most subjects are taught by the same *two male teachers* working as a team. *(They are supplemented by two other specialist teachers, usually also male.)* This means that strong relationships can be built up, and no-one is allowed to fall through the cracks. The boys are given high benchmarks, but also intensive help to reach those standards. Innovative and real-world learning methods are added, to capture their energy and imagination. One day a week, the group goes out to deal with and study the real world.

As with The Rite Journey, there is a clear and specific study of becoming a man – how a man behaves in different situations, and how to be ethical and good. Boys discuss intensely the options open to them in their lives, and there is a remarkable level of sharing. Many boys I spoke to described the group as being *like a family.* They were part of a collective effort to help each other succeed in life.

Vital to the program is the enlisting of parents as allies. For their son to be accepted into the program, parents have to convince the teachers *that they will support their son in doing homework, attending classes, and getting through the year.* Text messages and emails link parents and teachers *on a daily basis,* which enables two-way communication. As one teacher told me, 'The airwaves between home and school are continually buzzing.' If there is a load of homework one night, the parents will know about it before their son walks in the door. Most schools today talk about teaming up with parents, but in NITOR this really happens.

> I have a plan for how my life will go. I know how to get there, and I know I will succeed.

When I visited the class in late 2009, the boys were completing their last week of school. The classroom was intensely focused on Science revision, and there was not a murmur of disruption, but the atmosphere crackled with masculine energy. There was a sense of striving, but also of vulnerability in boys who normally might have not attempted such a level of work. The commitment was: 'we will get everyone through'. 'Disengaged' as a criterion for entry meant that there were boys of both high ability who had been desperately bored, and boys who struggled with learning, and always had. *In NITOR they got the help they needed.*

I interviewed the boys on-camera about how the year had gone. Here are some answers they gave:

I loved it. I hated school up until now; I wouldn't even have gone on to Year 10. Now I am planning to finish Year 12, perhaps even go further on.

NITOR is like a family. We look out for each other. The teachers are like big brothers to us. I will really miss them. I won't ever forget this year.

I learnt how to be a good man. You have to be a role model for other people. Not everyone knows how to do the right thing – you have to show them.

I have a plan for how my life will go. I know how to get there, and I know I will succeed.

What I liked best about NITOR is that they make you work hard. You get to like working hard and getting good results. If you don't understand, they explain it to you.

I know where I am going with my life. In Years 8 and 9 I was going nowhere.

While NITOR was going ahead with these 27 boys, the rest of the Year 10 students proceeded as normal, in co-ed classes with no special changes. Did other teachers resent or envy the NITOR program? It didn't seem so – they were delighted that a whole cohort of the most disruptive and unreachable boys had been taken from their classrooms. It was a win/win. The program costs extra to deliver, since often there were two teachers working with the NITOR group at a time – if not teaching, then planning and organising the weekly field trips, community projects, and parent liaison. This amounted to around $60,000 over the year, or about $2,000 per boy. While not insignificant, this was a mere fraction of what it costs for each student to be in a year of high school. And what really matters – these boys succeeded!

The results were spectacular. All of these boys passed their end-of-year exams. They each had concrete and achievable plans for their futures. Their parents were profoundly grateful. But above all, they emerged as young men who could look you in the eye, speak clearly and authentically about their own concept of being a good man, how they were implementing that, and their sense of responsibility to help others make it too. They had internalised hundreds of hours of interaction with men who were almost as close to them as their parents, who knew them inside out, and who had made a personal commitment to helping them build their lives as men. Slated for failure, the boys had *bypassed average* and turned into exceptional young men.

All that afternoon, as I interviewed the boys, I kept thinking – *this is what education is supposed to be.* It was moving, inspirational and, in a quiet way, revolutionary.

Contact details for The Rite Journey, Rock and Water and NITOR, along with other such programs, are listed in the 'Contacts and resources' section at the back of this book.

Image 13

Boys and cars

Scott Rankin *is a playwright, youth worker and activist. Sixteen years ago Scott founded the organisation Big hART; performer Robyn Archer recently described them as 'the theatre company I admire most in the country'. But Big hART are nothing like your average theatre* *company – they work and live in places where life is hard, and their purpose is to create change in people's lives.*

I had heard about Big hART's work with young men who are at risk of dying on country roads. At the start of a three-year project on Tasmania's northwest coast, there existed a trifecta of needs that all interlocked. Teenage mothers giving birth as young as fifteen or sixteen, and struggling to see their life getting anywhere. Old people, losing the ability to cope, terrified of young people and of crime. And young men, often the partners of the teenage mums, who had the highest death rate in Australia from road accidents, and non-accidents – the recently acknowledged propensity of young men to commit suicide by car.

Young men are the group in society that are most often seen as a problem, as an accident looking to happen. Yet the fact is that they are astonishingly restrained, given what many of them are dealing with at home and school. Australia-wide, 96 percent of young men never come to the attention of the police. Of the 4 percent who do, 3 percent never re-offend. Of the 1 percent who do, half stop at that. That leaves 0.5 percent who become long-term offenders, in and out of court, in and out of jail. It's worth investing in this group – a single person rendered quadriplegic in a car crash or bike accident costs the economy millions of dollars (that is, if 'ordinary' human pain alone doesn't convince you).

Youth work is the usual response, but it's costly, and the next generation may need it all over again. Scott and his colleagues, Telen Rodwell and Bronwyn Purvis, figured they could do better. While a youthworker looks at improving self-esteem, alternatives to boredom and alienation, Big hART's approach involves young people in ambitious projects in the arts, requiring substantial skill development, which re-integrates them into their communities.

In the Drive project, a group of teenage boys worked to create a documentary for television, telling the stories of recent fatal car accidents in their area. They traced the people affected, interviewed them, and edited the story creatively and sensitively. The parents of the dead boys, family and friends and the emergency workers who had hauled the bodies out of the wrecks, talked about how they were affected, what had been the legacy.

The footage is gut-wrenching to watch. A mother talks about getting the phone call and racing to the accident site. Her son's body had already been taken away; she fell to the ground, running her hands through the bloody gravel, trying to feel his presence one last time. These stories need no sermonising to make their point.

There were huge sensitivities involved in dealing with people in so much pain. Working as a team needed patience, compromise, holding oneself in check, and handling conflict. An enormous range of technical and literacy skills had to be mastered by boys who had barely coped with school, and had addictions and mental-health problems to deal with.

The point of the work was its impact on the community as a whole. Watching the finished product, the used-car dealer who sells powerful cars to naive young men, the Rotary member with no time for the 'nohopers' of his community, the teacher who writes off the potential of a young girl who will be a fantastic mother – all begin to change.

Big hART aims to trigger self-healing in communities, and more inclusive links between old and young, well-off and struggling, politicians and those they are paid to serve. Pride replaces shame, and a love of life replaces an attraction to death.

Talking to Scott turned my ideas about road safety on their head. Road deaths involving drunken and despairing young men don't arise in a vacuum, they are *an indicator of a sick or a healthy community – one that ignores, or cares for its young.* Young men who have avenues to self-respect, and have good adults guiding them, take better care of themselves and treat others with more respect, too. Tougher laws and safer roads and cars help, but they are not enough. Letting young men know they matter, building strong relationships between them and the wider community, and helping them belong is really the only answer, and it's not actually all that hard.

In a Nutshell

- Boys need active care and teaching to help them turn into good men. They have to '*see* good men to *be* good men'.
- Schools are where we still have community, and they can be the places where boys are taught about adulthood, with teachers and parents working together.
- *The Rite Journey,* a twelve-month program of training in manhood, with initiatory stages and a special

curriculum in being a good man, is being adopted in many schools.
- *Rock and Water* uses martial-arts thinking to train boys and girls to be safe, and to prevent violence and bullying, by knowing when to be like water and when to be like rock.
- *NITOR,* developed in a secondary school in suburban Melbourne, is a redesign of the tenth year of school. It involves assigning two male teachers to a class of boys for a whole year, supported by parents, to achieve both good marks and an empowered attitude to life. A single-sex program within a co-ed school, offering closer and stronger relationships with fewer teachers, this might well be the new revolution in raising boys.

Image 14

SIX

The five truths of manhood

'The purpose of man is to look after all the life.'

David Mowaljarlai

In all this talk of making fine men, we need to know – what does a good man look like? That's a big question, and takes a lifetime to answer. But for me it comes down to just two words. He should have *backbone* and *heart*.

Backbone is the ability to stand firm, endure, be true to his word, and sometimes *put himself last,* especially under circumstances of great need or stress. A man with backbone is someone you can count on. This quality was more recognised and aspired to in the older-style man of the early twentieth century. For the right reasons, and in the right circumstances, he would sacrifice his life.

But this kind of man was incomplete. The men of the first half of the twentieth century were often emotionally 'wooden'; their wives found them difficult to know or deal with. And since the expectations were so high, many men simply fell off the pedestal.

What the new man, the post-Vietnam era male brought to the situation was heart. Men, of course, always had heart, but now it could be shown – affection in the family, grief and concern, love and compassion in private and public life. You could talk to the new man; he was more real.

But a problem arose with the new man: guided by his feelings, which are changeable things, he was often slippery, uncommitted, narcissistic (Narcissus was the Greek god who fell in love with his own reflection). The 'sensitive New Age guy' was not someone you would look to in a car crash or a bushfire, or even in a hard time in a marriage. For a truly good man, we need some of the old qualities too. *Heart AND backbone.*

Men are now being asked to be more intimate and more sensitive.

However, we don't actually want men who are weaker – just men who can shift gears when needed.

To have backbone and heart is not impossible, and every action we take with a growing boy from babyhood to manhood builds towards this goal. Our cuddles and comfort give him heart, our sternness and expectations that he behave well and pull his weight give him backbone. But to finally knit this all together seems to need a kind of jolt, an intensive and marked transition which requires the help of a wider group of our extended family or community. This is initiation.

But something is still missing. The thing we have lost, the ingredient we men ourselves seem to lack, is the inner secrets, the *teachings* for becoming a strong and solid man. That is what this chapter is about.

Initiating ourselves

A lot of humour, and even anxiety, hangs around the idea of male secrets, initiations, and 'sacred teachings'. There's an air of mumbo-jumbo, of misappropriated bits of Indigenous culture being mimicked without proper understanding. Of silly men dressing up.

Then there are the toxic and profane initiations – 'hazings', as they are sometimes called – where groups of young men in schools or the military humiliate and assault younger men. Across town, in the 'neighbourhoods', proving yourself by stealing a car, knifing or shooting someone, are key aspects of gang culture. Initiation persists as an idea in our culture. We all understand the idea of a proof of entry, of earning one's way to a new level. We just don't have many good ways to do it.

The core idea, though, *that a process can be constructed* to carry you out of boyhood and into manhood, has regained currency in recent years. The fact that all old cultures, without exception, had such a process suggests that it may be a necessary part of the human pattern. As we have seen, schools and communities are looking into how this might be at least set in motion with teenage boys. And since most adult men today had no such opportunity, we are hungry for what we have lost. So it's important to ask – what is the core process? What is the essential teaching that a man takes so deeply into his being, so that he no longer lives and acts in a boy-like way? *What is the heart of manhood?*

> What is the heart of manhood?

What I am going to do in the next few pages is risky, and something of a gamble. I am going to spell out what are thought to be the key understandings of a mature man, which differentiate him from the uninitiated, boy-in-a-man's-body, which is the state of most men today. In doing this, I want to warn you that *I may not be doing you a favour* – in fact, it might be that reading these next few pages does you lasting harm.

Why do I say this? Because there are some things *that words cannot teach.* Reading something is not the same as living it, or learning it. By reading something in a book, you may be fooled into thinking 'I know that', and so fail to take the journey or have the experiences that actually get you there. *When we think we know, we sometimes don't look any further.*

For thousands of years, these secrets had to be earned, by passing through physical ordeals, fasting, vigils or deeds of courage, and they were taught directly by elders who knew your individual weaknesses and strengths, and could customise the message. They were not just abstract ideas, but direct and intense experiences designed to drive the message indelibly into the hearts of young men, to transform them. It is a pale shadow of this to simply set down words in a book.

Nonetheless, because this is such a critical time in our history, I believe such risky measures may be justified. Perhaps sufficient men reading this book will have made their own journeys, and endured enough struggle and suffering to be at the edge of readiness to 'go to a new level' of living. It's just possible that some clarity and insight might help you to knit together your own learning, and bridge the gap to being a better kind of man. So let's give it a try.

Some people are special

Let's start with what we know. *There are special people.* Everywhere in the world, in organisations, causes, neighbourhoods, in your own life, you come across them – men or women who stand out because of their exceptional humanity and their exceptional effectiveness.

These are the men or women who pull things together, and lead by the appeal of their personality, their warmth, commitment and ideals. They are more full of life, more at ease in the world, more part of the flow of the universe, and as a result have a great impact for good. Sometimes these individuals emerge in public life: Barack Obama promises some of this character, Martin Luther King certainly had it. Burmese political prisoner Aung San Suu Kyi, Former Irish PM Mary Robinson, former Australian Governor General Sir William Deane, Tim Costello, Peter Cundall, David Attenborough, Indian activist and author Arundhati Roy ... We've already mentioned Nelson Mandela. But it's not about visibility –

many superb human beings are known only to a few friends and colleagues.

Did these people just arise? Were they born this way? Did their lives always go smoothly, so that they were successful all along? No. In fact it's very important to understand that it was usually *quite the opposite*. Almost always, *these people had their greatness born in suffering.* Something happened in their life that should have broken them, but instead it transformed them. These people were *initiated,* but not usually in a formal way; rather, a combination of life events taught them something so fundamental that their grasp of life's meaning was taken to a new level.

Almost all outstanding people were, at some point in their lives, *broken*. And because of this, they opened to a deeper truth and understanding. As Richard Rohr describes it:

> *The larger-than-life people I have met ... always have one common denominator. They have all died before they died. At some point they were led to the edge of their private resources, and that*

breakdown (which surely felt like dying) led them into a larger life.

What does 'a larger life' mean? We will come to that soon.

Boy versus man thinking

Arne Rubenstein, founder of Pathways to Manhood (see 'Contacts and resources'), points out that a boy's psychology, though it has lots of positives, generally tends to be self-important, brash, and concerned with immediate gratification. It's all about 'me'. For a boy to become a man, something has to happen to move him out of self-centredness. All human communities in the past saw this, and dealt with it concertedly; this process was what we call initiation. Initiation was about shifting boys to men by showing them, sometimes forcefully but never unkindly, that *there were things more important than their own pleasure,* converting them into men who could care for and protect others, whose lives were lived for the common good. This was not just indoctrination; the aim was not to enslave or diminish. In initiation, the wildness, creativity and intensity of the young men were *enlarged,* not hammered down. They were *brought into a web of shared purpose,* so that the women, children, and the natural world on which they depended would be enhanced and protected by the young men's presence. We wanted them to be brave, but for a reason; energetic, but with a purpose; fierce, but in protectiveness.

This was the pattern for hundreds of thousands of years, but then, in a matter of a few hundred years, it was almost completely lost. Today, it's only by luck or chance that the combination of a shattering experience, matched with the right kind of support and knowledge, breaks someone through to the level that all men and women were once able to reach. When *life* initiates you, as opposed to a carefully managed process being provided, it's a rough ride. Formal initiation was rough enough, since it was designed to shake you out of complacent boyhood into total disorientation, prior to reconstructing you along very different lines. Hunting and killing a wild beast, ritual cutting or scarring of your body, making long and arduous journeys – these practices acknowledged that some kind of suffering was needed. Today, we encounter devastating reality, but it's random, and without support only some of us make it through. *That's why really alive and mature people are so rare today.*

It's time now to unfold what the teaching of mature manhood might contain. How we can reach manhood ourselves, even though we had no elders to initiate us. Before that, though, there are two important pieces of reassurance to give you. Firstly, being extraordinary, being an outstandingly effective and valuable human being, *is available to anyone.* There is a process for getting there. And secondly, if your situation has been desperate, lost and painful, this is not without purpose. Suffering is not something to be sought, but it is a vital ingredient in breaking out of ordinariness, an ingredient of transformation. It is *a wound that can be turned to gold.*

> For a boy to become a man, something has to happen to move him out of self-centredness.

Five awakenings, five truths

Richard Rohr is a Franciscan monk, well known for his men's retreats and writings on initiation. Rohr is not always a comfortable fit amongst the hierarchy of the Catholic Church: he often remarks that organised religion seeks the safe and secure, whereas sacredness is always a wild, fringe and disruptive force of liberation.

Rohr points out that for all hunter-gatherer peoples, stretching back over 300,000 years, initiation was the most important spiritual practice they had. It is the oldest religious tradition of the human race, 'before the church, temple or synagogue'. He makes a persuasive argument that *all religions are built on this foundation* in that they encapsulate what is essentially an initiation story. Abraham, Jesus, Buddha, Mohammed, Krishna, Lao Tsu, the goddess figures of prehistory, the

Indigenous story figures – all made initiatory journeys, and their stories lay down a template for ordinary men and women.

Initiation centres on the most pressing spiritual task of any culture – *making the young wise enough, soon enough, that they might join the tribe as superb and contributory human beings.* Hunter-gatherer culture was a life-or-death business: they could not afford dysfunctionality. When the wild mammoth charged, everyone had to know and do their job. Each young man and woman had to be intensively trained. The human species had no fangs or claws; we were weak and small. What allowed us to prevail was our extraordinary ability for social cooperation. *We became the dominant species on earth for one reason alone – our outstanding ability to teach our young.* Not just at superficial levels – that these seeds, in this season, can feed or heal you – but also at deep levels – of how to be wise and good.

It's important for us to understand that the sacred dimension for our ancestors was practical, not just some imaginative enrichment for long nights around the fire. Nor was it, as we often are taught, a fanciful way to deal with the anxiety of a random universe. These people were not anxious, they were masterful. *The sacred was coded wisdom, it was the thing that kept people alive,* that governed their relationships to all their food sources, land, water and each other.

Rohr has explored this deeply from both a Christian and a universal point of view. He has distilled his thinking and writing over 30 years into what he believes are *the core messages of becoming an adult male,* the five insights that carry us from boyhood into effective manhood. These are the individual truths that young men need to confront, grieve over, and eventually celebrate as ultimate liberation. As you read these, you will see that they are shattering in their implications – your life can never be the same when you take them in. They are the keys to freedom in this world. Here they are.

The five truths of manhood

> 1. You are going to die.
> 2. Life is hard.
> 3. You are not that important.
> 4. Your life is not about you.
> 5. You are not in control of the outcome.

The five truths are, as you will probably notice, exactly opposite to what the consumer society takes as its operating assumptions. Most people, and all young people who have not yet been cracked open by life, operate along the complete opposite lines to these five truths. *When we fail to accept these truths, we become a culture of perpetual childhood.*

So let's take them one by one.

You are going to die

For most of history, the smell, touch and sight of death was ever-present. We killed animals with our own hands. People saw, washed and prepared the bodies of their own family members who had died. Communities could be decimated by famine or disease. Even then, for the young and fit, and especially for boys – with their heroic sense of invulnerability – it was hard to imagine that this could happen to you.

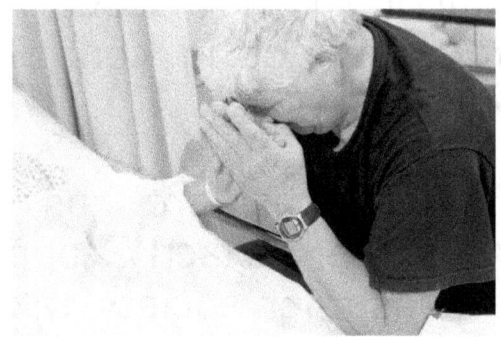

Image 15

It's a shame that death is now so hidden away, because *death is a teacher.* If you knew deep in your bones that you were going to die, that you might not even make it to nightfall, would you live the way you are living?

A father I know, a policeman, doubtless influenced by the young deaths he had witnessed in his job, took his son to a morgue when he turned eighteen. It wasn't a forced or brutal thing; the father explained what he wanted to do, and why, and it was a choice freely taken. But he was able to

stand with his son, and look at and touch a dead person. Not someone smashed up in an accident – it wasn't to frighten or jolt, which would have been an abusive and counterproductive exercise. It was simply to show – this is what death looks like. It's real. Game over. A person can be alive one minute and then be gone, just like that.

I have heard this same recollection from people who have been in wars or bad accidents, or simply had a loved one die, and spent some time with the body. *Until you see death close up, you don't really believe it is real.* We especially find it hard to conceive of our own death, and shy away from contemplating it. Yet we must face this. If we did, we would live with a different intensity; we would especially never waste our lives – whether through taking risks with safety, or with purposeless drifting, or with harmful activities. We would treasure every minute.

In West Africa, when people say goodbye, or make a plan to meet again the next day, they always preface it with 'God willing'. They know that life is fraught, that nothing is certain. 'God willing' acknowledges this; it does not skirt over the reality that our lives rarely go to plan, even as to whether we live or die. It gives a certain intensity to things, and may explain why African people are *often so much more happy and alive* when circumstances would not seem to support that.

If it was utterly clear to you in every fibre that your life might end at any time, how would it change the way you live? If you realised that your time in this world was short, might it change what you attempt to do with that time?

Life is hard

What our parents, teachers, and the TV in the corner all emphasise, every second of every day, is that *things can be managed.* That a cruisy and smooth life is possible. And not just possible, but something you should actively and relentlessly pursue. Just 'buy this, maintain that, insure that, save this, plan that', make good choices, and *you will be okay.* This isn't wrong to teach, or to attempt, so long as you understand that it will never be enough.

> Worthwhile things are hard. And they are risky.

What you have to understand is – *you won't be okay.* It may be possible to completely cut yourself off from life and reduce any kind of risk, but even then – who knows! Many things that make up a good life – being involved in the world, loving people, caring about what happens – expose you to risk and hardship. Worthwhile things are hard. And they are risky. Sickness and random injury will affect you and/or those you love. Deaths will happen, along with bad luck on a personal or planetary scale. You can't prevent this.

You have to make a choice. If 'easy' is your criterion, expect to be bored. If full and rich living is your goal, expect some pain. You can prepare for this, and triumph over it – not all at once, but as you accumulate more wisdom and experience. You can do this by *taking your sense of yourself beyond these ups and downs.* By resting in the ultimate joy of being alive, and not following the ins and outs/ups and downs with your whole heart, you will be able to step back from even your own heartbreaks. Richard Rohr puts it like this:

> *Hard and soft, difficult and easy, pain and ecstasy, do not eliminate one another, but actually allow each other. They bow back and forth like dancers, although it is harder to bow to pain and failure.*

Image 16

What he means is that our emotions are based in the relative. Even little children notice this. The ebb and flow of joy and sorrow, the seasons of life, the necessity of pain and suffering, are profoundly important to understand. The Book of Ecclesiastes in the Hebrew Bible contains one of the most moving pieces of writing in human literature: 'For every thing there is a season ... a time to weep and a time to laugh, a time to mourn and a time to dance.' When we grasp the transience of all these things, then we become free.

When pain stops, we feel joy. Therefore, it is the pain that makes the joy possible. Kahlil Gibran says, 'The deeper that sorrow carves into our being, the more joy we can contain.' When we understand this yin/yang pendulum, we can stop trying to freeze things in one place, since that will never happen. We can place our peace of mind somewhere that is not dependent on fickle emotion. Emotions are important – we have to feel them and let them do their healing work. But they are not where we should locate our wellbeing.

In 2004 an earthquake of magnitude 9 occured deep under the Indian Ocean. The earthquake continued for 8.3 minutes, and was so violent that the whole planet moved back and forth by several centimetres. The uplift of the seabed sent waves rushing at over 500km an hour towards coastlines all around the Indian Ocean. On reaching shallow waters these waves slowed down but lifted to almost 30 metres in height and surged ashore, killing almost 230,000 people.

Five years later, in Haiti, another earthquake killed 250,000 more.

It's that kind of world. There is no fairness, no deals we can strike with God to make everything go as we want. Fasten your seatbelt, eat healthy food, and be wide awake, but don't assume that this will always keep you safe.

Get used to the idea that effort, disappointment, suffering and loss all are equal parts of human existence. Then you will not be shocked or disillusioned. You will get on with it in the hard times, look forward to the good times, and enjoy them when they come. Underneath it all, a quiet joy will grow, that to be alive is glorious, whichever way the wind is blowing.

In the lovely and liberating book, *Tuesdays with Morrie,* the protagonist is dying from muscular dystrophy. He is active, cheerful and nurturing of his students and friends to the very last. But he explains to the interviewer that for half an hour a day, first thing in the morning, *he abandons himself to tears, grief and despair.* Then, having gotten that over with, he gets on with living.

A child is swept and overcome by the emotions of the moment. A grown man does not base his assessment of things on something as fickle as his own emotions. He feels those emotions fully and deeply, but then lets them go. He is interested in what will help.

You are not that important; your life is not about you

Our non-importance is a difficult truth to accept, because it contradicts what our brain tells us. As self-preserving mammals, we feel important to ourselves. Indeed, unless we prioritise ourselves to a sufficient degree, we do not maintain mental integrity or health, as any mother of small children knows. But one day we have to awaken from our boyhood thinking – that we are wonderful, significant, heroic figures, and our self-aggrandisement and gratification is the goal of life. We have to make other priorities, for two reasons. One is purpose – selfish living is a miserable kind of existence. The second is that we will be at odds with the rest of the human race, who do not share our wonderful opinion of ourselves. The strutting, preening and grasping man is a joke: *he thinks he is James Bond, but the world sees him as Mr Bean.*

The transition out of self-centredness is a normal and natural part of growing up. Small babies and toddlers feel themselves to be the centre of the universe, and the role of parents is to adapt to them, because this is what ensures their survival. Human babies are very dependent. A mother (in most cases) focuses on her child intently: she needs to interpret and meet its every need for several years. The better she does this, the more secure and loved, and therefore loving, the small child becomes. The problem is how to transition out of this. We aim for this gradually, teaching toddlers to take no for an answer, teaching primary-school children to get along with others, wait their turn, share and care. But finally, this shift has to be made absolute. This is what happened traditionally in initiation into manhood, usually at fourteen or fifteen years of age.

> Our non-importance is a difficult truth to accept, because it contradicts what our brain tells us.

At fourteen, the boys were often ritually separated from their families by the older men, taken away and taught a new way of thinking.

The Lakota people of the North American prairies actually forbade their sons from speaking to their mothers for two years following their initiation. It was as if they feared that the strong and warm mother–son bond would pull the boy back into boyhood. Living close by, they interacted with gifts and messages through intermediaries. When that time was over, a special ceremony re-united mothers and sons. But now the sons were men, and the relationship was friendship, not dependency. The Lakota were notable for the strong equality of men and women, and this respect-based relationship may have been one of the reasons for this.

In our world today, mothers and sons often remain in an awkward relationship in adulthood, the son not wanting to slip back into boyhood, the mother feeling sorrow that they cannot enjoy each other's company as before. Getting your son back, as an adult friend, is a great gift. When the men do their job, helping the boy to manhood, then the women benefit from the maturity and emotional independence of the young men.

The message of initiation was, at least in part, that *the world is not your mother.* If you go on thinking of yourself as special, you will come to a sticky end. It's time now to discover the joy and pride of giving, not taking.

Your parents might have harmed you, inadvertently, by going too far in either direction. If you were indulged and spoiled as a child, you will carry this delusion into adult life – 'the world revolves around me'. If you were neglected and left to your own devices, then a kind of savage self-preservation instinct might have cut in, so that you learn how to look out for 'number one' with cunning and a mistrust of others. Children who have spent their whole lives in daycare, competing for adult attention, rarely feeling special, will often show this kind of brittle social adroitness; they make allies rather than friends, and form relationships for the advantage it brings rather than out of a love of closeness or caring. Affluent families often combine the two errors, both materially spoiling and emotionally neglecting their kids, leading to self-centred and somewhat psychopathic offspring. Indigenous societies were deeply loving and indulgent towards the under-sixes, but increasingly expected responsibility and contribution from the six-to-fourteens. From fourteen onwards, they expected adult behaviour, though this always included fun and celebration.

Manhood is more fun than boyhood. There is so much more to be experienced when you set aside self-indulgence for the bigger adventure. There are billions of lives, human and non-human, on this earth. You can join in and make it all work better, and make strong connections with others along the way. But put yourself first, and you sink into the slime. Nobody will care. The joy of life comes from *belonging.*

Even shyness, self-consciousness and excessive humility are forms of self-importance. You have to shift your focus from yourself and onto the job in hand. When you sing, speak, build, teach, manage, lead, follow, or do any kind of work, realise that you are doing it for others. The difference this makes is enormous. You can take joy in the joy of others. That is the real reward.

From the burgeoning field of 'happiness studies', some clear results have emerged. These are that when we achieve a material goal – a new car, an expensive house, an exotic holiday – our pleasure and happiness peaks for a few minutes, and then immediately begins to decline. Even after winning the lottery, we rapidly return to the same level of worry and dissatisfaction that is our character.

What brings joy to life in a lasting way seems to be nonmaterial – being involved with friends and family, and seeking their wellbeing; moving outwards to looking at the world's needs. For example, whenever a crisis strikes, an earthquake or tidal wave, accident or war, an astonishing army of health professionals, aid workers, scientists and engineers from many developed nations around the world simply up stakes, volunteer and go to help. Aid organisations like the Red Cross or Medecins Sans Frontiers depend totally on this. Some people do this their whole lives. They are very happy people.

The kind of happiness that people bring just grows stronger. Once you discover the joy of service, you will not go back. Being *unimportant to yourself* is the beginning of freedom.

You are not in control of the outcome

This is the big one for many men. Not just the control freaks, but the good men, the ones who try to remake the world and improve it. Let me tell a rather extended personal story to illustrate this.

The SIEVX Memorial – a personal initiation

In 2001 my own life reached a crisis point. It was not that things were personally difficult – at least no more than normal for a parent of two teenagers. *My concerns lay in what had happened to my country.* In the aftermath of the 9/11 terrorist attacks in the US, fanned by carefully ambiguous political statements and rabid radio talkback hosts, the country's fears had escalated into something approaching a panic. The solution then proffered by our government, the way to 'make us safe', had been to imprison helpless and vulnerable refugee families fleeing Saddam Hussein's brutality, and treat them harshly – to 'send a signal' to others. Several thousand refugee families were dumped into hastily-built concentration camps in the desert and on remote islands.

I was a psychologist known worldwide for teaching about and caring about children. Nothing was closer to my heart than the situation of young mothers and babies. I watched as my own country destroyed young families' lives. The detention centres were not managed by Australians, but contracted to a US prison company. The conditions were horrific. Just once instance: women could not give birth in the centres. They were snatched from their families and flown in small planes to hospitals in Perth or Adelaide, shackled to beds, given no translators or explanations, in some instances given forced caesareans, and then dumped back in the hot and airless camps. Some simply went mad from stress, lay in their own excrement, and could not nurture or feed their babies, who also suffered developmental damage as a result.

In the midst of this, a single event took place which was beyond bearing. A refugee boat with over 300 mothers and children, and some 100 fathers, organised by people smugglers working with elements of the Indonesian military, sank, causing 353 deaths. Australia had a naval vessel in the area, and was intensely monitoring the region. Australian agents were working onshore with the Indonesian police and were aware of, possibly even involved in, the voyage. Nothing was done to rescue the people, most of whom survived the actual sinking but progressively died over the next 20 hours in the water. When fishing boats discovered them, just a handful were still alive to tell the tale.

A small group of us, meeting in a church in a country town, decided to build a memorial. Four years later, I found myself in Canberra, having spent those years, and a great amount of time and money, on the memorial, which was about to be built.

The concept for the memorial had come from a national schools competition we had conducted in 2003. It called for 353 painted wooden poles to be created all across Australia, each bearing the name of a dead refugee parent or child, and artwork from a school or church group depicting their own community welcoming that fugitive spirit to a place of safety on our shore. A site had been chosen on the lake shore in Canberra, and we had the support of the ACT Chief Minister, the ACT Parks, Sir William Deane, the Iraqi Ambassador, and churches and schools right across the land. Then four weeks out, the federal politicians woke up to what we were doing. The erection of the memorial was forbidden!

I lay on a motel bed in suburban Canberra, desperate. A team of volunteers and staff from across the country were in caravan parks and hotel rooms all over the city. Three hundred heavy wooden poles were travelling in trucks and trailers from as far away as Perth and Christmas Island, Tasmania and Cape York. Busloads of school children, contractors, rows of rented toilets, marquees, sound equipment...

My stomach knotted itself into a rigid piece of stone. I kept breathing, thinking furiously, searching for how to proceed. We had great people, contingency plans, amazing networks of support, but the personal responsibility involved just overwhelmed me. Gradually I forced myself to breathe deeper and deeper, and to think it through. Fear of failure was at the core of my anxiety. Then, a kind of psycho-physical event took place. My abdomen suddenly let go of all its tension, softened and relaxed. My mind at the same time grasped something fundamental: what we were attempting to do was A Good Thing. We had discussed it with thoughtful and wise people for over five years. People I deeply respected had praised and helped shape our efforts. Whether we succeeded or failed was not the question, or at least not something we could control. To quote the Blues Brothers, we were 'on a mission from God'. I needed to take no more responsibility than to do my best, but fallibility and frailty were part of that.

The next day, 2000 Canberrans and others showed up at the memorial site, and 600 of them held the poles upright in a powerful and moving ceremony. A Tongan choir sang, news cameras ranged down the line of resolute, angry, deeply moved young people, survivors and relatives, Middle Eastern people, retired couples, school students. We made the national news. Tens of thousands of people, who had previously had no idea, learnt the story of the SIEVX deaths. We had played a small part in a national awakening. By the elections of 2007, refugee issues were neutralised: ordinary Australians had woken up to the humanity of people with funny clothes, and Prime Minister John Howard lost his government *and* his seat.

The thing is, even if we had failed, it would have been okay. Because you only do what you can. The thing is to do what is *right,* or even what you hope is right, while being open to guidance and help from every quarter. A commitment not to know what to do, but to keep on seeking that, is all that the universe asks of us.

Failing at doing the right thing is not failing at all.

Note: In 2007, the SIEVX Memorial was finally erected in its completed form. You can visit it today at Weston Park, Yarralumla, in Canberra. For video footage of the site, and of the spontaneous ceremony described above, go to www.sievxmemorial.com.

Image 17

There is something very important to understand about

initiation. *It is not about standing on your own.* The five truths can easily be misconstrued as merely saying, 'Life sucks. Get over it.' The only rational answer to this, which many people take, is to dig oneself a hole somewhere and crawl into it – a response that doesn't help you or anyone else.

The purpose of initiation was to carry a young man or woman *into the adult community,* and the process presumes that community to be a cohesive, strong and lifelong network that will support you until one day you are an elder, too. Initiation is a *welcome to the world of the adults* who love you and value you, and will be there for your whole life. It's this and only this that makes the hard messages bearable. Building the community is the most important step, otherwise young people will never trust enough to leap over the gap.

The five truths are bearable, because we are never alone, even if we have a totally secular view of the world. Living for each other, setting aside self-importance, embracing mortality, we can make it.

It's not about us, it's not in our control, it will involve suffering, and we are going to die!

This is truly a joyful message!

IN A NUTSHELL

- The concept of initiation is ancient and proven in stepping boys into manhood.
- Exceptional human beings always seem to have had some difficult and testing period that awoke them to the depths of life.
- Richard Rohr and others have delineated five learnings that comprise the secrets of understanding being a man. These contradict all the assumptions that boys normally make about their own importance, effectiveness, invincibility, control and eventual fate.
- A man does not live for himself.
- An experience of overwhelming responsibility brings a lesson in trusting larger forces.

Image 18

SEVEN

Being a real father

'When your child seems to deserve affection the least, that's when they need it the most.'

Kim Payne, Simplicity Parenting

It's a sunny spring morning, and he is at the beach with his small daughter, exploring the rock pools. She is searching blissfully for crabs in the crevices, chattering to them and rearranging their social lives.

Without noticing it, she has moved further and further under a shelf-like overhang of rock. Suddenly, she stands upright and hits her head very hard on the underside, sharp needles of rock impacting with her skull. She wails, tries not to wail, then wails some more – a scream almost – as the pain intensifies. He runs across to her, feeling a swirl of responses. The ghosts of his entire ancestry spring up on the beach beside him offering things to say...

'You bloody stupid kid, why weren't you more careful?'

'Come on now, it's not that bad. Stop making that racket!'

'Oh geez, it's my fault, I should have watched out for you.'

He manages not to say any of these things. Instead, he scoops his daughter into an enveloping hug, and after a moment gives her head a rub to numb the pain a little. She seems comforted, and calms down a little in his arms.

Later, as they walk back homewards, her hand slips into his. He feels good, pleased to have gotten it right for once. Her hand in his says, 'Thank you.' His hand says, 'Yes, there is pain in the world, but I will be here.'

What is a father?

What does fathering mean? Listen to the language we use every day and it will tell you a lot. If we talk of 'mothering' children, we get a picture of nurturing and spending long hours in close, sensitive contact. The word 'fathering' means something quite different. You can 'father' a child in two minutes in the back seat of a car! At its most extreme, a father is just a sperm donor, nothing more. Lately, though, we have begun to challenge this idea: research is finding that active fathers make a huge difference in the lives of children. Today the idea of a 'male role model' is widely embraced. But it was a close shave; we are pulling fatherhood back from the brink.

There are plenty of books out about fatherhood, from the weak-joke victim kind to the busy executive variety – 'the one-minute father'! What this chapter aims to add is the deeper, inside story of wise fathering, and some practical advice that goes beyond the usual.

First, though (in case there's an earthquake or fire and you don't get to read the rest), here's the core message: loving your kids is more than a vague feeling of benevolent kindness. Love is something you *do.* Some of it is boring (shopping for shoes, keeping track of homework, waiting for them to come out of karate class). Other aspects grow on you and add beauty and depth to your life. Discovering you can bathe a baby (solo), or get her back to sleep at 3a.m., is a great feeling. A little older, and the interaction potential grows – listening to their chatter and endless questions, reading to them, having favourite ritual games and activities, like turning you into a bucking bronco. Soon it becomes a life-large project, as you realise how your care, teaching, fun, spirit and strength make their lives flourish and grow.

Before you know it, the 'great time paradox' of fatherhood will hit you – that while some days seem rather long, the years flash past. You start to want to put the brakes on, realising that your time with them is limited and coming to an end.

> Fatherhood can easily be the best thing you do in your life.

At some stage your children begin to outpace you, become smarter, quicker, stronger, sometimes wiser. But you are growing, too, and you will be of help to them until the day you die. It's possible for childless men and women to find equivalents, and they certainly should, but what a gift it is to have and be part of a family. The saddest thing about the single, the lonely, the homeless, is not their situation, but the fact that they are without a clan, that press of small bodies and laughter and argument and need that makes you exhausted but happy to be alive. Fatherhood can easily be the best thing you do in your life.

If there is no dad

A happy family is the dream all parents have. But pulling it off can be extremely tough; lots of dads don't make it. Divorce is probably the number-one danger. We already talked about how to stay married in earlier chapters, but here let's add – your kids would prefer that you do. More than one man I know has, in a deep, despairing moment in his marriage problems, wandered into his kids' bedrooms and seen them sleeping peacefully. He realises this security and peace depends on him not breaking up the family where they have lived their lives. And he decides to give it another go.

That's the crunch in parenthood: we don't own our own lives for at least a time, we've donated them to a good cause. Not all marriages can be safely kept together, but unless yours is violent and horrible, or a complete emotional nightmare, your kids would like you to try.

In struggling and damaged families, fathers are often the weak link that breaks first: the father leaves, or causes so much harm that the mother leaves him. John Embling wrote two books, *Tom: A child's life regained* and *Fragmented Lives,* about problem kids. John's masculine nurturing ability was the main tool he used to save kids from homelessness, violence and imprisonment. Here are his thoughts on fathers:

> *I spend most of my life with children, young adults, mothers – but where are the fathers? I have seen so many young children who*

need men in their home lives, men who are capable of psychologically meeting their needs. I feel a sense of profound loss, of defeat, of inhumanity, as I see men devoid of personal contact with their children. Their loss, the loss of something central to human process, is also our loss. Something is being crippled, and all the money, technology, bureaucracy, professionalism, ideology in the world won't make it right again.

Not all dads are a positive in their children's lives. But on average, given a half-decent male trying to do his best, the benefits might really shock you. The research picture is stunningly clear. If there is a father in the home, then statistically:
- both boys and girls have higher self-esteem
- they do better in school, and stay on in school longer
- they become better qualified and are more likely to be employed
- they are less likely to have trouble with the law

- they are less likely to be victims of assault, rape, or sexual abuse
- girls are less likely to experience early sexual intercourse or teen pregnancy
- boys are less likely to be violent or belong to a gang, and
- boys and girls are less likely to have problems with drugs or alcohol.

Remember, this is the overall picture, and some fathers would make all these factors worse, not better. But a caring father who lives in the home, or is close by and stays closely involved, makes a very great difference. Dads should be proud of what they do.

> Dads should be proud of what they do.

Dropping the old roles

There is a natural difficulty with fathering in the twenty-first century. Many elements you wish to bring to parenting your children – kindness, consistency, involvement – you may have never received from a male figure yourself. You are trying to invent fatherhood from scratch, a difficult task.

A good first step is to clean out the attic of your mind, where you will have old 'videotapes' of how your father used to do it. In his book *At My Father's Wedding,* John Lee describes four kinds of defective father that you might recognise:

1. *The man who would be king*

This was the man who returned home from work to be waited on by his wife-servant and seen-but-not-heard children. He was king of the house, and ruled his castle from the recliner. His family tiptoed around, careful not to 'bother' him. The only time this father got really involved was to dish out punishments or pardons. This was also the 'wait until your father gets home' dad.

My dad had an over-developed attachment to his roof. He talked about his roof a lot, and referred to it constantly when I dared question the king's decree for me. 'This is my house. You live under my roof. As long as you are under my roof you'll do as you're told. When you get your own roof you can do whatever you want to, but while you're under my roof you'll do what I say when I say it.'

'Damn,' I thought to myself, 'I can't wait to get my own roof.'

2. The critical father

He was full of put-downs and nitpicking, driven by his own frustration and anger. This father was certainly active in the family, but in totally negative, frightening ways. 'Is that the best you can do?' 'Can't you get anything right?' 'You stupid idiot, look what you've done!' Whatever was frustrating him – his job, his lack of success in life, his hopes for his children, even his difficulty in expressing his love – all turned into an acid which ate away at his family's wellbeing.

I was addressing parents at one of Australia's most

prestigious schools, whose principal was a famous ex-sportsman, a charismatic, intense man. The topic was fathers being absent from their children's lives. I could see him becoming agitated in the front row, and sure enough, after a minute or so, he could not contain himself. 'I wish my father had been less involved in my life. He damn well ran it!'

3. The passive father

This man gave up all duties, responsibilities and power to his wife, backing down also with the kids, his boss, relatives, society, the government and so on. This kind of father would make Homer Simpson look strong and determined. Unable to stand the heat, he would retreat into a newspaper, TV, alcohol or his garden shed. His kids grew up hating him for his lack of backbone.

Their mother would fly into insane rages, smashing the room

up, shouting and lashing at the kids with a jug cord as they cowered among the upturned chairs. The kids somehow understood this, tolerated it. But what they found hard to forgive was that their father just let it happen, sidled out into the yard. He never protected them.

4. The absent father

This man might have been a capable, even powerful man, but not in the family arena. He was off having a career, leaving early and returning late at night. On the night you were conceived, he was thinking about something else. He wasn't at your sports events or your school concert. He might have paid for all kinds of goodies for you, and even been courteous and kindly if you chanced to meet him in the hallway. But he wasn't any use to you as a father, because a father has to be there.

Was your father one of these types? If he was, be alert to the danger of dropping into that style of parenthood.

You may need to reprogram yourself. One way to do this is to look around for men you admire in real life, or even in books or movies, on whom you can base your fatherhood style. If they are real men, see if you can spend time with them, watching and asking questions. At least actively decide: that's the kind of father I want to be. And in a tight spot, ask yourself, 'What would he do here?'

By the way, the all-time favourite male character in literature, according to many surveys, is Atticus, the father of Jem Finch in Harper Lee's *To Kill a Mockingbird.* Gregory Peck played him in the excellent film of the book.

Being more self-aware is always the best strategy. For example, if your father was the angry, shouting and violent kind, then notice when those buttons are starting to be pressed. What is the first physical sign you are losing your cool? Can you step out of the room and chill out when that happens? Breathe three breaths, or count to ten? A good clue is to never, ever act impulsively or from an unexamined feeling (unless you are jumping to push a child out of the path of a bus!). Take a moment or two, and you will always have a better idea of what to say or do.

Whatever our parents' style was, auto-pilot for most of us is idiot-pilot. Think before you speak. Don't yell at kids when you are too angry to think straight. Never say things when you are upset. Always breathe, deep down in your belly, and go quiet for a while until you have a chance to think. This will minimise the chances of 'bad Dad' leaping out.

Creating a mood

Sometimes it's the simplest, most obvious things we overlook. A father, to his partner and children, is a powerful presence, and that can be powerful for good or for bad. For one thing, he is big. We easily forget that from a child's point of view, and even into the teens, a father is a physical threat if he is not committedly gentle, respectful of personal space, and eschews completely the use of loudness or an overbearing manner. Secondly, while many couples share the breadwinning role today, the father usually provides at least half the income, and often all of it. Should he choose to make this a source of power, he can do so to the great disadvantage of his partner (and kids), since the way she contributes, though huge in impact, cannot be measured or withheld in the same way.

> A good dad makes the family feel safe in the world.

Because of these powers – brute size and financial wellbeing – a man has historically been a considerable hazard in family life. Not only his behaviour, but even just his moods can create the entire atmosphere of the family whenever he is around, and even when he is not. Think about this from a child's point of view: you don't have any power, you can't leave, you are small, you have no safe refuge. A child's life is like a bedroom with a door swinging inwards and no latch. The mood of the father comes flooding in, and there is no defence.

Imagine your child has done something really dumb, dangerous or repeatedly defiant. You are raising your voice at them. Shouting is something we all do on impulse, and occasionally it's needed to get a child to take notice. But if you must do it, do it *with your eyes open.* See the child. (We can all remember the childhood experience of an adult 'losing it' with us, and raging on and on, out of control. It's terrifying.) As soon as your child shows, by a widening of the eyes, the slightest flicker that they are getting the message, then *ease off.* Make your voice much quieter. Ask if they understand what you are telling them. If they will change. And then let it go.

The only sense of control and safety a child has is that which is granted by parents showing respect and care.

Always check – am I angry with this child, for this reason, or is something else bugging me? Like my life? Kids can be a convenient lightning conductor; they even help by noticing we are stressed, and adding to it for good measure. But they don't deserve to be a dumping ground for our anger at our job, our sex life or lack of one, our having found a new dent in our car that morning...

Kids have to choose to be good, and you want them to be cooperative out of respect and fairness, not out of fear. Fear and respect are miles apart; only bullies confuse one for the other. If you show that you are noticing your child's nonverbal messages of surrender, and calm down right then, they will love you for it.

There's something else that really helps: prevention. Kids have a huge wish to be helpful, so as you prepare to go into a stressful situation – a supermarket, a holiday, a visit to relatives, Mum in hospital – talk to them about specific help that they can give. Give them jobs to do; make it a team effort.

A good dad makes the family feel safe in the world. A bad one makes the family feel afraid, mostly of him.

A home that feels good

Parents can consciously work to create a vibe, a feeling that permeates their home and all they do together. Good dads often lighten things up. They are like the conductors of the family's emotional music. Is the family mood dial set to 'hassled'? Full of anxiety and small needless fears? Is it resentful? Or is the home a place of positives? Do people hug each other in the mornings. Does Dad always make pancakes for Saturday breakfast? Do people put on good music and dance about to it? Do you have really great birthdays? Drop everything sometimes and go to the beach at sunset? Are mealtimes a place for relating funny things that happened, catching up on everyone's day?

Often the most politically aware, enviro-conscious, idealistic parents create a miserable mood for their kids. They fulminate at the politicians on TV. They watch the SBS News at mealtime, a rolling litany of massacre and misery. They tune into documentaries about endangered everything. Magazines on famine and death lie about the house. They surround their children, in other words, with fear and concern they are not able to do anything about.

Yes, the world is in danger, in a mess. But first you have to learn to love life. There will be plenty of opportunity later to protect it.

Most often, the single greatest enemy of love is hurry. People are just too busy. It feels like the home has no walls, the world is always crashing in – phone calls, emails, people dropping by, people rushing out, the television always on. Fathers can decide to change all this.

The work hazard

A while back, a toy company wanted to market a family of dolls called 'The Heart Family'. They trialled the sets, which comprised (naturally!) a mother, father and three children. The test children, in numerous samples, took the father doll and set him aside. Then they played with the mother and children. When asked, 'What about the father doll?', they replied, 'He's at work', and left the doll untouched in a corner. Father's work had no substance or meaning, and he was rarely used in the make-believe play. (Eventually, of course, the problem was solved: the father dolls were sold separately with big muscles, armour and a gun!)

Your work can be a danger to your family. What children get from a career father is not his happiness, nor his teaching, nor his substance, but only the leftover scraps of his life and, mostly, his mood. And at seven o'clock at night, that mood is often irritation and fatigue. Work, parenthood, couple time and self-time are the four legs of your life, and it takes real grace and conscious choice to keep them all strong.

Both boys and girls need fathers who are around, but for boys it can be critical. It's likely that boys are programmed to need several hours of male contact every day. This can come from schoolteachers, Scout leaders and sport coaches, but for the most part, most days, this means you.

It's a considerable challenge to find out how to have this much time, and still earn a living. But it helps to know that no amount of income will overcome the effects of having a dad who isn't around enough.

Boys are so hungry for male input that they will look elsewhere if you don't provide it. Teenage gangs are made up of boys whose fathers are either absent or have withdrawn emotionally. Whether it's the twelve-year-olds on BMX bikes after dark in the shopping centre, or nineteen-year-olds raging around the town in cars, all are missing out on the same thing – good men to guide them. Binge drinking by young males is a national disaster right now. Huge numbers of young men wander in and out of clubs and pubs all night, off their faces with alcohol. Why they drink is one question, but the bigger question is, why are they there in the first place? They should not be in these same-age groups, bored with each other and hopelessly failing at connecting with girls beyond quick sex in an alleyway. At this age, young men should be around older men and women, doing better things, having opportunities to meet the opposite sex without being blinded by alcohol.

> No amount of income will overcome the effects of a dad who isn't around enough.

When all that dads, uncles and other men do is work until they drop, they don't organise the activities and places where the young can belong. Sports groups, music, performing arts, outdoor adventure, four-wheel-driving, fishing, barbecues and expeditions are all part of a healthy adolescence and young manhood. Someone has to provide these, and steer things along. If work has sucked all the juice out of you, you will just sigh with fatigue at this idea. But it's pointless to feed, clothe and expensively educate a kid who then gets killed, hooked on drugs, or goes to jail because you were too busy to walk alongside him on the difficult path to manhood.+++

Peer groups – for you

Just back from a five-day hike around Wilson's Prom, I am asleep in my van at Tidal River campground. I don't even realise it's New Year's Eve. I'm awakened by the sounds of fighting and yelling. I listen. Is this something that needs a man? Then I begin to make out some of what is being yelled. One of the young men, totally drunk, wants to race his motorcycle up Mt Oberon to celebrate the New Year. His friends have hidden his keys. He is berating them into giving them back. They are telling him how much they love him and that they want him alive in the morning.

Not all peer groups are bad for you.

Peer-group pressure, which affects all children, can push your kids into bad choices. All kids want to belong, but some are desperate and will do anything to fit in with the group, including things that are criminal or dangerous.

Family therapists have discovered something important that can really help: peer groups only exert a dangerous influence on those who have a poor relationship with their same-sex parent. A girl who is not close to her mum, a boy who does not get along with his dad, looks to the group to be a surrogate parent. A teenage boy who enjoys the company of his father and his father's friends will be more his own man. He will also have had those talks and discussions that mean he can say to a group of friends, 'That's a really dumb idea. Come on, you guys, take that girl home, she doesn't know what she's doing/Let's call a taxi, we wanna get home safe/That guy didn't mean it, leave him alone.'

It's the fathers who need a peer group. This especially matters when your son reaches his mid-teens. From the age of fourteen, boys are programmed to want to listen to other men, not Dad. So you need a bunch of dads and sons to do things with. You should aim to join or create some kind of activity group, where the men are caring, responsible, and interested in the kids' wellbeing.

Heriot Sailing Club is a hand-built but comfy tin building in a cove on a wide reach of the Tamar River. Several dozen people of all ages can be found there on any weekend. I went there to learn to sail, but what I learnt was how people care for each other's kids. Mums took their ten-year-olds there to learn, but it wasn't a drop-and-run thing, you could spend the day. Loud-voiced, watchful men buzzed about in rescue boats – you couldn't drown if you tried! The more interpersonally skilled were teaching, guiding, making sure you knew your jib sheet from your tiller. Nobody was ignored; everyone was offered a sail, a coffee and a chat.

I talked recently to a father who had become a Scout leader. The emphasis on safety, mastery of equipment, fail-safes, back-ups and protocols for avoiding every kind of hazard – though it somewhat damped the sense of adventurous danger – was impressive, and infected the kids with an earnest enthusiasm for doing things right. Boys love this kind of thing. We hear occasionally of young people coming to grief in the outdoors, but we don't realise that thousands of them are out there every weekend doing it in total safety, because caring adults have taught them well.

Don't leave fatherhood too late

People used to have their children young – late teens or early twenties. These days the age is more like the mid-thirties and beyond. That's a huge change. In response to medical warnings, women often worry about their 'biological clock' running out, as two risk factors – increased infertility and the risk of a child having Down syndrome – increase dramatically after thirty-five.

But recent research is finding that dads, too, should not wait until they are too old before having children.

Abraham Reichenberg, an assistant professor of psychiatry at the Mount Sinai School of Medicine in New York, has reported on studies that show an increased risk of brain disorders like schizophrenia and autism in children born to older fathers. Both disorders have a genetic component and involve subtle brain changes.

Reichenberg's team studied more than 300,000 children born in Israel. One set of government records showed the age of each father when a child was born, and usually the age of the mother. 'In fathers who were 40 years or older, the risk for autism was almost six times higher than in the offspring of fathers who were younger than 30 years of age.' The mother's age didn't seem to matter. The analysis of the information showed a clear trend; the most likely explanation is damage to or mutation of the sperm of older men.

Another complicating problem for couples who delay parenthood is that fertility treatment itself tends to damage the babies produced, in small but significant ways. Professor Mary Croughan, of the University of California, studied 4,000 women and their children aged up to six years. She found that the risk of five serious disorders – autism, cerebral palsy, mental retardation, seizures and cancer – was 2.7 times higher among children born to women who experienced fertility problems, compared with those who did not have difficult conceiving.

Bipolar disorder (once called 'manic depressive disorder') is also emerging as being linked to older parents. The offspring of men 55 years and older were 1.37 times more likely to be diagnosed as having bipolar disorder than the offspring of men aged 20 to 24 years.

The offspring of older mothers also had an increased risk, but it was less pronounced than the paternal effect, the authors note. For early-onset bipolar disorder (diagnosed before age 20), the effect of the father's age was much stronger, and there was no association with the mother's age.

Even IQ is slightly lower in children of older dads. The average score on the Stanford Binet Intelligence Scale was nearly 2.2 points lower for children born to fathers aged 50 compared to those born to fathers aged 20. But this has to be put in perspective: older parents are usually better off financially. Positive factors such as having good nutrition, a stable home environment, good education and unstressed parents all improve with age, and can easily have a more positive effect on ability than a mere 2.2 points.

Still, the advice is increasingly – don't wait too long. Harry Fisch, MD, director of the Male Reproductive Center at Columbia University Medical Center, says that testosterone levels begin to decline slowly from age 30. Ideally, men should father children 'sooner rather than later,' he says. 'The twenties and early thirties are ideal.'

A good start

Just about to have a baby? Here are some ways to get fatherhood off to a good start.

You can get started as a dad even before your kids are born. During the pregnancy, if they hear your voice often, they will soon distinguish it from their mother's and any other voices. They will turn to face you once they are born, recognising that familiar rumble. When they are small, hold them against you so they will also feel your voice. A man's voice resonates deep in his chest and vibrates through a held baby, in a way they will come to love.

If you can be at their birth (which is a really good idea), take them into your arms, have your shirt open. Do not use soap, deodorant or scented cosmetics of any kind, so that your child bonds to the natural smell of you. Babies have a fantastic sense of smell. They will imprint your unique odour signature, which will reassure them when they wake up in the night (and they will not complain about your smelly feet when they are teenagers).

Don't be separated from your wife and child in the hospital. (Or, if you are up to it, consider a homebirth.) Sleep in the room, care for the child so your wife can get some sleep. Of course, respect her wish to have time with the child alone, too. Do not let nurses take your child to a nursery when it can have its parents' own care. That might be necessary in an emergency, but otherwise it just confuses the child's attachment patterns and disrupts feeding.

Really encourage and support breastfeeding. When a mother breastfeeds, she produces oxytocin, the 'love hormone' that floods in when we make love, or laugh together, or even sit down to eat with friends. Oxytocin helps a mother love her baby. Breastfeeding also gives great immune protection and gives baby's brain fatty acids that cannot be replicated in formula. Mums whose husbands support them in breastfeeding tend to breastfeed longer and better, and babies do better as a result. (On the other hand, don't make her feel a failure if she isn't able to. But make sure she gets support from a lactation expert. It's a knack, and some skilled guidance really helps.)

Organise some time off work (try for a month; three if you can) so that the early days can be unhurried and you can get established as a family, with less risk of loneliness or depression sinking in. And teach yourself to cook!

Watch for competitive feelings

On the cover of *Families and How to Survive Them* (John Cleese and Robyn Skinner's book on families), there is a cartoon almost everyone can relate to. A man is sitting watching his wife breastfeed the baby. The mother and baby are smiling at each other blissfully. The man is sucking a dummy and looking most put out.

When a new baby arrives, watch out for, and accept, competitive feelings if they arise. Your wife loves you as well as the baby. But her hormones have switched her into

> 'devoted mother love' instead of 'hot romantic love', enabling her to care for your child, and to love doing it. Support her – find a few minutes a day just to 'link up' with her, and be patient. She'll come back to you.

Dads and daughters

The newest discovery in fatherhood research is the remarkable effect that dads have on daughters. Girls face some powerful new dangers, and dads can be a protective bulwark against these if they understand what is going on.

In the last few years, a new problem has emerged which become the number-one concern for everyone involved with girls. This is the problem of 'premature sexualisation'. Through a combination of two factors – the reduced time that girls have with mothers and other older women, and the huge onslaught of media images and low-grade TV and advertising – girls have begun, from as young as three or four, to think that they have to be 'sexy': slim, coy, flirtatious and physically available to boys, in order to be valued and loved. An obsession with looks and body image, clothes and cosmetics, diet and exercise, has pushed many girls into deeply miserable and sometimes dangerous places. Far more girls are anxious and unhappy now than has ever been the case in the past.

Image 19

In particular this has affected the age of first sexual intercourse. The number of girls who have multiple sexual partners before the age of leaving school has doubled in the last six years. Few of these girls are happy or fulfilled with these sexual relationships; having sex is just something they think they should do to be loved. Almost every girl now dislikes her body and her face, and believes that being physically attractive to boys is more important than a career, having fun, having good friends, playing sport, or just simply taking time to grow up.

Dads have a part to play in this that can be incredibly helpful. As the opposite-sex parent, Dad is the 'practice male' for a growing girl. If, from an early age, he shows a strong and reliable interest in her life, reading, talking, playing, taking her places, she will decide that she is interesting and worthwhile. A dad who, on a Saturday morning trip with his daughter, doesn't rush home but stops off for a hot chocolate with her and chats, or plays basketball or walks the dog with her every evening, sends a message: 'You are good company', 'You are smart', 'You are interesting'. Having an involved father has been shown to prevent premature sexual involvement with boys, and make a girl manipulation-proof. 'My dad thinks I am great' is strong armour for a girl to wear around.

The other action which fathers and mothers can implement early is a dramatic reduction of toxic media in the home. Decide right away to never have TV or the Internet in kids' bedrooms (it increases anxiety and sleep problems, and greatly increases their exposure to inappropriate content, both sexual and violent). And to not have the TV on in the home unless it's to watch a specific program. Those homes where the TV goes on in the morning and stays on till night expose girls to a barrage of subliminal pressure about weight, looks, behaviour and damaging unhappiness with who you are. Don't buy magazines for young girls that are just advertising vehicles to get them using make-up and worrying about fashion. Don't spend the weekends in shopping malls, or treat shopping as recreation. Find healthy and happy relaxed ways to be with your kids, and keep the corporate manipulators away from them for as long as you can.

Dads and sons

There are very specific things which good fathers do for boys. In fact, dads have always done these, but not until now did we know why they mattered.

Little boys love to wrestle. Uncles, dads and big boys have always rough-housed with little boys, and nobody has ever understood why – women especially! We now know that some important lessons are being learnt in this fun activity. The first is 'not hurting'. Inevitably, a child wrestling on the carpet will hurt an adult by being too boisterous, not careful enough with an elbow or a knee. If this happens, the father stops the action, and says clearly to the boy, 'Your body is precious and so is mine. We need one or two rules so no-one gets put in the hospital. Like no kneeing or hitting. Can you handle that?' (Say this with a challenging voice, chin stuck out. Don't make a joke of it; it has to be dead straight.)

> Your body is precious and so is mine.

The aim is to coach them in how to be energetic, excited and lively but always safe. A potent lesson is being learnt here. When the boy is grown up, he will almost inevitably be stronger and larger than his girlfriend or wife. He must know how to take criticism, experience strong emotions and, at the same time, never use his physical strength to dominate or hurt her. The boy learns to contain his strength from the example of a father who never hurts him and who doesn't allow him to hurt others.

Winding up and winding down

There is a unique pattern of play that fathers all over the world seem to demonstrate. I'm grateful to Alastair Spate, who described this pattern to me as follows:

> *Imagine two parents on a living-room floor with a two-year-old lad and a pile of blocks. The mother encourages the child to play with the blocks and at least construct a pile or some sort of rough*

structure. Typically, at some stage, the father will transform himself into a roaring monster-cum-bulldozer, knock over the bricks and provoke peals of delight in the child. From then, the two males 'wind up' in challenge and response, giggling and hooting, rivalling each other to make the biggest mess.

When the father eventually senses some disapproval, or at least concern, in the mother, he begins to 'wind down' the play until a breathless equilibrium returns to the room and the boy rests in the arms of either of the parents.

This sort of play is very much the father's specialty. The crucial thing is the winding down. Here a father teaches his child, through play, the mastery of his energy and angers, sets the limits of aggression and how to stay in charge of one's emotions and not be flooded by them.

Most readers will have seen the uncontrolled inner and outer rages and depressions of the *underfathered boy, whose first experience of male limit-setting is likely to be the police or the truancy officer in early adolescence – and by then he is literally a marked man. (Or marked and not yet a man.) He never learnt through this uniquely fatherly play how to become the master in his own house of angers, dreams, yearnings and energy.*

And you thought you were just playing! 'Winding oneself down' turns out to be a vital, life-saving skill. This is another gift a good father can give.

Discipline

In the bad old days, fathers were often the disciplinary 'bad cop', the 'enforcer'. The fact that they were away from the house all day made them scarier. 'Wait till your father gets home!' was the last-ditch threat of exhausted mums. Today we have the opposite problem – wimpish fathers are everywhere. They leave discipline to their wives or, worse still, undermine them: 'Let the kids be – they aren't being that bad'; 'Just relax, honey, it doesn't really matter.' (Such men are in for a short marriage and a terrible sex life!)

Women and children need men to be at least equal partners in discipline. Boys especially require a certain good-natured combativeness in order to get the message through. Men who are comfortable with their masculinity enjoy this matching of strengths. They can do it without feeling threatened and without the same sense of exhaustion that women may feel from being 'hard' on children.

There is another reason why fathers need to take a tougher role. The feelings of a mother for her child are primarily tender, and the child reciprocates this. If a great deal of disciplining is being done by the mother, especially if it is negative and critical, a boy can start to feel that his mother hates him. Many mothers tell me, 'Every time I open my mouth, it's to criticise.' A boy can feel the mother-love eroding. If the father is doing his bit, the mother relaxes, feels supported, and is less cold or harsh as a result. You can pick at a glance those women who feel backed up by their husbands in the home. They are more relaxed, warm and feminine. Women who have to do all the tough stuff – argue with the builder, battle the kids and make the decisions – look hard and tired. Their body language says 'my husband is too weak'.

If the father talks firmly and clearly about what is and isn't acceptable, and reinforces this with a non-violent but firm follow-up – then the wife is able to relax, and can remain more loving. This isn't to say the role division is all one way; both partners need to do both. Unless the father also has a loving and involved role with his son or daughter, then his discipline will not work.

The essence is to get engaged, eyeball to eyeball, and be definite – so that children can state their case but are also made to listen to yours. Even when you are being stern, kids still like it deep down: they know you are involved.

I talked to some Year 12 girls about the growing pressure on girls to act sexier younger

and younger. They agreed that this was a serious problem among friends, some of whom had gotten mixed up with boys far too young, through being poorly supervised and allowed to stay out late at night, and had their lives unravel as a result. The girls had noticed a clear divide among parents – those who wanted to be 'friends' with their daughters, and as a result were afraid to draw limits or boundaries; and those who understood that a parent sometimes has to be unpopular. These girls were clear: they actually wanted parents to set curfews, know where they were, and be strong in supervising them.

Adolescents may sound very logical, but they are not able to handle strong sexual pressure, alcohol or driving cars without good supervision. Kids may grumble, but they actually feel more secure and loved when parents understand they are not adults yet, and need external limits. Dads and mums can back each other up in this, and parents who align can help each other be strong and clear.

Knowing a boy's stages

There are three stages that all boys seem to pass through. Little boys from birth to six stay very much in their mother's world: they are learning to love life, and she is at the centre of that. A dad can do a lot with small children – care, teach, read, play and guide – but compared to a mum he is like 'light entertainment'.

Then, at six, boys change – they seem to notice they are male, and families all over the world observe the boy starting to move his interest towards his dad. This is important for several reasons. The boy knows that he is turning into a man, and he wants to learn how it is done. Also, it's important for the boy to begin to feel emotionally independent from his mum. This is a gradual experience, and not a sudden change – the father is added, while the mother keeps up her role. (Psychologists still have many male clients who were sent to boarding school at age six.) Being able to exist away from female comfort and support, to experience the slightly more robust, slightly more conditional love of a father, means that a boy is able to find his independence, to feel safe and at home in the world of men. The result of this is an important one – he knows he can stand alone without being mothered, so when he begins to relate to girls and women as a young man, he does so as an equal. He will be less likely to want to be mothered. This is a great relief, for both mothers and future partners. A fully-grown man makes a much better partner.

> The peak years for fathering are from six to fourteen.

The peak years for fathering are from six to fourteen. After fourteen, a dad and mum are still important, in both supporting and setting boundaries, but a new element is needed. Fourteen-year-old boys seek out male mentors.

A mentor for your son

Even the best fathers cannot raise their sons alone. Fathers need help from other men to complete this final stage. In tribal situations, the whole male community got involved with the teenage boys, training and initiating them. A father could count on all kinds of help, and boys could count on positive input – usually more relaxed and accepting than fathers manage.

A boy in his mid to late teens needs other men for three reasons: to teach him skills, to give him a sense of worth, and to take him out beyond the family walls. In the old days, a mentor was the person who taught a boy his trade or craft for life. This arrangement took the heat out of the father-son relationship, which can get very tense, as anyone who has taught their teenager to drive will know!

If you have sons, it's brilliant if you have a group of male friends whom they can be around, so that they begin to feel accepted in the adult male world. Often sons have interests that you don't share, however hard you try.

There will always be deeply intellectual fathers with athletic and extroverted sons, and vice versa. This needn't be a problem if the father finds good men among his acquaintances who can fill the gaps, and so create a balanced adolescent experience. Whenever a boy seems to be unmotivated, at home or at school, look to a lack of male role models as the cause. As mentoring expert Joseph Palmour puts it:

Image 20

A boy needs help to learn about his own gifts and identity, and help to learn how to identify someone who has mastered the skills that are the birthright of his nature. [Boys'] lives seldom expose them to mature men doing things of such quality as to inspire a boy's emulation ... In this light, we should not be surprised that our teenagers have grown apathetic about preparing for roles that are either invisible to them or that exercise no charm over their imaginations.

Wise men understand that the myriad activity groups around which people organise their leisure time serve a more important purpose. A fishing club isn't really about fishing, or a cricket club about cricket (though part of the role involves treating these things as being of extraordinary importance!). They are really just ways that men can care for each other and take boys into tutelage, give them positive messages, and so provide a vehicle for character growth and maturation.

What single mothers can do

Today there are millions of mothers raising sons without a man in the house. They mostly do a fantastic job, but it's uphill and fraught because they are trying to be both mother and father.

Single mothers are usually very alert to the need for male role models for their sons. Once they find a way to supplement this need, many problems of young sons – such as over-shyness or over-aggressiveness – disappear. There is a lot you can do if you are a single mother of boys. Visit your sons' school and ask if they can have a male teacher next year. Choose the athletic, musical, Scouting avenues that have good men in them. Be choosy. Select on the basis of, 'Are these the kind of men I want my son to turn into?' That is what 'role model' means. But be careful – sometimes sexually abusive men prey on fatherless boys, exploiting their craving for male affection.

Despite the risks, boys need men, as the following story illustrates dramatically.

> A mother in a Tough Love group (a form of self-help group for embattled parents) told how her fourteen-year-old son would simply not get out of bed and go to school in the mornings. Several men from

her group offered to come, as a team, and rouse her son from bed to get him off to school each morning. This they did. Imagine the boy's surprise! After a couple of visits, they only had to be 'on call'. The boy got his act together. He protested, but he also seemed kind of pleased.

Single mothers can raise boys well, but not alone. They need the help of a wider network. If you are a dad, your son will have friends with no dad. Invite them along when you go to a concert, a camping trip or a sports match.

If you are divorced

Increasingly, parents who divorce are learning to do so responsibly and to share parenting for the benefit of the children. If you are an estranged father, or a father relinquishing a child for adoption, or even a sperm donor, the thing to remember is that, somewhere, your son is waiting, with all kinds of mixed feelings, to know you and know your side of the story. If the hostility between you and his mother is an obstacle, then you should work to drop this on your part. Let him know that you are available when he is ready to sort things out.

> Being a whole man involves living the bigger life...

Sometimes a son living with his mother will unconsciously start to make it so difficult for her that she will consider letting him go to his father. On occasions, to everyone's surprise, this can be just the right thing for 'finishing off' a young man's development. If a father sidesteps this responsibility, the boy's soul may be deeply wounded. Some fathers just vanish from the family scene following a divorce. Since this is most likely done from a position of hurt – out of hostility to the mother – it is very unjust to the child. A father has the power to bless his children's lives and the power to greatly damage them, depending on whether he maintains or loses contact. For men there is, potentially, enormous satisfaction and peace of mind if you take on your proper role here – and being a better father can compensate for the feelings of failure with the divorce. Some men have told me they only got close to their children after they divorced their wives.

Being a whole man involves living the bigger life, the long game, looking to the future and knowing what will make you proud on the day you die. Nothing quite beats parenthood for this kind of opportunity, or this kind of danger and challenge. It's a very manly thing to do.

IN A NUTSHELL

- Loving kids is about what you *do,* not just a warm, good feeling.
- If there is no dad, kids' lives are much harder.
- We were shown some very bad models of how to be a dad – it's important to dump these from our repertoire.
- A father often sets the family mood because he is big and powerful. Work at sending a message of safety, lovingness and good fun.

- Your job can be a danger to your family – it pulls you away from parenthood.
- Dads keep boys out of trouble, and help girls set high standards for boyfriends.
- Dads help boys learn to manage their physicality, to stay safe.
- Discipline can be done with calmness and strength, and this helps mothers to relax around teenage boys.
- Dads need other male friends to help with mentoring their teenage boys.
- Single mothers can raise boys well, by understanding the need for good men in their lives.
- Divorced dads can still be good dads; sometimes they become better dads as a result of divorce.

Image 21

EIGHT

Meaning

'There is no passion to be found in playing small. Don't settle for a life that is less than you are capable of living.'

Nelson Mandela

Donald Miller was lucky. At 32, single and living in a shared house with friends, he wrote a bestselling book, a series of reflections on his own life called *Blue Like Jazz.* People loved it – it was honest and funny, everyone recognised themselves in it. Money poured in; he had it made.

Then an interesting thing happened. Some film producers arrived at his home to begin working on a movie, based on the book. They settled down to work with him on the long preparation that a film takes, and realised they had a problem. Not to mince words, his life was boring. Miller had intelligence, humour, a good heart and a complete lack of direction. Since becoming rich, he had spent most of his time in bed. Tentatively, they shared this insight with him. Miller suddenly saw that he was a successful nobody.

The film-makers explained to him what makes a good plot for a movie, the arc of drama and resolution that makes people watch right through and feel uplifted when it's over. In Miller's case, the ending was a good one – he got rich and famous at thirty-two. But a good story needs more than that. If you think back over any good film or novel, it always begins with a character, a hero, whom the audience likes and cares about. Early on, this character has to do some good things: save a child, be nice to his mother, at least have friends or a pet. If he is just selfishly going about life, feeding his face, who cares if he lives or dies? What we admire in a human being is their *caring.* If they care about others, we care about them, because we sense that this would be a good person to live or work alongside.

Almost all movies establish the goodness of the lead character early on, and those that don't, that set out to deal with the badness of people (or even the blandness of people), tend to be box-office flops, unless they get some kind of redeeming point happening fast.

A likeable hero is the first step, but that's still not enough. Early in the storyline, he or she needs a quest. A purpose. The hero needs a goal that they really want to achieve. Buying an expensive car won't do it. Finally having that holiday in Europe? Well, everyone does that. The goal has to be difficult, worthwhile and unique. Getting the girl is a common challenge, but getting the girl when you have no legs, or are being chased by drug-company gangsters across Africa – that's a story worth telling. There have to be insurmountable obstacles, so it really looks like you are going to fail. You struggle with those obstacles, there are some twists and turns, you finally triumph, and everyone cheers and goes out into the sunshine.

It was in thinking about this that Don Miller made a simple but explosive connection. If his life didn't make a good film, then it probably didn't make a good life. Without direction, without worthwhile goals, without significant challenges, his life was empty. He began to wonder – can you edit a life? Can you improve the plot of your own existence, so it's a life worth living?

Miller figured all this out. In a remarkable act of self-help, he decided to give his life a better script. Instead of leaving it to chance, he would become a good person, do good things, take on mighty tasks. His book, *A Million Miles in a Thousand Years,* tells the story of how he did this, with considerable success. I highly recommend it.

> All good therapy is based on helping people to realise, 'We are living a crap story!'

Your life is a story

Many of us would be in Miller's situation. Who would want to watch the movie of our lives? So it's useful to ask the question – am I living a good story? For most of us, the missing plot is related to goals. We either don't have them, or they are so ordinary that an audience would start chewing the chairs. Partly it's cowardice: most worthwhile goals are difficult ones; the easy ones have already been taken. But difficulty is not the criteria for something being worth doing. (Remember the Monty Python sketch about teaching crows to fly underwater?) Worthwhile goals have to have meaning, in terms of impacting other lives and contributing to the human race's journey. Making a difference means just that – altering the way things are – and there are many forces supporting the way things are, many powerful vested interests.

Rich, nasty people rise to the top as much today as they did in the Dark Ages. They just have to be a little more careful about PR now. Also, to do more good than bad, you will have to overcome your own limitations and weaknesses, and this will often involve struggle – a hero's struggle. To achieve great good, you will need to team up with others, to face obstacles and discover surprising allies. And finally, sacrificing and risking all, you may one day achieve what seemed impossible. Hooray!

Finding the plot

Realising that your life is a story has a profound, sometimes shattering effect, but a good one all the same. We all live stories – sometimes borrowed stories from the stock footage provided by the culture, sometimes stunningly original ones. Knowing this, and choosing rather than having your story happen by accident, is the secret of personal liberation. All good therapy is based on this: helping people to realise,

'We are living a crap story. Let's change it!'

When we are young, we think life is about having fun experiences, making buckets of money and getting the most beautiful girl; we seek success in conventional terms. But eventually we realise these goals are not working out (or we reach them, and they don't make us happy). Some men stop trying then, and drift for the rest of their life. They may drift into a job, a marriage and a family, but it's drifting nonetheless. Their lives will lack passion, their families and workmates will find them boring, no-one will miss them when they are gone.

Other men keep on trying to figure this out, and because the universe tends to reward sincere effort, these men gradually begin to experience an awakening. They realise, one day, that it's all about meaning. Our lives have to add up to something, and only we can choose what that something is. Meaning is something you can't see or touch, but it is more real than houses, cars, skyscrapers or jet planes. It lasts longer; it impacts the world more. It shapes the future. Live long enough and you will slowly realise that meaning is the only thing that matters. As Donald Miller found out, if you have a worthwhile life, others will find it inspiring and interesting. *You* will find it inspiring and interesting. You will be happy to wake up in the morning. Life will be an adventure. When you die you will die happy and proud, and people will be moved and affected by your life's story. You will have a wonderful funeral. (Miller, at the end of his book, wisely points out that life is not quite like a movie. Movies have a big finish, and everything is resolved. But in real life there's always something else coming along – more like a long-running 'soap' than a feature film.)

What is 'meaning'?

Imagine a busy main road in the suburbs, perhaps like one you travel on every day. Two taxi-cabs pull up at the lights. In one of those cabs, the driver is Sudanese. He is tall, startlingly black, and laughing and talking with his passenger, a middle-aged psychologist heading for the airport. This taxi driver has a past, though the two of them do not venture there. But he also has a present: there are photos of his two daughters on the dashboard, and he talks animatedly about their lives. One is now at university, studying nursing, still living at home. This man is working, in the most lowly-paid of jobs, to feed his family and give his children a secure and happy life. He talks about the Sudanese community in Australia, the get-togethers and extended community support, the music and culture they preserve, the food, the celebrations. When he drops me off, he will continue to grind through traffic, transporting the drunks, the vomit-in-the-back- of-the-cab party girls, the racists, the businessmen who barely acknowledge his existence. After ten or fourteen hours of this, he will collapse into his humble, spartan home, his loving family will greet him, and he will fall asleep, happy.

In the cab alongside this one, also waiting for the traffic to inch forwards, a taxi driver scratches himself, swears, and shifts the radio dial between a racing channel and a talkback host. (The talkback host secretly received large sums of money from a large bank and began talking positively about banks and banking, markedly reversing his previously scathing position. In short, an already rich man, his life built on the trust of his uneducated listeners, has sold them out to the big end of town.) The cab driver nods in agreement with the racist statements of the radio man. He talks desultorily with his passenger about his divorce, the bitch his first wife is, and how ungrateful his kids are. It's hard work to find the heart of this man.

The outward activity is the same: two men drive cabs. But the meaning could not be more different. Every traffic light, every fare, every minute of the day for the Sudanese man is an act of purpose for a clear and worthwhile goal. He has brought his family from torture and death in the desert, through terrifying obstacles of international borders with no money or means, to a strange and alien country. He will see his daughters walk onto a stage and graduate to secure, beautiful lives. His life is a hero's journey. The second cab driver will die alone in a brick unit somewhere, or grouching at nurses in a crowded hospital ward, and no-one will care.

A matter of life and death

In 1990, a small group of school students and teachers hiked into a cave system called Mystery Creek Cave, near Hobart in Tasmania. The cave takes its storybook name from a bubbling creek that enters the cave mouth, follows it for several hundred metres, then completely disappears underground. It's a beautiful and exciting place to visit. The two teachers, a man and a woman, and five girl students spent a day exploring the dark caverns. Meanwhile, on the surface, heavy rain was falling. As the party clambered back towards the exit, they discovered that the creek had risen dramatically, and surging waters now flowed across their route. They faced a decision: should they remain where they were, until the water subsided? That might involve a night underground, and anxiety for their parents and friends. So they linked arms, and began to move through the waist-high water. But the current proved too strong; two of the girls and the woman teacher were knocked off their feet, and in seconds were swept to their deaths.

> It's not hard to save lives in the world we live in...

There was grief and shock in the school and community. The male teacher, much loved and admired by students and colleagues, was devastated. The louder voices were saying, 'It could happen to anyone', but locals and experienced walkers talked quietly about an error of judgement, that the weather forecast indicated rain, and the cave's tendency to flood was well known. That once trapped, they should have waited. The male teacher clearly sided with the latter voices. On a trip to Melbourne with friends a couple of weeks later, he slipped away and threw himself to his death from a high building.

If it's possible, the grief over his death was greater still. He was a young husband and father, a fine teacher who did so much for his students. The bereavement columns of *The Hobart Mercury* ran for several pages with messages of loss. The counselling community, of which I was a part, also searched its soul. This was a predictable, preventable death. We had to learn from what went wrong.

It's not possible to know the full facts of this young man's death, so what follows deals, in broad terms, with any situation where a perceived error leads to a terrible result. Error is part of human life, and we need to have a pathway out of crushing guilt. The Christian message is built around this, but every religious tradition deals with it.

When a man feels guilty, he has to be listened to: he is the one most aware of the circumstances, and of his own inner processes. Feedback from objective sources may help, but ultimately we judge ourselves. No intervention that did not take this into account could have been credible with the person involved. The starting point has to be, not 'You weren't to blame', but 'If you blame yourself, what does that mean?' The teacher might have felt that he owed the world three precious lives. If that was true, then would killing himself repay that? The answer has to be no. Dying just adds to the circles of grief: it wastes his life, and sends a message to young people that if life gets too hard, give up. The degree of emotional support and closeup contact needed to help a man stand with such remorse would be immense, though it has been done over and over throughout history. Redemption – earning forgiveness for past errors – is among the most ancient of our stories.

The logical answer must lie in living one's life to try and re-pay what has been lost. And, in fact, people do this all the time. It's not hard to save lives in the world we live in: you can donate a kidney or bone marrow. Thirty dollars will restore someone's sight. Imagine what a lifetime spent redemptively might give to the world. Tens of thousands of doctors, nurses, teachers, engineers, pilots and truck drivers live and work in tough places; they risk their lives because they can save lives by doing so.

You don't have to be seeking redemption to want to do good. The world asks questions of you every day. The TV news each night is mere entertainment; the real news is that 30,000 children die each day from preventable causes in countries too poor to save them. Climate change, forest loss, fishery destruction, soil erosion, disease, illiteracy, sex slavery – take your pick, all offer a lifetime of purpose. Closer to home are Indigenous issues, homelessness, kids without fathers, the mentally ill, families needing help, and so on. We are in the midst of a continuing human emergency. The human race might not make it. *There is no shortage of meaning on this earth.*

Nor inspiration. As author Terry Pratchett puts it, 'we have come from monkeys to the moon' – our species' adventure is a mighty one. We are only here because people made it happen. Someone worked, and sometimes died, to gain every positive aspect of your life – health, education, safety, travel, housing, protection from heat and cold, justice, clean food, clean air, water and soil. If you are ever feeling depressed, a bit bored or lonely, try visiting an Emergency room, or an inner-city police station, or a suburban high school, where kids either snatch a future or don't. You are needed somewhere right now. The human race is endangered, it's shoulder-to-the-wheel time. And those who do shoulder the wheel usually have the best, sexiest, laughing-out-loud time of their lives.

The circle of life

Discovering your life's unfolding purpose isn't something to panic about. Each stage of life builds towards its eventual destination; Mother Nature takes her time to create the competent human being. The young are supposed to have fun, explore – this is what makes their brains grow the best. It's alarming to see parents torment their babies with flashcards, or rush their toddlers to 'enrichment' classes, like prying at a rosebud to make it open sooner. Primary school should not be for worrying about your looks or your possessions. Even adolescence should be a time for dreaming, trying on many roles, guessing and probing the meaning and purpose of life. If we get too serious too soon, we foreclose on exciting futures that we might rise to if we spent a little longer building up our potential.

You have your whole life, and there is an unfolding that needs to happen. For a young man, meaning might seem to lie in the awesome sight of his girlfriend asleep by his side. For a new dad, it might be the trusting hand of a small child, the clear knowledge that her whole life depends on him to protect and provide. That feels like meaning enough. But what about other children, other women, other lives? The truth is, our horizons, and our contribution, never cease to expand. We always seek a wider story. The Australian Indigenous leader, David Mowaljalai, taught young men both black and white throughout his life. The culmination of his ceremonies was an initiatory message, and he stated it plainly: you are in this world to nurture and protect life. That is what men are for.

The big picture

Imagine a beach. It's long and flat, with firm, rippling sand, and the tide is out. You pick up a piece of driftwood, and walk along the beach, drawing a line as you go. You walk for a kilometre, then stop. You turn and look back at the line. That line is human history. The journey you have walked spans 300,000 years.

Some remarkable things are known about this line. From our mitochondrial DNA, the tracer of all our mothers' bodies through all of time, we know that every single human alive today shared one single ancestral mother, somewhere in the African rift Valley. There were thousands of her race – she was not like the biblical Eve, but she may as well have been. Through chance, only her offspring survived.

Absorb this for a moment: we all have the same mother.

> We knew our world, we lived in culture and story, we created and loved.

We also know that our species was far from promising in its early days. We lived on the fringes of the great herbivore herds, and were preyed on by the big carnivores. We were scavenging, rock-using little tribes that were smart and cooperative, but physically weak. It's a wonder we made it at all.

At Laetoli in Africa, some of the most poignant records of prehistory survive in a rock shelf, the earliest known evidence of our first upright ancestor, *Australopithecus afarensis.* The footprints clearly revealed in the rock show two people, one larger, one smaller, walking across an ash bed. They were within sight of an active volcano that had created the ash, and was still spewing smoke several kilometres to the west. The footsteps pause, draw close to each other, and turn to face the volcano. Perhaps one of the figures puts an arm around the other; they are standing very close. Then they walk on. *A. afarensis* were only a little over a metre tall, but they were on the way – they were heading to be human.

Now bend down and lay your metre-long piece of driftwood along the last part of the line. What are you looking at now? For a kilometre back along the beach, the line shows the time humans identical to you and I have walked upon the earth. And for all of that line that is uncovered, 999 metres, we were hunter-gatherers, moving with the seasons. Hunter-gatherers could feed, clothe and shelter themselves with, at most, two or three hours' work a day. We knew our world, we lived in culture and story, we created and loved. A child of twelve could identify 100 plants useful to her, and know their season, their processing, where they could be found. Teaching, cultural and religious activity was our most common use of time.

That is the uncovered part of the line. Now, the part the stick is covering, the last 0.1 percent, is the period of human settlement. Whether from invention or necessity, we discovered agriculture, a way to support far more people. Storeable grain meant the rich could live off the poor. In the deserts of Iraq and Pakistan, the first towns and cities were built. They were built by slaves. For the last 10,000 years, most human beings have had terrible lives. Empires have ruled the earth, we have laboured in fields and quarries, and only a lucky few could rise above the level of mere subsistence.

Now look down at the length of your hands: 15, 20 centimetres. That is how long there have been cities of more than a million people. That's us, that's now.

Image 22

This is the context to your life; in fact it's the *meaning* to your life. We are living in a relay race. The human race is headed for the stars, and for unimaginable futures of beauty and grace. But we have to get our part right. Our ancestors fought famine and disease. Then it was fascism. Then it was the imminent threat of nuclear war. Now it is whether we will bake the earth and make it uninhabitable for our grandchildren. There is always something. But each generation of our forebears has kept passing the baton. In the end it comes down to one thing: little babies being born, and whether they will thrive and grow. This is the work of men.

Living for others

Mohammed Yunus is a small man with sparkling eyes. He was born to prosperous parents in Chittagong, on the coast of Bangladesh, and as a child his mother often sent him to take food or money to poor families in his town. He experienced at an impressionable age *the joy of being able to help.* As a qualified economist, he grew sick to the stomach with his inability, through economics, to be of help to the millions of poor whom he saw, stick-thin and dying, in the streets of his country. He searched for a new paradigm. His name may be familiar to you – Yunus invented microfinance, lending tiny amounts of money to the poor women who were enslaved because they could not buy their own sewing machine, or bamboo to make chairs, or cotton to sew. He enabled millions of people to become self-supporting, educate their children, afford health care, and escape suffering and hopelessness. He won the Nobel Peace Prize as a result.

Yunus told a television interviewer that the 'eyeglasses of profit' were what the whole Western world looked through, and that *there were other ways to see the world.* Once we discover the joy of being able to free others, of helping to change the world, Yunus argues, we will never go back to selfishness. He had a word for the pleasure of doing good – he called it 'intoxicating'. Yunus brimmed with calm happiness, health and intensity. The interviewer was visibly moved. If you are a rich man reading this, or even one of modest means, this is the question to consider. *Would you be immensely happier if you were to spend the rest of your life doing good, not as a sideline but as your total focus?*

Back in the 1970s, a young, bespectacled man, a computer nerd, realised that the coming wave of personal computers would need a common basic software, and that the first to develop one would own the game. Bill Gates followed his hunch, got to work, and the rest is history. Lesser men would have stopped there, counting their billions and hugging them to their chest. Bill did something different: he decided to devote the rest of his life, and his money, to doing good. With his wife, Melinda, and colleagues like Warren Buffet, he has since spent billions of dollars saving lives, primarily through researching and preventing childhood disease. *They have alleviated more suffering, for more people, than any other humans alive today.*

Image 23

We can't all be Bill Gates (a cliché, but true). But the message here lies not in the scope, but in the joy of contribution.

This is the message at the heart of the book you hold in your hands: to consider how much good you can do in changing the lives of others. If you do this, you will experience deep joy, motivation and an integration of all the pieces of your life into a streamlined whole that means not a second is ever wasted. Live for others, and you will be freed of the prison of self. Your time in the world will be blessed.

This is the heart of manhood, the reason we are on this earth: to care for the lives around us in wider and wider circles as our ability grows. To do this humbly in brotherhood and sisterhood with others. To die knowing you built the future.

IN A NUTSHELL

- A good life is like a good movie: it has a hero, a purpose, a struggle and a resolution.
- Two taxi drivers do the same thing, but one has a purpose.
- A young schoolteacher loses his life through confusion about meaning.
- You are in this world to care.
- Human survival and destiny is the big story – you can be part of it, or you can run and hide.
- Men who are really happy and free are the ones who are nurturing the whole of life.

Image 24

NINE

Real male friends

'Now listen to me. You're going to make it. You know why? Because these are smart people who love you, and they've got your back.'

Aaron Sorkin, The West Wing

Two farmers stand in the dusty yard of a property. One is a neighbour, come to say goodbye, the other is watching as the last of his furniture is packed onto a truck. The farm looks bare – stock gone, machinery sold. Two teenagers stand by the car, the wife sits inside it, eyes averted. The two men have farmed alongside each other for 30 years, fought bushfires, driven through the night with sick or injured children, drunk gallons of tea together, and cared for each other's wives and kids as their own. They have shared good times and bad. Now, one is leaving, bankrupt.

He will go to live in the city, where his wife will support them by cleaning motels.

'Well,' says the mate. 'I'll be off then.'

'Yeah,' says the other. 'Thanks for coming over.'

'Look us up some time.'

'Yeah, I reckon.'

And they climb into their vehicles and leave. While their wives will correspond for years to come, these men will never exchange words again.

So much unspoken. So much that would help the healing to take place from this terrible turn of events. What pain would flow out if one was to say, 'Listen, you've been the best mate a bloke could want', and looked the other straight in the eye as he said it. Or if they had spent a long evening together with their wives, full of 'remember when...'s punctuated by tears and easing laughter. If, instead of standing stiff-armed and choked, they could have had a long, strong hug from which to draw strength and assurance. The farmer leaving the land will not find the opportunity for any of these supports, comforts or appreciations. He will be at massive risk of suicide, alcoholism, cancer or an accident, as he deals with his life alone.

Men, you see, don't have friends – at least not in those countries cursed with an Anglo-Saxon heritage. In Australia we have 'mates', with whom we share a straitjacket agreement on which subjects we never discuss. A subtle and elaborate code governs the ways in which serious feeling or vulnerability is deflected.

When I wrote the paragraphs above in *Manhood'* s first edition in 1994, they described an Australian man and an Australian style of friendship that had been constant for 100 years. In the time since, men here have undergone a quiet revolution in emotional openness. Today, politicians on TV talk about their struggles with depression. Soldiers and policemen on the evening news show real grief over events they are reporting first-hand. Men hug each other at airports and use the word 'love' without embarrassment, even about their mates. Younger men have deep and frank conversations with their friends.

This change has affected boy–girl relationships, too. Where once separate tribes of selfconscious young men and women stood at opposite ends of suburban dance halls, today's generation have close friendship networks of mixed gender, who can discuss any subject and give solid and good-hearted support to each other through life's ups and downs. Many young men are as communicative as young women.

But it's early days, and many men still find friendship difficult. So some maps are needed, some skills training in how to be a good friend, and that is what this chapter will provide. First, though, let's shine a light on the cliff-face once again, so we can see exactly where we are.

Proving you're a man

Little boys start out warm and affectionate. You will see them in the younger grades of school, arms about each other. At this age they are tender and kind to younger children, unfussed about being with girls, and able to cry over a dead pet or a sad story, get through their feelings, and move on. Their emotional health seems to be on a good trajectory. So what goes wrong?

> 'Proving you are a man' becomes a barrier to making friends.

We know that many boys don't get a lot of father-time. Also, we tend to segregate young children from older children in our schools and communities. This is an odd arrangement, since little boys love to be around older boys. So learning about male friendship from Dad or big boys does not happen as much as it should.

A same-age peer group of little boys in primary school easily becomes harsh, even violent. Because there is no natural leadership or nurturing from older children, the group is unskilled in cohesiveness and lacks real protection. It easily becomes the law of the jungle – the kind of conditions portrayed in *Lord of the Flies*. The result is a very physical and intimidating pecking order.

Men's activist Paul Whyte uses a guided fantasy to help women understand what it is like to grow up as a boy. He asks the women to imagine if membership of their gender depended on their being able to physically defend themselves against other women. That is, if being a woman meant having to fight, physically, with any woman who came along and challenged you – and many did. If you couldn't do this, you would be beaten and accused of not being a woman!

Boys have a natural physicality, and enjoy some challenge and jostling for position. It's not always hostile; sometimes it's just confused. Paul tells audiences he got his start in men's work at the age of five:

> *Jimmy Stevens walked up to me. I smiled at him, and he punched me in the nose. He went to do it again, and I punched him*

in the nose before he could hit me again. We both stood there with tears welling up, holding our noses, and decided to be friends. Jimmy was my best friend for the next four years.

The problem was that the 'jostling' easily got out of control, and neglected boys (or those beaten at home or by the teachers) retrieved their self-esteem by beating up those smaller or weaker.

Today, while many schools are much safer, boys are still killed or injured in schoolyard fights, and in street fights, party and pub brawls every year. Most of these incidents involve some sense of threatened manhood, and the bizarre idea that violence proves manhood.

My father was made to leave school at age fourteen by his father, who found him a job in a car factory, sweeping and cleaning up. He decided to better himself, and secretly enrolled in night school. Each night on the way to the tech college, he had to vary his route to avoid gangs who might lie in wait. He started to smoke to

look tougher, and wore heavy coats to look more muscular.

Acting tough prevents being picked on – tattoos, aggressive-looking clothes, piercings, smoking, swearing, putting down other races or women. Often these traits are accumulated in direct proportion to how afraid a young man feels. Soon a young man has acquired a complete layer of bluff. But this role doesn't allow him to admit to fears or sorrows, discuss difficulties in relating to girls or problems at work or home. 'Proving you are a man' becomes a barrier to making friends. And so the problem just gets worse.

Proving you're not gay

Another barrier to men being good friends – going out for coffee, talking deeply about their lives, even going hiking or travelling together – has been the fear that others might think they were secretly gay.

> 'Proving you are a man' becomes a barrier to making friends.

The existence of homosexuality as a biological fact in most mammal species, combined with our long history of persecuting gay men, meant that all through the twentieth century the dread of being thought to be gay hung over the head of any boy who was different from the norm in any way at all. The risk was real, and ranged from being rejected as a friend (if you have him as a friend, you must be gay too) to being ridiculed, bullied, beaten or even killed. Our non-acceptance of gays took its toll on *every* man. It led to the self-censoring of any signs of warmth, creativity or emotionalism among the whole male gender. No-one felt free to be themselves.

Fortunately, this too has, for the most part, changed dramatically. Gay men and lesbian women fought for their rights in brave and visible ways. Greater acceptance led to even more people 'coming out'. Most people discovered that they had gay or lesbian friends, neighbours or family members, and the sky didn't come falling down. People wondered what they had been so afraid of. The side benefit, for all men, that came out of gay liberation was that, with the fear gone, they could just be themselves, have friends and express affection without fear of 'looking gay'. Not that there's anything wrong with that!

Growing up gay

Rodney Croome *is a household name in Tasmania. He is an activist for gay rights, who through his own courage and quiet dignity has won the respect of ordinary people and politicians. When he first started out, homosexuality was still a criminal offence punishable by 21 years in jail. Today Tasmania is a gay-friendly, diverse and inclusive place. Rodney received an Order of Australia in 2003.*

I grew up in a peaceful, friendly, traditional community, a dairy-farming district where the great changes of the twentieth century had had relatively little impact. Stability was what defined the place, not migration, war or upheaval. The people there had a strong sense of who they were and where they fitted in. It was far from perfect, but it gave me a sense of belonging.

All this changed when we moved to a nearby town whose industries were just beginning to struggle against global competition. The boys there were angry, violent and deeply insecure in a way I'd never experienced before. And their greatest insecurity was about sexuality. My white underpants, poor ball-throwing skills and interest in music – plus a hundred other little things that had been innocuous in my former world – now carried a terrible threat. That threat was of being called 'a fairy'.

I suffered that worst of labels for a few weeks after I was seen with my arm around a male friend, something no-one thought twice about where I'd come from. I learnt my lesson quickly, and adopted a mask to avert attention.

I know now I wasn't alone in copping this abuse or adopting this survival strategy. Former rugby league star Ian Roberts has said he adopted a tough-guy image to hide his homosexuality from others and from himself. Transgender rights advocate Martine Delaney says that, as a young man, she covered up her desire to be a woman with furious body-building, beer-drinking and car-racing. In her own words, she was 'the ultimate boy'.

Since my sporting skills and automotive interests were too low-level to hide behind, I concealed my sexuality behind an entirely different mask. I became a studious, uptight geek. What better way to hide my real difference than to adopt a diversionary one, and one seemingly without a sexuality? My mask worked; the jocks overlooked me. But my cover limited me no less than Ian's or Martine's. For many years, instead of facing life's challenges, I retreated behind a blank face or a pile of books.

I had no inkling then of the profound effect of the prejudices I experienced. Because of the isolation they feel, the abuse they suffer and the self-hatred they develop, same-sex-attracted teenagers are more likely than their straight counterparts to have conflict with peers and parents, abuse drugs and alcohol, leave school early, be homeless and seriously consider, or even commit, suicide. The statistics are even worse for young transgender people.

But homophobia also damages straight boys and men. Studies from Australia and overseas have shown the many ways heterosexual males limit themselves out of fear of appearing gay. In high school this can take the form of avoiding art, music and literature classes, or even under-performing generally because academic skill is seen as somehow effeminate. In older men, everything from expressing emotion to looking after your health can be curtailed by this fear. The film *Billy Elliot* highlights how homophobia forces boys to tie themselves into a narrow macho straitjacket. Unfortunately, not all boys and men are lucky enough to burst out like Billy did.

Fortunately, there is a way out of homophobia. When gay and straight men talk honestly about their experiences, then long-held fears, prejudices and resentments can quickly evaporate. Pretty soon they find they have much more in common than they expected. A good example is world champion axeman, David Foster. David is a hero in the area I grew up in, and a role model for many young men, especially blue-collar, working men. In 2007, in response to a nasty homophobic campaign against a local same-sex couple, David opened up about once being a bigot, the awful consequences of such bigotry, and about growing beyond prejudice:

Twenty or thirty years ago, I was as big a bigot as you could possibly find. A bigot is someone who is intolerant of others' differences, and when it came to homosexuality, the term 'bigot' fitted me perfectly.

Times change, though. You mature, you learn tolerance and acceptance of others, and you learn that the prejudices you had were irrational and uninformed. I believe we all need to be more tolerant and respecting of others.

What if one of your kids came home and told you they were homosexual? Would you accept it and support them?

I've known people who are no longer with us on this earth because their loved ones could not come to terms with who they were as a person and their sexuality. That's tragic.

A lot has changed where I grew up. Now same-sex couples have legal rights, and transgender folk have protection from discrimination. But most important of all, there has been a change of hearts and minds, especially among men. This has been because gay and transgender men bravely stood up and began telling their stories. It is also because heterosexual men like David Foster responded with equal candour.

After many years of feeling like an outsider and an outcast, I finally feel again the sense of belonging I had as a child on my parents' dairy farm. But this time it is a belonging based on a growing acceptance of my sexuality as a gay man, and the increasingly widespread belief that this sexuality is not what should define or limit me. My hope is that all men, gay and straight, are able to shrug off the masks and the straitjackets homophobia has forced them to wear, and experience the joy of being themselves.

Competition

Competitiveness, always wanting to be better than others, almost always stems from a childhood of seeking approval that never comes. Even winning, as many top athletes find, is not enough. If they are given enough love, boys and men do not have this compulsion to impress – they settle down to learning for its own sake, less concerned with being biggest and best. There are societies where competition is simply not a feature: in Bali, there are literally thousands of great artists, dancers, craftspeople – everyone is creative. There is no cult of celebrity. In Ireland, before television came, everyone sang, played instruments and danced. Competition is a scourge because it discourages us from having a go or being happy with ourselves. In the end, we don't participate, we just consume.

Men are naturally predisposed to compete, so it affects us more severely.

Everyone agreed that condoms were a great idea except for one thing – while men came in different sizes, condoms only came in one. Manufacturers had cottoned-on early that no self-respecting man would walk into a chemist shop and ask for a box of small condoms! The marketing conversation turned quiet at this point as each person made their own inner reflections. Finally someone hit on an answer: the smallest size could be called 'Large'! What about the larger sizes? The atmosphere became ribald at this stage. It was finally agreed, after many alternatives, that there should be three sizes of condom – 'Large', 'Huge' and 'Oh my God!'

Competition is the bane of men's lives. To this day, when I sit down in a public place – beside a swimming pool, for example – I relax and feel good if there is no-one else around. If another man arrives, I first run a check that he is no physical threat – that he is not about to mug me. No-one has ever mugged me or hurt me since childhood, but the feeling still lives. (Women understand this reflex, for different reasons.) Then I get to assessing whether he is stronger, has better clothes or is more athletic. If he is with a woman, I look for signs that she doesn't really like him! If the car park is within view, I check out his car for comparison with my own – a good guide to income and status, as well as taste. Even if he is friendly and a conversation starts, I consider in what light to best present myself (modestly!) – as important and successful. It's really pretty sad, this insecure obsession with comparisons.

My participation in many great discussions among men is helping me to change this pattern. Listening to men share their terrible experiences at the hands of other men or boys, through being short or fat, skinny or tall, redheaded or bald, lame or unwell, the wrong race, occupation or physique, has given me a sense of revulsion about judging, and a sense of brotherhood with all men. I see a gang of boys in the street, or bikers outside a pub, or noisy, self-opinionated, suited men in the city, with the eyes of knowing that inside each of them is a man struggling and insecure, no different to myself. I still take care around each group, but the judging, and even the fear, has reduced.

> It's really pretty sad, this insecure obsession with comparisons.

I am teaching myself to see other men as brothers, with good things to give and to receive. I have always felt this way about women, but why not men too? This is leading to a huge change in attitude and a huge boost in my enjoyment of half the human race. There are a lot of friends out there.

Beyond competition

Indigenous peoples across history have had the same problems with masculinity that we do, but they seemed to have given it more thought and care, and so turned it to more positive ends. The Xervante people of Brazil divide manhood into eight stages of growth. The men are grouped by age, and each peer groups stays very close throughout life. Each group is nurtured and helped by those in the next older group. Each year the Xervante hold ceremonial running races for each age group in turn. These races look like a contest but they are not: when a runner falters or trips, the others pick him up and run with him. The group always finishes in a pack.

In fact, it's not a 'race' at all in the sense we mean it, though everyone puts in a huge effort. It's a celebration of manhood – an expression of surplus vitality. This is a culture that has survived thousands of years by cooperation. They don't have to prove they are men, they *celebrate* that they are men. Marvin Allen says it beautifully: 'I defy anyone, anywhere in the world, to "prove" that they're a man'. In fact, it's a ridiculous concept. Women wouldn't entertain the concept of 'proving' they are a woman.

Male friends offer enormous comfort. They help to structure your time. They show you that you belong and can be cared for. Perhaps this is why men traditionally cook at barbecues – it's a declaration that 'men can feed you, too'. If you don't believe this, listen to the banter that takes place between men and women over the quality of the sausages and chops!

Research shows that a man who has a network of friends will have better health and a longer lifespan. His marriage will be happier. Friends alleviate the neurotic overdependence on a wife or girlfriend for every emotional need. If a man, going through a 'rough patch', gets help from his friends, the burden on his partner is reduced. If his problems are with his partner (as they often are), then his friends can help him through, stop him acting rashly and help him to find a constructive way forward.

A male-out—men supporting men in crisis

Some years ago, in a large government department in Hobart, a man in his forties was given a retrenchment notice. He had been a dedicated, professional worker, and his boss did not have the guts to tell him personally. Instead, this man and a dozen colleagues received a form letter in the mail.

The man took it badly. Reacting out of acute anxiety, he became irrational, went to a sports store and purchased a gun. At work, he locked himself in a room and shredded important documents. These actions greatly alarmed his colleagues, and his wife and young children.

Several of his friends conferred about what to do. They settled on a course of action. They went to his house, taking food and sleeping bags, and spent the weekend living there, while his wife and children were sent elsewhere. They rostered themselves so that someone was always awake and with the man –

who was too agitated to sleep much. By the Sunday afternoon, after much talking, crying and holding, the man thanked his friends for stopping him from 'making an idiot' of himself and began to make concrete plans for his future. The friends were careful to monitor him, staying in hourly contact and checking that things were in fact going well. His family came back home a few days later, and his life has progressed well.

The friends knew somehow that this was their job – it was a man's issue. Male friends can do these things, where wives and other women probably cannot. Other men know how you are feeling. Men have issues – about being a provider, for instance – which they feel in different ways to women. Only other men can help you learn about the ongoing process of being a man.

Levels of communication

Millions of women complain about their husband's lack of feeling, his woodenness. Men themselves often feel numb and confused about what they really want. But what if men's inarticulateness simply comes from a lack of sharing opportunities (as opposed to bullshit sessions) with other men? If men talked to each other more, perhaps we'd understand ourselves better. Perhaps we would then have more to say to our wives. It seems entirely possible that only in the company of other men can many of us begin to activate our hearts. Storyteller Michael Meade says that just as men's voices have a different tone, so do our feelings. We have more than enough feelings, but they are not the same as women's feelings. Once activated, we have no trouble expressing ourselves.

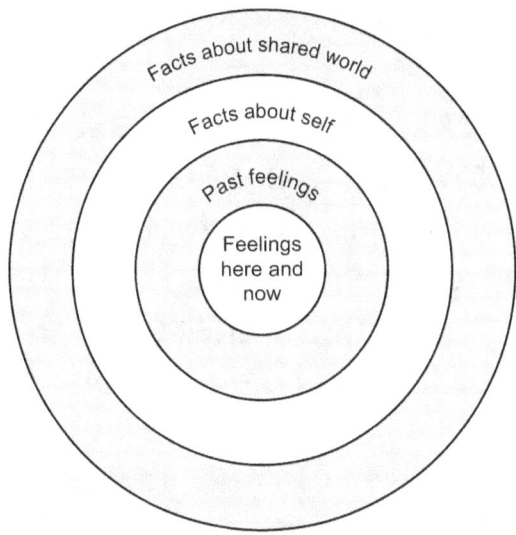

Image 25: The four levels of human communication

If you want to become a better friend, some skills and understanding can help. In the 1960s, the concept of levels of communication was mapped out as a series of concentric circles, as above: Outermost communication is about impersonal facts. 'It looks like rain.' 'There's a train strike tomorrow.' This is all in the public domain; there is no self-disclosure. That's why we talk about the weather with complete strangers – it's safe ground.

The next layer in is still factual, but includes personal information – 'I come from the country.' 'My father was an engineer.'

The next layer has past feelings – 'I hated it when we had to move to the city.' 'We had a rough time when my daughter got sick.' At this layer, you can feel the juice; there is a sense of getting to know the person on a real level.

Image 26

The final layer is the feelings I am having now. 'I am still shaking with fear.' 'I am so sad that he is gone.' 'I really appreciate you listening to all this stuff.'

> A mate who is a good listener is alert to tracking down what you are really feeling...

Friends are the ones we can talk at level four with. To help a friend really connect, you need to take the risk of going to level three or four. If you don't do this, chances are the conversation will stay superficial and the relationship simply won't have a lot of meaning. It will be shallow-rooted and easily die.

How emotions work

Men have often been mystified by them, but feelings themselves are actually a very logical business. They reflect simple biological states in the body, and are our mind's way of telling us what we need.

There are only four primary emotions, and just as with primary colours, all the others are made up of these four in different combinations. They are:
- Anger – the feeling we get when we are boxed in, ignored or trampled on.

- Fear – the feeling we get when things change too much or too fast and we feel unsafe.
- Sorrow – the feeling we get when a piece of our life, a person or object that matters to us, is ripped away.
- Happiness – the feeling we get when things are going right.

Complex feelings are always an alloy of two or more of the primary ones. For example, jealousy can be sorrow at someone not giving us their love, mixed with anger at the person who has stolen it away. Nostalgia is the happy feeling we get about feeling sad for what once was (feelings can combine in some very odd ways).

To sort out a problem, it's important to remember that there is usually one true feeling at the bottom of things. Both genders have characteristic ways of masking their emotions. Men who feel afraid – for instance, that their wife is unwell, or their teenager is taking too many risks – often cover this with anger, criticising her for not exercising, blasting the teenager for driving too fast ... This emotional substitution doesn't work very well; it makes people cranky. Being able to say 'I am scared' has a better effect: people feel your caring instead of your criticism.

A mate who is a good listener is alert to tracking down what you are really feeling, sometimes before you do.

> Two men sit at a bus stop. They have never met. Some teenage girls jostle past, laughing and shoving each other. The man looks over and says, 'Bloody kids, ay?'
>
> The listener smiles, pauses for a second, then says, 'Yeah, they are a bit of a handful.'
>
> The man says, 'Mine is, that's for sure.'
>
> The listener asks, 'She gives you a few worries?'
>
> 'Yeah, bloody always wanting her own way, wanting to go where she wants.'
>
> At this point, the temptation to say some platitude is huge – to go back to level one, generality – like, 'They're all the same, these kids. Who'd be a parent, ay?'
>
> The listener doesn't do this. He says, 'You're a bit scared of what she might get into?'

And then something amazing happens: the man dives into level four. 'Too right. And it'll all be my fault. It's just me, you see. My missus died when Sophie was just nine. I don't think I'm cut out for raising a girl.'

'You lost your wife?'

'Worst thing that ever happened to me. People just told me, "Pull yourself together, you have to be strong for the child".'

'That's really sad.'

The man gives a long look into the face of the listener, their eyes lock; something inside him is testing for real connection.

'It feels like it just happened yesterday.'

The listener doesn't say anything, he just looks right back. There are no words needed, just space.

Being alert to and respectful of feelings tracks you into the heart of the matter. This man will only be able to care for his daughter when he is able to grieve for his wife. A bus-stop conversation won't take care of this, but it's a start. You might feel like this has been of no help. But the fact is, this man needs to talk about his wife, not his daughter. When people told him to 'pull himself together', they were wrong. He needs to go *through,* not around. Sometimes people get stuck in feelings, but men mostly get stuck in not feeling.

Fun and friendship

The other reason for having male friends is to have fun – the kind of fun that is noisy, energetic, affectionate, ribald, accepting, careful underneath the playfulness, but shamelessly free from respectability or restraint.

I once attended a men's retreat in a rainforest valley in northern New South Wales. The attendees were extraordinarily diverse: there were dreadlocked young men and clean-cut city workers, teachers, doctors, old men, Aboriginal men, youth workers, a couple of recovering drug addicts, gay and straight men. An Adventist minister brought several men from his congregation. We listened and learnt, spent time in small affinity groups, swam, ate delicious food. We followed some ritual stories from a senior Ngarinyin Aboriginal man from the Kimberley, whose presence lent a gravity that was like an altered state of being. There was no alcohol, no drugs, and of course no women, though at the end we were welcomed back into the world by a group of women, in a final ritual that was emotionally quite overwhelming for reasons I cannot yet understand.

One night we created a concert out of our own imaginations. To this day I have never seen such amazing creativity, outrageous humour, poignant drama, or sheer beauty of storytelling. I felt that such a thing as 'genius' existed and had somehow been drawn down out of the heavens, inspiring the men to be so much more than

their everyday selves. I have been really free and happy perhaps a dozen times in my adult life, and this was definitely one of them.

Everybody needs to have friendship, especially young men going through the natural ups and downs of life. Friends of our own gender simply understand us better; they are our brothers. We can become part of something larger than ourselves and achieve great things.

> Friends of our own gender simply understand us better...

Some teenage boys near where I live did an unusual thing – they had enjoyed some camping trips on the banks of the Huon River, and decided they wanted to build a wooden boat and sail down the river to its mouth. Since they were young men rather than children, their parents gave the project their blessing. With the help of one of the fathers, they found a shed to work in, scrounged materials, worked weekends, saved money, and the boat gradually took shape.

Things did not always go smoothly between them. One young man often failed to match the monetary contribution of the others, and added to the insult by borrowing money from them for other purposes. Since several of them had taken part-time jobs to raise funds, they got angry after a while and decided to confront him: 'You aren't pulling your weight. You're using us!'

Because of the bond that already existed between them, and the firm but unaggressive way they tackled him, he did not storm off. He thought it over, got a job, and paid back what he owed. Character gets built in this way.

Another of the young boat-builders had trouble with overbearing parents with high expectations. The others noted his growing depression and consulted their parents about how to help. They decided to simply tell their mate up front: 'Listen, Dave, you only have to live with your parents for another year. Hang in there and finish school. Then your life's your own. You do what *you* want to do with your life. You can always live here in the boatshed!'

Image 27

Islands of seriousness in a sea of good times. Everyone's lives are eased, stabilised and supported by such friendships. Why shouldn't all men – young and old – have such a safety net in their lives? It could avoid all kinds of disasters. And why shouldn't we laugh more, play more, be teased out of our anxieties and pomposities? Friends are the very heart of a brave, happy and vibrant life. They need to be elevated in our priorities, and given the time and energy they deserve.

Men's groups

One problem with the whole 'self-help' and 'self-improvement' scene is the idea that we can change things all on our own. Contemporary man has been plagued by this illusion. When this solitary approach fails, we conclude that nothing can be changed after all, and give up.

To make personal change easier, it helps to belong to a community of men who are working towards similar goals. Even small groups of men who meet regularly and talk can give each other huge insights, enormous amounts of encouragement, and occasional kicks in the bum – all essential to keeping you open and moving towards liberation. If you want your life as a man to really get moving, then consider joining or starting a men's group. Here are some guidelines, if you are interested.

How men's groups work

In a lounge room not far from where you are reading this, it's odds-on that a group of eight or nine men meets every couple of weeks to talk about their lives. Their wives or partners are happy for them to do so because they like the results – happier, more balanced, stronger and more peaceful men.

I know of several hundred men's groups in Australia; there are doubtless many more quietly getting on with it. Overseas, the picture is the same. Therapist-turned-activist Guy Corneau has single-handedly founded 300 groups in Canada; and there are thousands in the US. They are also blossoming in the UK, Germany, South America and New Zealand.

The structure of a men's group is based on some key guidelines. There is no pressure to speak unless you wish to. There is an emphasis on hearing someone out, rather than interrupting either with argument or well-meaning advice (most people get plenty of this in their normal life). The emphasis is also on speaking from the heart, not 'discussing', 'debating' or 'theorising'.

Men's groups can be emotional at times. Something very freeing happens when a private space is set aside, when the rules are 'no bullshitting' and 'say what you feel'. If men know their stories will be heard and honoured, a great deal finds its way to the surface.

Men's groups are also very practical. The chosen topic of the night may be 'how to discipline your kids', or 'how to break out of an alienating career and make time to live'. It might be some frank discussion about sex, or it might be more crisis-driven – shoring up a man wounded from marital combat, or a man whose wife has just that week been diagnosed with cancer. I've listened in men's groups to older men talk about war trauma, honestly, for the first time after decades of silent suffering.

Young men find surrogate fathers and uncles in men's groups. The ethics of men's groups are strong – particularly about never supporting acting (or even speaking) violently to women, children or each other. Men's group talk has a style that is very different from women's talk – there's less tiptoeing, and less of a tendency to agree with everything you say.

Men's groups usually meet in homes, though occasionally they are church-based or meet in a health centre. Most are general purpose, while some are specifically for men with violence problems, or health or marital concerns. A group may close its membership once it is running, though some will invite new members periodically. The commonest way to start is to invite a few friends and begin your own. Some groups use a book (such as this one) as a discussion starter, or generate a list of topics agreed by members. Leadership tends to be rotated, rather than having no leader at all – acknowledging that men like structure and are goal-oriented.

Men's groups usually have rules (no put-downs, confidentiality) and there is a tendency to confront bullshit or irresponsibility. 'You're neglecting your bloody kids, mate! When are you going to wake up to yourself!' 'Well, sure you could leave your wife, but you'd be an idiot to do it. Why don't you talk to her and tell her what you're feeling?' 'You're tired, mate. You and your wife need a holiday.' And so on. You don't have to 'spill your guts' in a men's group – there isn't any pressure. Perhaps for that very reason, though, you soon find yourself hoeing in, prompted by the similarities of your own experiences with those being shared by the other men. You get practical tips for living, and feel you can breathe more deeply, all at the same time! It adds a sense of relaxation to your life (quite different from getting drunk or going fishing) because the changes are cumulative. Your life starts to make more sense.

Most men's groups reach a point where they organise to get away for some weekends. In groups where most men are fathers, activities are often planned to include the youngsters. Some groups, such as YMCA Explorers, exist specifically for dads and daughters, or dads and sons, to spend time together supported by some resources and structure.

Men's groups began because there was a need for men to look at their inner, private worlds. But a balance is springing up between introspection and action in the world. Projects like 'Uncle', which provide mentors for young men at risk, do prison visits, volunteer in schools, work with teenagers in 'men's sheds', set up youth groups, support dying men, help with older men's projects, work on overseas aid projects, and so on. Men who are mentally healthy don't sit on their backside for long. But what they do in the world is so much better for starting with self-reflection and having real emotional support.

'Males who are denied appropriate physical affection from other males while growing up become people who never mature. In fact many men who are so denied will strongly repress their need for manly affection. You can see these men in any football game or boxing match. They seem to thrive on the violent aspects of male contact, while distancing themselves from any form of intimacy.

When men are allowed to freely experience the love and support of other men, they begin to question competition in our society. This questioning engenders a willingness to engage in more service-oriented projects and activities whose aim is to nurture and protect the planet.

Here lies the power of the new masculine soul.'

Barry Cooney in *Wingspan*

IN A NUTSHELL

- In 30 years we have turned the corner from having mates to having real friends.

- The biggest obstacles to friendship are the toughness mask, and fathers who were cold and remote.
- Emotions are logical and have a purpose – they are nothing to be afraid of.
- Men need their friends in order to heal.
- Male friendship gives you courage, humour and strength to do more in the world.
- Men's groups can create a safety and support network that is rarely found in the big world.
- They can accelerate you to a braver and freer life.

Image 28

TEN

Finding a job with heart

There are four things which are ultimate, and one of those is a competent man.

Tao Te Ching

Work is love made visible.

Kahlil Gibran

In the 1950s my dad and I used to love watching westerns on TV. The raw masculinity of Laramie, Bonanza, and The Rifleman would thrill our Yorkshire souls. Even as a six-year-old, I noted the recurring plot devices in these cowboy soaps: the cougar that leapt out at the bad guy was a favourite, the rattlesnake another, but by far the most

horrifying was quicksand. Goodies and baddies alike might run down a trail, and splosh – up to their armpits and sinking fast. It looked like a terrible death.

I asked, 'Dad, is there really such a thing as quicksand?' (I hadn't come across it in the English woods.)

'Yep,' he said, not even pausing for breath, 'it's called a job.'

A 'job', the exchange of your life's time for money, is a very modern idea. As we know, for most of history people did not have jobs, they caught or grew their own food, clothed themselves, built their own shelter. Their 'workmates' were their friends and relatives, and there were seasonal rhythms of rest and work. Kate Grenville, in her beautiful novel about colonial Sydney, *The Secret River,* has one of her characters note of the Aboriginal people of the region that 'they were all gentry'. Especially compared with the hard-pressed white farmers, scratching a desperate living from the alien soil.

Anthropologists working across the world have made the same observation: hunter-gatherers usually met all their material needs with a couple of hours' effort a day. In work–life balance terms, they make us look such losers!

Today we assume a job is a necessity, and it probably is. *But we shouldn't accept this too passively or without carefully assessing the options.* A job is a huge thing: it takes up most of your life, unless you come to a different arrangement. And it can be a terrible trap: unless companies and organisations are prevented from doing so, they can literally suck the life out of their employees. Their goals for you are not the goals you would have for yourself.

For men seeking to be whole and to live a larger life, the work question is one of the most important of all.

Finding your true work

When we are young, we are given 'storm warnings' from time to time by the adults in our life. They are phrased delicately, but kids are perceptive, and can feel the chill winds blow. 'What do you want to do when you leave school?' Being asked this for the first time can be a nasty shock. 'Leave school? You mean, this doesn't last forever?' The future comes like a threat, because deep down *that's how we see it as well.* Adulthood doesn't sound like fun.

> 'What will be my life's work?' is a vital question for every man and woman to ask.

In talking to young people about their future, there seem to be several viewpoints. A large number see having an income as the main focus – 'I can get my own car, buy lots of stuff.' Others are more sober, even somewhat afraid – 'I will need to have a job. I hope I can find one that I like.' Only a smaller proportion of kids see a career as a positive goal in itself: 'I really want to be a [vet, nurse, teacher, mechanic, movie star].' That number reduces even further as the reality gets

closer. By seventeen, a certain depressing kind of young man is nominating accountancy, law or IT. It's rarely for the joy of it.

There is something wrong when young people view their future through the lens of either consumerism or frightened conformity. Our lives should inspire us; young people need to be roused up to dream of greater things. Is it possible that, as parents, we have totally let our kids down? That we have unwittingly slipped onto their ankles the same manacles we have worn all our lives, and refused to tackle with them the big question – *why are we in this world?*

The main task of adolescence is not to worry or flinch from life, but to explore what our real work is to be. *Our life's work and a job are not the same thing.* Work is larger, and it is a matter for our soul. Our work is the place where our hearts, minds and talents all meet, *the thing we are made to do.* Or, to use more spiritual language, the thing *you were put on this earth to do.* Nelson Mandela's work was to defeat apartheid and white rule in South Africa – he didn't get a salary for that. Neither did Gandhi for liberating India. Jesus, as best as we can tell, quit his job as a carpenter to campaign against the enslavement of his countrymen and countrywomen. (Perhaps he left someone irate about not getting their chairs on time.) The point is, *none of these roles was a vacancy advertised in the job listings.*

You might argue that these men were the greats of history, that it was different for them. But that is to miss the point. *It's because they thought this way, and lived this way, that they were great.* Jesus explicitly taught that every man and woman should do the same as him. So did the Buddha, and most other spiritual leaders throughout history.

'What will be my life's work?' is a vital question for every man and woman to ask, and to answer many times as life proceeds, since all the factors and variables keep changing with our age and stage of life. *What purpose will I gladly give my energies to?* The second question – how will I live, feed myself, support a family, if that's what I choose? – is important too, but it should only ever be the *second* question asked.

The question should come not as pressure, but as an invitation to careful and slow reflection. What is your soul drawn to? Music? Science? Educating? Healing? Activism? Growing? Making? Building? The practical issues come next: how can you do this and be able to eat, have shelter, support a family? Merely living, even affluent living, is not the goal. The question is, *living for what?*

The question of a job then becomes the practical challenge: how can I do what I wish, what I see is needed, and at the same time support myself and be able to live? Both points need answering. It's the order you answer them in that is crucial – as is how much of your soul's direction you are willing to trade away. Sometimes people sell themselves for pretty poor fare. What we think we 'need' to live can be astonishing.

If I look at my friends' lives, I am amazed at the range of

material needs that people consider 'necessary'. Some live in humble cottages in country towns. Some live in million-dollar beach houses. One drives a 3-tonne, late model SUV, another a ten-year-old Corolla. Some send their kids to $12,000-a-year private schools, others get involved in the local high school's committees, canteen, working bees and sports days. Some have holidays in the Seychelles, some go camping in a tent. There is an unavoidable tradeoff here: having more stuff requires more work, so the price has to be assessed. How much (lost) time with your children did your car cost? If you are rich and have little time to live, perhaps you have misjudged...

We should aim for the free-est, largest life we can live, where our ideals, our understanding, our emotions and our bodies all point in the same direction. If we at least know what we really think matters, then even if we fall short, we know that we have tried. Some people work hard in jobs they don't like, but find time to volunteer overseas during their vacation. Some people work part-time so they can follow their dream of music or art or writing. Some take turns with their partner to be the breadwinner so that each can pursue a dream, even if that dream is 'just' full-time parenthood, or to make a really great food garden, or to start a business they always dreamed of.

If we don't pursue our true work, we are really just eunuchs – comfortable, castrated slaves. Finding what our true work is, is the key to standing at our full height as men.

A changing landscape

A hundred years ago, 90 percent of us worked on the land. Australia, the US, Canada and New Zealand were agricultural giants. (A century earlier still, so were England and Europe.) Then came Industrialisation: we flooded into the cities and towns, machines did the harvesting and tilling and we were needed in the factories and mills. Later came two global wars that were essentially clashes between industrial empires over raw materials. From the 1950s on, manufacturing migrated inexorably towards Asia, and white-collar work became the predominant form of employment in the West.

Throughout the industrial era, social institutions still held sway. People belonged to churches, and to clubs and associations. Everyone walked to work. Communities were close knit; there was meaning and connection beyond that given by the job. It was just bearable to hack coal a mile underground, among good friends, with the choir, the chapel, and the weekend dance to look forward to.

But workers were also very vulnerable and, in the tradition of earlier agricultural movements, trade unions now sprang up to oppose abuses of the working man. Through long and bitter campaigns they ended child labour, created the old-age pension, clawed back the working week to 50, then eventually 40 hours. 'Eight hours to work, eight hours to learn, eight hours to sleep.' Now a man could earn a family wage – his wife and children did not need to join him down the mine to 'make ends meet'. By the 1950s they owned a modest house and car, and went camping at the beach for three weeks in the summer. This was a time that, for all its cultural sterility, still ranks highest in all the surveys of happiness and contentment.

Then 'economic rationalism' arrived. Working hours grew longer. In particular, the need for both parents in the family to work became more and more pressing. Two-income families could outbid single-income families at house auctions, and house prices rose massively.

All the predictions made just a decade earlier – of a new age of leisure through productivity and automation – proved to be spectacularly wrong. People earned more, but spent more, often on non-essential consumer goods. *We shifted from involvement satisfactions to consumption satisfactions.* We didn't want to be free, we wanted to be wealthy. Where a quarter-acre *block* was once the goal, now a quarter-acre *house* – five bedrooms, three bathrooms – was what a young couple wanted, and they wanted it *now.* Instead of Lorne or Coffs Harbour, they vacationed in Phuket or Fiji. And sometimes just for the weekend.

> We should be happier, but *something is undermining us.*

No word characterises the changes of the twentieth century as much as that slippery term, 'progress'. Progress is a 'sleight of hand' word: it creates the impression that change is always good. In reality, of course, it's far more complex.

Visitors to Istanbul are told how the Bosporus Strait, the broad waterway that glistens beside that lovely city, has two currents – a warm one on the surface, flowing out to the Mediterranean, and a cold one, down below, flowing back towards the Black Sea. Progress is sometimes like that.

From the 1960s to the present, we have made huge advances in material wellbeing, health, opportunity, equality, prosperity. Yet underneath this, a cold current has been running the other way. People are falling apart – family breakdown, increased depression, anxiety, mental and behavioural problems in children and young people ... We should be happier, but *something is undermining us.* We've lost our compass, and this is somehow tied up with work.

Choosing to be slaves?

In a powerful book called *Willing Slaves,* journalist Madeleine Bunting investigated the workplace culture of Britain and why in a time of unprecedented prosperity, so many people felt miserable and burnt out. Bunting quickly realised that the greatest single factor harming people's happiness today was the impossible pressure of work. She found that work culture had become more stressed, more insecure and more manipulated than ever.

The most memorable accounts were of the UK supermarket chain ASDA, where checkout workers were regularly assessed by company spies posing as shoppers. Each checkout worker was rated on the warmth of their smile and their use of scripted chat to make buyers feel that it was a sociable, community experience to shop at ASDA. Not friendly enough – *black mark for you.* Even the emotional world of the staff was being colonised to increase profits.

From the humblest supermarket to the swankiest office suite, when work is set up this way, people react fearfully, compete with each other, and feel terribly alone. It's like *Big Brother* on TV, wondering who will go next. And yet we keep coming back for more.

Bunting observes that magazines, and government campaigns, continually tell us we need 'work–life balance', as if we just need better 'time-management skills' and a little more grace and poise. Jolly circus metaphors are usually invoked at this point – walking a tightrope, juggling, looking good in lycra ... Men and women alike feel deficient if we can't manage to maintain a marriage, care well for our kids, run an efficient house, keep the boss off our backs, and stay good looking at the same time. This doesn't sound like balancing so much as being roped to wild horses.

The question just has to be asked – *what if it's simply not possible* to work a 50-hour week and be anything like an adequate parent? What if two jobs takes a devastating toll on anyone's marriage? What if a society where everyone works actually collapses because no-one is doing the caring any more?

A great deal has been lost in the last 30 years. Our lives have been whittled away; much that safeguards and gives value to living has been eaten out by the need to work. The corporate ideal of the wage slave/consumer has replaced citizenship, humanity, community, and freedom itself. We have given away what Japanese or Nazi invaders could not take from us by force. We have traded our lives for a flat-screen TV, an SUV and six days in the Maldives.

Image 29

The problem is not work itself

Work is not a bad thing. Men love to work, to do things well and with energy, to be in a team, to make their mark in the world. Work done well is stimulating, exciting and rewarding. There is a greater human endeavour going on, and being part of this is what makes us fully alive.

The question is, *what* work? Meaning is everything: you have to believe in your own role, its importance to the overall picture. And you have to believe in what your employer is doing. This is rather more difficult.

Viktor Frankl, who wrote the classic *Man's Search For Meaning*, drew his observations from his years in a Nazi concentration camp. He noticed that when people had work to do – even digging holes in the frozen rocky ground – they were better off than those who did not. However, when the work was meaningless and empty – at one stage the guards made the men simply move piles of rocks from one place to another, then back to where they'd been – the suicide rate soared. People just gave up.

Primo Levi, another powerfully articulate survivor of the Holocaust, observed how the POWs laundering and ironing army uniforms devised a special source of job satisfaction. They carefully took lice eggs from the clothes of their fellow prisoners, who had died of a highly infectious typhus, and inserted these under the neat collars and linings of the Nazi officers' shirts and jackets. Today this would be called 'adding value'.

In the death camps, meaning and purpose became everything. They were enough to lift men above the unendurable hardship and fear of annihilation to a place of transcendence. Robert Bly, speculating on the modern workplace of today, asked whether the reason few men ever take their children to work was that their work did not have much meaning; its value could not be explained. That *deep down they were embarrassed at its pointlessness.* If you don't believe in your job, it makes it very hard to stand tall, even in your own mind.

Rating your job

As we saw in the taxi-driver story in Chapter Eight, work can mean very different things. It can have purpose in itself, or it might serve another purpose. We might work for free if the values involved are right, or work for less in order to have a job we believe in.

> What matters is that *you* find value in what you do.

The UK government recently created a one-year practical degree program for people in other professions to become schoolteachers. The result was that some thousands of men in mid-life shifted out of jobs in engineering and IT because they wanted to do something *more meaningful.* Many of these men underwent an income drop of about 50 percent. They are much in demand because schools feel an acute need for more good men in the lives of children, and the men I spoke to from the program reported a great increase in job satisfaction. Money isn't everything (although we should pay teachers more).

The checklist below can help you evaluate the meaning and value in your work. The list is not for comparing between individuals. What matters is that *you* find value in what you do. The checklist will help you pinpoint what might be missing in your current job, and how to change it or choose another that might make you happier. The list is not limited to paid work, as many useful roles exist outside the workplace.

How meaningful is your work?

1. Do you do your share?

This begins early. Even a six-year-old can contribute around the house. A teenager living at home can be a major asset to the family – cooking meals, shopping, doing yard-work, looking after the younger kids. *Being useful is the best source of self-esteem.*

2. Can you support yourself?

It's always good to be self-sufficient, if you can be. Drawing a welfare cheque or unemployment benefits may be necessary, but self-respect comes from self-reliance, and getting back to this when possible. If you are financially dependent on the community, using your time to help others will make you stand taller. If you are raising a child, you can already stand tall.

3. Is your job one that allows you to improve the lives of others?

Teachers, nurses, police officers and firemen have an immediate beneficial effect on others' wellbeing. Other unglamorous jobs, bus drivers, shopkeepers or doctors' receptionists, for example, also have an important impact on the people they deal with.

I ring the surgery in trepidation; it often takes three weeks to see a doctor. I try to be light-hearted with the receptionist while also conveying my panic: 'I have a lump where there shouldn't be one.' She doesn't miss a beat – 'Okay, you need an appointment today, as it's Thursday, and a scan straight after so we can have your result before the weekend. Can you be here in two hours?'

When I arrive in the waiting room, I notice what a sociable place it is. This receptionist puts out a vibe of welcome, and people needing lots of treatment clearly see it as a second home. She tells me later she has worked there for 20 years. (I was okay, if you wanted to know.)

4. Are you a provider?

Helping to put a roof over the heads of, and food on the table for, other people is a very great thing. You make it possible for your partner to devote more of him- or herself to loving and teaching your kids when they need it the most. Having time for small children lays down emotional wellbeing and love of life that will be lifelong. (Note I am not assigning gender roles in these sentences!)

Alec drives iron-ore loaders at Port Kembla. He is an intelligent and imaginative man; he finds the work boring and uninspiring. But the work schedule is four days on, four off, and the pay is superb. He does it because it gives him ample time with his family – it does not intrude on him living his life the rest of the time, and on balance it's a good exchange. His life is going well.

5. Do you create an infrastructure for the work of others?

Does your job create other jobs, provide management and structure, or opportunities for other people? Your work or business may provide a niche for others that otherwise might not have existed.

My boyhood friend, 'Speedy', left school at the end of Year 10, along with 80 percent of kids in those days. He apprenticed as a toolmaker, did excellent work, rose to be manager, *bought the firm,* and employed dozens of people and trained many apprentices. They made car parts, and the doors inside shopping centres – careful and intricate items that they specifically designed to solve unique problems like sloping floors. His sons are now policemen, and at 50 he sold the firm to go 4WD camping. Meanwhile, I am still at work!

6. Do you train and develop other people, enhancing their lives and futures?

We all need mentors and father-figures, not just bosses, in the workplace. We need men and women who take pleasure in our progress and success. Being a mentor to younger people can be the most satisfying aspect of any job.

    7. Does your work help or harm the world, its people and its life? Doctors have an ancient rule – at the least, do no harm. If we all applied this in our jobs, it would be a different world.

    The chemical weed-killer atrazine can trigger soft-tissue cancers and disrupt hormones, in even the smallest concentrations. It has no safe level, and is banned in most developed countries. Near where I live, a helicopter company used to fly out to spray atrazine on thousands of acres of forest each year, contaminating every major water catchment in the State, at times spraying homes and people directly. Tasmania has the highest cancer rates in Australia, and the very highest are those in regions that are most forested.

    Every job has its ethics. Would a caring shopkeeper refuse to sell cigarettes – to anyone? What would an ethical real-estate agent look like? A movie-maker needs to ask, what kind of movies does the world need? The ad man, what kind of ads? A journalist, what kind of news items? A real man has to look at these questions. It isn't enough just to be successful. You have to ask, successful at what?

8. Does your work use your unique abilities and talents?

Some people are just right for their jobs. Their natural abilities are used to the full. We feel best when we are 'flying' along, with our talents and skills being used and stretched. How many potential surgeons, dancers, artists, teachers, counsellors and writers are wasting away in some other job? Don't settle for less than what you really could do.

Dave is a farmer. His father and grandfather managed the same land, and he likes to think he cares for it the best of all three. He has planted shelter belts and implemented water-conservation measures, set aside

> creek banks and built up the soil. He works long and hard, and sometimes the farm makes so little money that he would be better off pumping petrol. But his son comes home from school and they muster sheep together in the long evenings, his wife loves the peace and beauty of farm life, and they are part of a close-knit community. He has a life that he loves.

Here is a joke I heard when working out in western New South Wales. Two farming friends buy a lottery ticket. Turns out it's the winning ticket: they each get $5 million. They discuss what to do. The first outlines his plan – to buy an apartment complex on the Central Coast, collect the rent, then go on cruises and live at the beach for the rest of his life.

'And what about you?' he asks his mate.

'Oh, I reckon I'll just keep on farming until it's all used up!'

Chasing the wrong things

Let us be absolutely clear: some people don't have a choice. They do miserable and lowly-paid jobs, and even then don't earn enough to get by. But these people are not the majority, and they are probably not you. You have the education and literacy to have a choice. If more of us made better choices, then society would not be such a greed-driven, me-first rat race. We would vote for politicians and policies (like free public transport) that made everyone's life more liveable. Our individual greed does collective harm. Living with less is a virtue.

Image 30

The less time we spend working, the more we have for the caring, sustainable human sides of life – visiting sick relatives, running youth groups and Scout troops, cooking and growing good food for each other, being peaceful and available to our children and teens, and the children and teens in our community.

Some friends of mine live in an intentional community, a cluster of about twenty houses in a lush valley, with a shared meeting hall and gardens, in northern NSW. The residents include old people, couples, singles and young families with children. To cut back on shopping trips, they have a fully stocked cool room with all the basics, for which everyone pays a share and takes what they need.

I ask, 'What about families – do they pay more, since they eat more?'

My host smiles. 'No, that's the point.'

> Just getting our working lives under control would be a good start.

Just getting our working lives under control would be a good start. In France the government legislated for a mandated 35-hour week, and discovered that there were improvements in health, child wellbeing, marital happiness, fitness and participation in the community. In Utah, a four-day week has been implemented – offices and businesses now close on Fridays. Among other benefits, oil consumption has fallen by 20 percent. Madeleine Bunting writes about firms that implemented family-friendly hours – no work after 5.30, no weekend work – and reaped benefits in reduced burnout, happier staff, and better work outcomes. They increased their customer base by being reliable, friendly and doing better quality work.

Flexible working hours are the next big issue in the workplace. People really do want to have control of their lives.

Where we are going

It seems increasingly likely that, in the next few years, the globalised economy will fail. In 2008 this came very close to happening. Many experts, especially in resource fields like oil, water and agriculture, feel this was just the foreshock of a larger collapse.

We have built a whole planetary economic system on two false premises – inexhaustible resources and infinite growth. It was only a matter of time before a critical ingredient ran out; most people expected it to be oil, water or food. The spectre of a baking earth through a chemically-altered atmosphere barely entered our heads.

Only two scenarios are possible – a rapid and unprecedented adaptation to *new ways of doing things,* which are much less resource-intensive; or a chaotic descent back through history, a new dark age of violence and collapse. Few people yet grasp how serious things are, and those who do are deeply distressed at their inability to convey it.

None of this is really a new problem. Civilisations always collapse on themselves; it just hasn't been on a planetary scale before.

The bestselling Asian book of 2008 was a semi-autobiographical novel called *Wolf Totem,* by a Chinese dissident named Jiang Rong. As a young man, Jiang Rong was a Red Guard, but he was also the son of intellectuals, and he realised he would soon be sent to the country, perhaps for the rest of his life. Seizing the initiative, he packed a chest full of books, and exiled himself to Mongolia. There he lived among nomadic herders, becoming gradually integrated into their way of life.

Mongol people worship Tengger, the sky god, who overlooks all living things. They are acutely aware of the balance of the elements in their environment – the grasslands, the grazing animals, and the wolf packs and other predators that hunt them. They refer to this entire system as 'the big life', and to themselves and other creatures as the 'little lives'. They reason, with total ecological awareness, that all life depends on the big life staying in good shape. They fight the wolves, but not too hard, as the wolves control the rodents and antelope, who compete with their herds. They need just enough of these other prey to keep the wolves in shape. And, above all, they need the grasslands to thrive and grow, and not become desert. To the north, the vast Gobi Desert is an object lesson – this too was once grassland. *Wolf Totem* is a tribute to the wisdom of this ancient way of life. It's a pretty good analogy for the rest of the planet, really. We had better look after the big life, or our little lives will soon be at an end.

Making sure that we take the adaptation pathway and not the road to economic collapse means a mighty shift of priorities and behaviour. But we have made such shifts in the past. In World War Two, almost every individual changed their behaviour to be more self-sacrificing and cooperative with their neighbours and friends, because the danger of invasion was so real and immediate. Interestingly, many people remember that time of danger with great warmth for the friendships and community spirit.

> People discover that there is a richer life that money can't buy, but effort and caring can.

Having real community is a joyful thing, because it is more sociable, slowed-down, satisfying and creative. The Internet is already doing this community-building job, and bringing the breakdown of mass-media conglomerates as people use blogs, create local news networks and publications online, and share their DVD collections! Local produce sold in farmers' markets bypasses the supermarket chains, people share food from their gardens, and meals are cooked for the old or sick. Neighbourhoods become safer. Email greatly magnifies grass-roots power, such as organising actions for campaigns and boycotts. As affluence declines, neighbourhood revives, and people discover that there is a richer life that money can't buy, but effort and caring can. We all become more unique in person and place.

Find work you believe in. If it involves building community, feeding people, harnessing energy from the wind and sun, living with less, networking and decentralising and protecting the earth's delicate life-support abilities, then you will be part of the main game – the big life.

Image 31

IN A NUTSHELL

- A job can easily be a kind of slavery. Even if comfortable, we are often 'comfortable eunuchs'.
- We have to find what our real work is in the world, and then how to make it possible to live from it.
- Getting these questions the wrong way round means we waste our life.
- Men like working, if the reasons are good.
- There are six good reasons to work: being independent, supporting a family, creating an economy, mentoring, using your talent, and changing the world.
- The world economy is not going to last long in its current form. We need to get started on a new one.

Image 32

ELEVEN

The journey down

*'I have always known that at last
I would take this road.
But yesterday I did not know
it would be today.'*

Narihara, 13th-century Zen poet

Nothing sets us up for problems quite as much as the idea that life is an upward journey. We are taught to expect constant improvement, so it's easy to feel a terrible failure when setbacks occur, in career, health, family or finances. The older traditions take a different view. They teach that, in an authentic man's life, we need to be defeated by greater and greater forces, because we are trying to do greater and greater things. Psychologists working with men have noticed that having things go badly, while hardly something to say 'Whoopee!' about, often means that you are about to break through to a new level. There is something in a man's psyche that means suffering is the greatest teacher, that only through crisis do we really change and grow. This chapter is about the importance of having your life sometimes fall apart. It is about finding your direction, and purpose, when you are seriously lost.

In the conventional mainstream thinking, the tamed-man suburban viewpoint, there is a plan for a man's life – everyone knows what it is. It's a six-point plan: you find a girl, get married, have kids, work, retire and die. In between, you have holidays, buy bigger and better furniture and cars, take that trip to Europe and perhaps that cruise to Alaska. Then it's the old people's home and cancer or a stroke. Hopefully not dementia.

By the early 1990s, a few men had begun to ask if this could not be improved on. In fact, quite a few began to look down the track into their future, and choke. (This was called a 'mid-life crisis'. Everyone prayed you would get back on the rails.) The search for a better and more meaningful pathway through life began to heat up, and many writers and groups of men across the world (and the women who loved them) began to investigate ways of deepening the journey, letting the train go off the tracks and run free in the meadows.

Some looked towards new psychologies, others looked back to anthropology and ancient wisdom, and both these directions bore fruit. Now we will examine some stages of adult growth, and some pathways that might suit you better than the one you are on. The main point to remember: the path to being a whole man does not always involve building success on success, on a smooth, upward flight. The path to real manhood sometimes travels down.

A hard day's knight

Before there were schools or universities, or even books, cultures still trained and prepared their young with careful intensity. Their lives depended on conveying wisdom across the generations, and they used one favourite medium – the story. Stories were told almost every night: they were recalled and retold by the elder men and women, and some stories took months to tell. Some of these stories had such resonance that they persisted for thousands of years, to become the mythologies of all the great cultures.

Fairy tales were not always amusements for children, and nor were their occupants always sparkly and cute. Most stories from European culture had their origins in pre-Christian times, when we lived in ferocious warring bands, held our ground against invaders, farmed the earth and ventured for meat into dark surrounding forests. We made jewellery of astonishing beauty, traded across the globe for silks, wines and precious gems, and spun a culture that was no less rich for not having written a word. When collectors like the Brothers Grimm set these stories down in print, they had already percolated through 1000 generations of people who thought them worth passing on. Stories were a different and deeper method from instruction or exhortation, and they allowed plenty of choice for interpretation, for taking what suited you. To use a modern phrase, they worked on many levels.

> Quite a few men began to look into their future and choke.

We can only clutch at fragments of these, but it's fun to try. For our purpose here, let's take just one single fragment from the thousands of stories still known. It's a good one, and it gives you a hint of the treasure that lies waiting.

In many old and rambling stories, three different knights make their appearance: the red, white and black. (Centuries ago, youngsters hearing these stories, half asleep by the fire's red glow, would think, 'Aha, it's those knights again!' and pay more attention.)

A knight is a mounted warrior, and he belongs to many traditions – from the Japanese samurai through Genghis Khan's cavalry to King Arthur's round table. He is also a metaphor for the individual man, as is obvious in the way he seeks always to find an ethical path through a long and difficult quest. The red knight, the white knight and the black knight always occur in that same colour sequence, because they were a progression of type. It's not a big leap to see that these represent *the stages of a man's growth.*

The red knight is, of course, the angry young man or teenager. And angry for good reason, a rebel *with* a cause. At this age, if we have anything like a heart, something stirs deep in us at all the world's wrongness. No longer a dreamy child, we sense the world closing on us and we don't like how it looks. Hormones are as much behind it as our sense of right and wrong, and both play equally valid parts. Most men can remember this phase when, at 17 or 22, we lashed about destructively, drove a car 500 kilometres for no reason, fought with those we love. Maidens and dragons may have featured in all this.

The red-knight stage isn't bad – it's an energising, a breaking-out. But it lacks focus or direction; it's *more about what we are against than what we are for.*

Then, gradually, we settle down, we find our place in the scheme of things, we become more *white.* We learn rules, begin to focus our efforts on study or career, making or doing. We become more what the society wants in a man. Girls may sleep with red knights as part of expressing their own wild phase, but they *marry* white knights. In our white-knight phase, we men become safe, organised, purposeful. And dull.

These stages are all necessary, *they can't be skipped.* Like Siddhartha in Herman Hesse's magnificent tale, we have to try all the different ways of life before we can truly renounce them. It's important to *graduate in redness,* and then in whiteness, otherwise you cannot really move on. Then, as life works on us, its complexity and suffering eat away our ego's armour, and we begin to sink into the black. The black is deep, forgiving, subtle and wise. The Man in Black knows what is what.

Here is a wonderful example of what I mean.

> During the American Civil War, a distraught mother broke into the White House, woke President Lincoln from his sleep, and pleaded for the life of her son. A young soldier, he

had been posted back to Washington on a long train journey from the front, in a standing-room-only carriage, without sleep. The following night he had fallen asleep at his guardpost and *was to be shot the next day.* (Falling asleep on guard duty was a capital offence; right into World War One, we were still shooting our own soldiers for disciplinary infractions.)

Lincoln's words are recorded: 'Well, I guess shooting him wouldn't help him much.' He called for paper and a pen, and signed a reprieve on the spot.

Robert Bly tells this story in *Iron John*. He speculates: 'a Red Knight president would have howled, "Get this woman out of here". A White Knight president would have said, "Madam, we have to have rules".' Thankfully, Abraham Lincoln was a better man than that. A black-knight president, he had 'moved beyond blame'. He had a sense of humour, and of compassion.

Australian Prime Minister Kevin Rudd is still clearly in the white-knight phase and, perhaps through the loss of his father in childhood, may have missed the chance for a red-knight phase altogether. He is moral and thorough, extraordinarily hard-working, but lacks passion or heat. Not heart, *heat.* He fence-sits on climate change, and on taking a humanitarian stand on refugees, when the people are hungry for bold and compassionate leadership. He tends to prevail by boring everyone to sleep. US President Obama suffers the same difficulty: he is a good man, but does not yet have the emotion needed to match the intensity of danger we are in. He believes emotion is dangerous, whereas the emotion of the black knight is wise but implacable and *intense in the preservation of life.* This kind of emotion people can trust. But there is hope for every man; blackness seeks us out.

The Time of Ashes

In ancient times, if a person encountered grief, loss or despair, they would do something which would appear to our eyes very odd. They would dress in the roughest clothing or 'sackcloth' and smear their body with ashes from head to foot. They would wear this as a sign of trauma for many days. Often they would carry this ceremony out accompanied by friends and family, moaning and shrieking in a very public display of their life being in collapse. People not only understood this, but honoured it; in fact a man who encountered loss and failure but did not go down into a Time of Ashes was regarded with deep alarm, even scorn. People would stand clear of him, waiting for lightning to strike.

In the shallow optimism of our culture we make no room for necessary failure, and so when it happens, our denial, with the aid of alcohol, drugs, and diversion, grows deeper and deeper. We need to recognise that the Time of Ashes is a part of the healthy growth and deepening of every man. When we accept this as not a bad thing, but a powerful and painful journey to the next level of wisdom, then some of the pain is lessened, and underneath our cries and groans is a sense of purpose unfolding, a strengthening of spirit.

We are taught that adolescence is the big transition of life, as if there are no other important journeys. No-one is even close to being a fully-grown male before turning forty. And at each stage, something large has to happen to kick it along.

Young men are prone to be cocky. They have an optimism which is charming but shallow – since it has never been tested. They are inclined to think they are invincible. Eventually, though, all men learn that not everything works out in this life. The late thirties seem to be the time that this often happens. The trigger can be anything. Perhaps a baby is stillborn. Or your wife stops loving you. A once-sturdy father shrivels and dies before your eyes. A lump becomes cancerous. A car accident smashes up your body. Or your carefully built career tumbles like a pack of cards. Suddenly there is shame, error and grief all around you. Welcome to the Time of Ashes.

> In the shallow optimism of our culture we make no room for necessary failure...

In my mid-thirties, the trigger for my journey downwards was a miscarriage – an abrupt end to a much-wanted pregnancy. When my partner felt the contractions after only three months of pregnancy, I swung into auto-pilot, being the caring and competent husband. I drove us to hospital calmly and safely. I remember crouching beside her, soaking in the shower room at the hospital, catching in my wet hands small pieces of our hoped-for child. Still seemingly unaffected, I carried off a two-day seminar straight after this.

Then the impact came. I sank into a black hole that lasted for many months. To this day, I barely understand what happened. I can only guess that my sense of optimism and confidence evaporated in the face of powerless grief. I became unlovable, self-absorbed, barely wanting to get out of bed. My moods served only to push away my partner, who was handling her own grief as she had been forced to as a child: alone. I drifted towards non-being.

The consequence of this was that I sought out healing and direction in completely new ways. I did it by working on myself. I sat with men and women, sought their help, stopped being the boy-genius therapist and began to be the broken beginner-man. It was such a relief. It was this experience that prompted me to start writing **Manhood**. *I might not have made it, and I did not want other men to suffer alone.*

You do not have to experience total devastation in order to grow into a mature man, but it helps. To discover that you are not all-powerful and that your dreams may well not come true may be enough. Thus you make the journey down. (If you fail to learn the lesson the first time, then down you go again!) When you are young, you judge people for being weak, for failing, for being beyond their ability to cope. You think, 'I would never let that happen to me.' You fail to realise that we all have limits, and we all are at times desperately in need of help. We are utterly dependent on each other. Once you have been there, you know that; you at last have empathy. Finally you get the message, and only then do you grow from a feckless boy into an open-hearted, compassionate man.

Healing through healthy shame

An old man and a younger man are on a long camping trip through the desert. For several days the young man is somewhat tense and quiet. The older man notices this and settles in to wait. Finally, one night beside a quiet waterhole, the younger man begins to talk.

He is the manager of a fruit-growing property, and in the winter, six months ago, he backed a trailer over his three-year-old son's legs. Disaster was narrowly avoided – the ground was muddy and wet, and the toddler's legs were pressed down into the mud. Miraculously, he was only bruised and shocked.

The young man was distraught for weeks. Close friends and family told him not to worry, it could have happened to anyone. He recovered somewhat, but could not put the incident out of his mind. Even on this trip, a much-needed break, he was still experiencing flashbacks and cold sweats.

The old man remains silent. He does not reassure or minimise the feelings of the young man, who sits also silent, feeling the familiar knotting in his gut as he once again relives the experience.

'Exactly what did people say to you?' the older man asks eventually.

'They said it was an accident. Not to blame myself.'

'Hmmm.' The old man is quiet again for a while. There is only the crackling of the fire and the sound of a night bird far off.

'They're wrong then,' he says all of a sudden, so that the young man is jolted from his reverie.

'Wh – what do you mean?' he asks.

'It was a really stupid thing to do,' says the old man. 'You're lucky the young fella wasn't killed.'

The young man is suddenly glad that it's dark around their small campfire. His face flushes and hot tears begin to run down his cheeks.

'I thought my wife was looking after him. We'd just had a fight. I started the tractor. I never looked. I was thinking, "it's her bloody job to keep the kids inside", and I never looked.'

The young man pitches forward onto the sand, wailing out loud. The older man moves alongside him and puts one hand on his arm. The young man seems to continue his curving fall into the old man's chest, holding on and sobbing great, gulping sobs.

After a time, the sobbing stops. He becomes aware of the texture of the older man's shirt against his cheek, sits up a little, and looks at the starry desert sky. A deep calmness settles into him; he is calmer than he has ever felt.

We need things to go wrong

Carl Jung is said to have taken misfortune in an interesting way. Whenever a friend reported enthusiastically, 'I've just been promoted', Jung would say, 'I'm very sorry to hear that, but if we stick together I think we will get through it.' If a friend arrived depressed and ashamed, saying, 'I've just been fired', Jung would say, 'Let's open a bottle of wine; this is wonderful news. Something good will happen now.'

Every man needs an ashes time in his life, to discover that, in spite of all optimism and effort, one is still vulnerable.

Former Australian politician John Brogden was a fast-rising star. He had been Opposition leader in New South Wales, pitted against the immoveable Bob Carr. Now, with Carr's resignation imminent, he was widely tipped to become premier of the nation's most populous state – and he was only 35 years old. Then, at a large social gathering in the Sydney Hilton, he became intoxicated, harassed a number of women, and made an offensively racist comment about Bob Carr's Malaysian-born wife. It was a private event, and might have gone no further, but the details were leaked to the press by another faction within his own party. It was front-page stuff. Within three hours of the revelation, Brogden apologised publicly and resigned from politics. Some days later, *he made a concerted attempt to take his own life.*

John Brogden talked about his experience at the inaugural Happiness Conference in Sydney, where he was warmly applauded, because today he is a different man. He is an active spokesperson for 'beyondblue', the national depression-fighting body, and national patron of the Lifeline counselling service. He is doing useful and effective work in many roles far removed from politics.

There are thousands of similar stories. Malcolm Fraser, one of Australia's chilliest prime ministers, who reigned over an era of 20-percent youth unemployment and famously said, 'Life wasn't meant to be easy' (which sounds like one of Rohr's five initiatory truths), travelled from being a privileged and insensitive 'blue blood' to one of our most humanitarian voices – for refugees, for overseas aid programs; a tireless worker and a crystal-clear voice for justice. To this day he is seen as a flagship example of a man who found his heart.

> Malcolm Fraser is a flagship example of a man who has found his heart.

This is the gift of ashes. A man is broken. His arrogance and self-pride make the fall all the more painful to bear. Suddenly he knows how it feels. If he can make that impressive and redemptive leap, if he doesn't snap shut his armour but stays open to the scorching bath of shame, the experience will change him, will wash away the dross and the pretence. He has made the journey down. He no longer looks disdainfully at the poor, handicapped or defeated. He realises they are just like him. His capacity for compassion deepens enormously. The ashes time completes what has begun in adolescence – the making of a real man.

A map of the journey

Psychologist Erik Erikson was born at the very start of the twentieth century, and died at the very end. He was a beacon of good sense who rose above the Freudian murk of his day, which was threatening to disappear up its own railway tunnel. But he also saw that there was more depth to life than the 'rat-psychologists' were proposing.

Erikson set out a map of life that was coherent, purposeful and easy to understand. He saw each stage of life (he counted eight) as a dilemma to be solved. There was a natural tension built into being a baby, toddler, teenager, married man, old man, etc., which had to be figured out before you could move on.

His stages were:

Babyhood – trust vs. mistrust (do my parents love me?)

Toddlerhood – autonomy vs. shame (can I do things independently but still accept limits?)

Preschool age – initiative vs. guilt (can I do things independently but still get help when I need it?)

School age – industry vs. inferiority (can I feel capable even if I am not good at everything?)

Adolescence – identity vs. confusion (what kind of person am I going to be?)

Young adulthood – intimacy vs. isolation (can I make a good relationship with someone?)

Adulthood – generativity vs. stagnation (will my life be purposeful and creative?)

Old age – integrity vs. despair (can I keep and develop my values while physically falling apart?)

It's a fantastic map because it tells you what should be happening when. (For example, a seventeen-year-old is probably still finding out who he is and what his direction is in life. This would be a bad time to pair up with a partner, because he has not yet discovered himself.)

If you stick with the goals and 'graduate' from each, you end up, in sequential order, hopeful, strong-willed, purposeful, capable, your own person, in loving relationships, caring for the world, then wise and useful, till the day you die.

As a man approaching 60, and also wearing out rather fast, the eighth stage now holds my attention the most. I was from the generation that grew up on 'do what your feelings tell you', and the feelings I mostly had at 55 were to go and have a long lie down. Then I discovered a long-hidden iron deficiency – I had been tired and in a brain fog for almost eight years, and numerous medical tests had found nothing. Then a simple organic iron supplement transformed my life, and gave me back my mojo. But I had learnt something from those wasted years – what old and useless felt like. I didn't like it at all. I decided not to go there again. Now I spend about 40 minutes a day in maintenance. Yoga, tai chi and Feldenkrais are all great technologies for fighting off old-and-crook. I have always meditated (otherwise my brain is not somewhere you would want to live). And jogging and resistance training complete the picture. I'll be honest: while some of these are a joy, others are a bore. But I have a reason for them now. I want to do more good in the world, as well as have a lot more fun. And you need a working body and mind to do that. So I am fighting against death and decrepitude, as if my life depends on it!

The body is a great coach at this age. With aches, pains, feeling flat or depressed, moving yourself about – gardening, bushwalking, swimming – will always help. You are a big mammal, and you need to be active until you drop.

Image 33

Men and health

Professor John McDonald, *who has contributed the following text, is Professor of Primary Health Care at the University of Western Sydney.*

In the last decade, governments, health providers, and people generally have become more interested in male health. Last century, the feminist movement brought attention to the issue of gender and health. The benefits to women can be seen today in the many services and health programs designed specifically for them.

The women's movement had to struggle with 'women's health' being reduced to clinical concerns for the reproductive health of women. Likewise, male health has been dominated by concerns around the prostate and, more recently, erectile dysfunction – both important, but only part of a much bigger picture. This medicalisation of men's health has often been accompanied by repeated assertions that 'men don't take care of themselves', 'men don't seek help when they need it' and the like. Generally, this has been done in a blaming tone. This 'culture of negativity' around male health has influenced a lot of thinking and policy: blaming men for their poor health diminishes the caring extended to them. One striking example is that five men a day (at least) kill themselves in Australia; Dads in Distress, an organisation set up to help separated fathers, has said that if it were five *whales* a day and not five males, there would be a greater national empathic response.

At last, though, we are beginning to see a more rational and compassionate view. This has come about in part from a growth of interest in the 'social determinants' of health, a movement spearheaded by the World Health Organization. This has meant acknowledging the context of people's lives and a scientific appraisal of the factors affecting health and wellbeing. Work, stress, the social gradient (where we fit in the ladder of society), social inclusion and exclusion are all examples of these social determinants, and provide a useful entry point to look at male health. One example is that of work, employment and unemployment: men working to support their families and anxious not to be made redundant; men working in health-threatening jobs, which may be the only employment they can find; men finding the adjustment after retirement hard and stressful. All these issues need to be looked at when dealing with men's heath. Much behaviour – such as smoking or drinking, having a poor diet, not having the time or energy for exercise, having poor self-esteem or a lack of social support networks – can arise from the pressures on men's lives.

A 'social determinants of health' approach allows us to acknowledge the importance of personal behaviour (including violent behaviour) but also to see this in the broader context of their lives. For example, men do attend health services less than women, but the context of their working life goes some way towards explaining this.

Some Australian circumstances may have relevance for the wider world. National male health conferences have been run in conjunction with Indigenous, Aboriginal and Torres Strait Islander male health conventions, and we see that there is much to be learned from Aboriginal approaches to health, including male health: a more spiritual and holistic view of health, consistent with a social-determinants approach, underpins Aboriginal philosophy, and there is a respect for 'men's business' as separate from women's business.

Image 34

Australia has proclaimed an official Male Health Policy, only the second country in the world, after Ireland, to do so. The preparatory documents stressed the social determinants of male health and also the importance of 'male-friendly' health services. Both these elements allow us to move away from the narrow clinical perspective of men's health (or rather illness), as well as from the 'blaming men' approach. We can now think of building the health of men and boys across their lifespan. Instead of asking why men don't come to services, we should now be asking, what can services do to make themselves more accessible to men and boys? What are we doing about access for men who work 8–10 hours a day? What are we doing to help young fathers be better at fathering? What are we doing for isolated elderly men (the group most at risk of suicide)?'

It looks like we can build male health more rationally and compassionately!

Retirement is for wimps

It's worth mentioning here that, along with the invention of paid work, came its corollary, retirement, the consolation prize for a life spent doing something you don't like. Retirement made sense when we worked with muscle and sweat, and simply wore out and could work no more. It seemed a humane ending to a life of hard slog. Retirement was the life goal of generations of men, to finally stop and be able to enjoy what you had earned.

However, like snow-covered mountains seen from the desert, it was all in the yearning. When they reached retirement, many men hated it, and did not live very long in it.

As we have noted throughout this book:
- *activity* is what we are made for
- *purpose* is what we live for, and
- *belonging* and *enjoying* are the juice of life.

So why would anyone give this up?

The trick, then, is to organise one's work so that it transitions progressively into a balance that suits the age you are. You might work hellishly hard as a young single. Cruise somewhat when you have babies and toddlers. Ramp up again when they are at school. Ease back when the teen years come, and maybe even take a year off for an around-Australia camping trip with the family. Then get into more philanthropic stuff, less concerned with money, in your fifties. And when you pass 60, shape up a nice mix of paid and unpaid, wisdom-using, effort-avoiding, creative, useful and helpful eldership. With some fine tinkering, this can continue until the day you die.

Image 35

The main message here, though, is – never retire. You won't like it, it will drive your wife mad, and if you believed in your work, why would you quit when you were just getting good at it?

IN A NUTSHELL

- Men do not usually learn much through things going well. It's pain and disintegration that are the greatest teachers.
- The three knights in old stories – red, white and black – represent the stages we pass through.
- Kevin Rudd is a white knight. Abraham Lincoln was a black knight. Perhaps this will change.
- Men's lives sooner or later go through a Time of Ashes. This is when we graduate as fully human.
- Shame and grief are the best teachers.
- Each age has its challenges. Old age is when your life proves itself a success or failure.
- Whatever you do, don't blow it and retire.

Image 36

TWELVE

Spirit

'Sometimes I go about in pity for myself, and all the while a great wind is bearing me across the sky.'

Ojibwa proberb

Readers outside Australia may not know about Michael Leunig, a tousle-headed cartoonist/philosopher in his sixties who holds a unique place in the country's soul. For almost 40 years, the piece of paper most likely to be found stuck to a fridge door or an office noticeboard anywhere in the country has been a Leunig cartoon. He also writes columns and books – sometimes angry, always beautiful. Most days the quality papers carry a Leunig work, summing up the mood and vagaries of the day.

Leunig's cartoons 'took a different road' long ago, from being political and current-affairs-based towards a cosmic, whimsical commentary on life and the world of the spirit. Leunig cannot stomach either the values or the sensory overload of the modern world; he lives in a rural community, far from the city. Nonetheless, his voice and contribution remain at the centre of national life.

Just one example: astonished and appalled at the onset of the Iraq war – that in the modern world we could countenance the violent invasion of a sovereign country, causing 100,000 civilian deaths and up to 3 million refugees – he made it a personal quest to never let us forget it was going on. Day after day, he reminded a nation that wanted to just get used to it, or even feel patriotic fervour, that this was about harming real, terrified, innocent people. Some wondered if he had lost his sense of humour, but he was just *keeping vigil.* When it was over, he returned to cartoons about ducks, the moon, intimacy and the search for truth.

In one of Leunig's early cartoons, back in the 1970s, he portrayed a small figure kneeling and praying to a cardboard box. A scornful intellectual type then strides up, stamps on the box, crushing it flat and, after mocking the kneeling figure one more time, struts away. In the third frame, a remarkable thing happens: the kneeling figure simply *folds the box back into shape, and goes on praying.*

This cartoon always disturbed me. I took it to be denigrating both the figures in it. But then I noticed a detail in the way it had been drawn that had previously escaped me: the serenity and humility of the praying man once he had reassembled his box. *It looked like he had won the day.*

I have often asked myself the question embedded in that cartoon – is this what spirituality, and religion, are about? Pathetic belief in an 'imaginary friend' – a caring god in the sky; pious clinging to a ridiculous and outdated supernatural mythology? Or is something going on here that an informed and rational person (someone like you or I!) could respect?

A whole industry has developed in attacking the idea of God or spirit in life, and given the current shape of religion, this seems well deserved. From the pedophile rings that passed for some religious orders, the bigotry against women and gays, the credit-card mega-churches fleecing meaning-hungry suburbanites, back through the long histories of bloody division and persecution, the willing participation in slavery, conquest and genocide ... To wish for a world with 'no religion', as John Lennon did, is a tempting thought.

Giving up on religion, or condemning it to scorn, is understandable on the face of things. But somehow, this never quite happens. Just as we are about to throw out the putrid bathwater, people keep discovering a pristine, lovely and bawling baby, and it all begins again. And even if we give up on religion – the container – we return again and again to spirit – the content, the experience of unity beyond our own skin that somehow redefines every act we take and every thought we think.

> To wish for a world with 'no religion', as John Lennon did, is a tempting thought.

Today there is, among intelligent and active people, a sustained and growing interest in things of the spirit. Sometimes this locates itself within organised religon, and sometimes outside of it. There has been an explosion of interest in Buddhism, as well as the deeper aspects of yoga. We have seen gentler and more sophisticated forms of Islam emerge, much as Christianity did, from its mediaeval roots. Judaism is flourishing. And always, strongly represented among the most progressive, courageous and effective social-justice activists, environmentalists and political figures, you will find people of faith, who draw from spiritual roots their ideas of human worth and the sacredness of 'God's creation'. These people are not fools. They have a high level of personal effectiveness, and often of physical courage. Something is working for them. It cannot be explained by delusion.

A gentle antidote

Spirituality is as old as man. In the pre-literate ages of the human race, religion did not just add meaning to life, it *was* life. The sacred was our worldview; we inhabited a spiritual landscape. This was the reason that the hunter-gatherer culture lasted 300,000 years, something no 'civilisation' has ever done. Their response to the natural world was utterly realistic, though depicted in magical terms of animal spirits, hunting taboos, and sacred sites. Like the Mongol concept of the 'big life' mentioned in Chapter Ten, the spiritual language embodied an acute environmental awareness. (Today we call ourselves realists and believe in consumer credit, democracy and everlasting oil.)

Then, 4,000 years ago, the age of empires began, and things went downhill. Most of humanity became slaves and serfs in continent-wide domination systems. The hunter-gatherers were rounded up in chains. From the Mesopotamian to the Aztec, the Roman to the British Empire, it was the same story. Only a tiny handful of people were free or treated well; the rest were human livestock.

But then an odd thing happened. As the great slave-based empires rose, so did value systems that opposed the dehumanisation, that preached the value, and equality before God, of all human life. In the Western lineage, it was the Roman Empire that oppressed us, and Christianity was the response. We forget how radical it was for Jesus to have women in his retinue, to praise the Samaritan and befriend the tax collector, to confront the high priests and trash the temple courtyard – the New York Stock Exchange of his day.

Islam played the same role. Mohammed affirmed that all people must be cared for and treated well. The Buddhist king Ashoka founded an India-wide empire based on kindness, non-violence and compassion. Religions were like an antidote, a gentle but still powerful moral force against the brutality of their age. When it all turned to chaos, it was the monasteries that remembered medicine, science, art, culture, history; that kept a light burning in the darkness and cared for the sick and lost.

The sacred world

At the heart of all religions is the sacredness of life – the idea that we are all one, we all belong, we are all one family. US writer Alan Watts very accurately summed up the physical truth of this, noting that we don't *come into* this world, we *come out* of it, the way that leaves come out of a tree.

Our ancestors sat around fires and looked at the stars and, with lively intelligence, asked the very same question we do – *what the hell is this all about?* They saw, just as we do, that this universe is miraculous, in the sense that its very existence is a mystery that cannot be understood. Our brain has to normalise things in order to cope, but we should never lose hold of the fact that our very existence is wondrous.

This is the great dilemma of being human: physically we are not so different from a bird or animal, and yet, unlike an eagle or a bear, we have a sense of time, we know there is space beyond what we can see. We know about the ongoing story of our species, and this gives us pause, and perhaps even purpose. We are small but we are huge. People who grasp this, and relate to it through tradition or through their own independent thought, begin to act less like animals and more like something very different.

The Taoist monks, the fishermen in Galilee, Aung San Suu Kyi confronting the vicious Burmese generals, Gandhi meekly taking on the British Empire, Jimmy Carter averting war in the Middle East while his citizens' concerns never rose above shopping. Dietrich Bonhoeffer returning to Nazi Germany where he knew he would face torture and death. The ending of slavery. The emancipation of women ... *Religious underpinnings and spiritual perspectives lent reason and transcendent strength to most of those who delivered the human race from its nightmares.* That religion also caused many of those nightmares is not to take away from this.

Big brain, big vision

What makes us human? Proportionally, we have larger, more complex brains, but does this create a new level of neurological functioning? Can we best understand ourselves as spiritual beings, in that we can begin to *grasp the totality?* We are *'the eyes with which the universe looks at itself'*, as one writer put it. While the big picture is hard to keep in mind, those who do so are living at their highest potential. They are more *realistic.*

It's a practical problem: if *we are all one,* how can we live in the way we do – buying products made by slave labour, heating the earth up in ways that will cause famine and death across the globe, robbing our children of forests and clean oceans? To do so is like slashing at our own arms, stabbing our own eyes.

Furthermore, if we are part of God, then why be afraid of death? Why be anxious? Why not rise to our greatest heights in the face of it?

Spirit is the highest dimension of our life. If we acknowledge that we need to nurture and develop this capacity, just as we should nurture our athletic, artistic or intellectual life, what would that mean? We men value our sex life. We are learning to have an emotional life. *How might we develop our spirit life?* How might we make space or time to allow in a sense of mystery? The transcendent? How can we be open to intervention by the greater life into our mundane plans and ambitions? As twenty-first-century men and women, would we function best in the world with a spiritual core to our lives? I believe so.

Some men (including me) meditate. This simple calming of the brain can rapidly create a mental spaciousness that allows far more of the sensory totality of the world to wash into us. We think better, bigger and more holistically. Some men spend a few days around the time of their birthday each year in solitude, in nature, just waiting for the mud to settle out of their minds so the light can shine through again. Some men record their dreams. Some write a daily journal. Some paint, write poetry or make music. Some go on retreats or pilgrimages – there are long traditions of self-healing, for others have trodden these paths before us.

Here is a favourite poem of mine that conveys how simple it all can be.

'The Peace of Wild Things' by Wendell Berry

When despair grows in me
and I wake in the middle of the night at the least sound
in fear of what my life and my children's lives may be,
I go and lie down where the wood drake
rests in his beauty on the water,
and the great heron feeds.

I come into the peace of wild things
who do not tax their lives with forethought
of grief. I come into the presence of still water.

And I feel above me the day-blind stars
waiting for their light. For a time
I rest in the grace of the world,
and am free.

How spirit works

I love computers. I am old enough to remember the days before they existed, and cannot ever take them for granted. I had them all – a Sinclair, a Commodore 64 ... But I remember my first glimpse of true love, a $10,000 Apple Lisa computer at an electronics show. It was the first computer to ever have a 'mouse'. And there on its crystal-clear screen was something new and wonderful – 'icons', little pictures on the screen to represent files, programs and data. Today these little pictures make everything possible – without them, computers would be useless. The folders, files, applications and software are available to us by clicking, opening and dragging these icons about. We take them utterly for granted. But there is something important to remember. *These images do not exist, and nor does the content, text or pictures they call up.* There is nothing resembling an actual folder, photograph, movie or file of text anywhere inside your computer. There are only electrons, streaming or being held in place on drives and chips. The icon is *our interface with the unknowable inside of the machine.* Those icons are illusions of dots and dashes that fool our eyes; *they don't exist, but they work.* Hold that thought for a minute, while we bring in another thread.

In the movie *Contact,* written and directed by astronomer Carl Sagan, a spacecraft carrying a young woman scientist is sent down a 'wormhole' – one of the energy flows known to exist in the universe between galaxies. She arrives on, of all things, a tropical shoreline. A figure approaches her: it is her dead father. There is no suggestion that this really *is* her father, or really a beach, but rather that the beings where she has washed up have delved into her brain and arranged a reassuring figure to create the least anxiety while she takes in some startling facts.

She knows this, but is in awe of it nonetheless. (It's an enormously moving scene in the film: her widowed dad had raised her and nurtured her interest in astronomy – he had metaphorically *brought her there.)* She cannot remain there; it's a brief trial contact between civilisations. But there is one more mind-spinning revelation that comes out as a throwaway line as she is preparing to be sent back to earth. The mode of transport, the corridor along which she was brought there – how was it created? The beings, via the image of her father, tell her they have no idea. Some *other* civilisation created it, they merely came across it. The sheer vastness of creation begins to sink in.

Where are we headed here? It's the idea of the aliens creating an image to talk to her, an interface bearing her father's voice and appearance, an *icon.*

Image 37

Concepts of God

Little children think of God as a person in the sky. So did the peasants of the Middle Ages. The sky is a good place to put God: it reminds you of the bigness of things, the infinite bounds of the universe. I have sat in thatched huts in the rainforest of Papua New Guinea and heard old men talk about the sky gods, the creation forces, the nature spirits. I did not feel superior or scornful of their world view – these were handles on reality, and the only measure of a handle is how well it grips. God in the sky, God in the earth, God in us – these are our poetic attempts to grasp something that just cannot be grasped any other way.

Your concept of God is extremely important to examine. The God that some writers like to reject is not the concept that most Christians, for example, actually believe in.

You are beginning to comprehend things when you realise that there is nowhere that God isn't. He/she is not separate. But that means s/he is not anywhere in particular, either (atheists and spiritual people agree on this, in a sense), and is certainly not a being or identity. God isn't a superhero or a giant father or mother sitting apart from things and looking on. And he is certainly not the vengeful psychopath sometimes portrayed in the Old Testament.

God is *not there,* but only in the same sense that an email or a document on your computer screen is not there. Your idea of God is the tip of an iceberg that is very much larger. It's not even enough to say that God is in everything. (This is the concept of *spiritus,* the Latin word for 'breath', and also the root word for 'inspiration'.) It's that God *is* everything. Or, put another way, that everything adds up to something. As the ancient Vedic scriptures of India teach, we are one.

The concept of God as a *being* is enormously useful as a poetic explanation of something beyond words, a human interface, a clickable icon that taps into something you could never understand; or, more importantly, never manage or access any other way. There is nothing false about this. A rock is not there, either, nor a car or a bullet. If we saw realistically, without the benefit of sensory simplification provided by our mammalian eyes and sense of touch, then a rock would be a zinging cloud of particles. A car would be something you could pass right through, like the invisible radiation cloud after a nuclear blast. Reality is real, but it's just not the way we perceive it. Our perceptions are short-cuts, 'handles' on the world we occupy.

We've always known this slipperiness about reality, that there is more than meets the eye. Poetry can grasp things that logic cannot. Music can, too. The prehistoric painters of those beautiful antelopes and lions in the caves in Lascaux, France were grasping it. The spirit of antelope-ness and lion-ness leaps from these paintings. *Everything* has spirit, a deep-down essence to it which is its real truth. The beauty of physical love cannot possibly be understood just by watching it: what looks like pornography can have the deepest sacred meaning to those involved. JRR Tolkien responded with this 'essence' when accused of writing 'mere' fantasy. (They should not have spoken like this to a man who had survived the trenches of World War One.) 'Do you mean,' he wrote, 'that lamp posts and kerbstones are more real, more important, than heroism, sacrifice, striving together with friends?' Meaning is the only durable thing; everything else falls away. Tolkien hated industrialisation, the loss of community, the death of nature, the death of imagination. No wonder he is so popular today.

> I give thanks for what has come my way, because when you appreciate your life, it deepens.

Every morning when I wake, and every night when I relinquish the world again, I pray. I pray to God. I do not think there is a man in the sky listening, or even a woman. I think there is a pattern to the universe that is powerful and generative, a pattern that reaches and touches everything. I pray to change not God, but myself. I use a personal icon to bring myself back into tune with larger forces. I do not think these forces are going to take care of me, but I think that if I am aligned with them, my best self will manifest in me, I will have a focus that is not my own dismal and frightened selfish needs. Joy and unity will characterise more of my days, and I will be part of the great journey of life that has marched down the eons.

I give thanks for what has come my way, because when you appreciate your life, it deepens. I give thanks for my life. I ask for help with what those I love need from me, and how I can best provide this. I celebrate the caring and laughter and beauty of the people, the animals, plants, oceans, winds and mountains that surround me, and I fall asleep appreciating what, one day soon, will all be over for me, but will continue nonetheless into immeasurable time.

IN A NUTSHELL

- Spirit is a way of looking below the surface to the totality of what lies beneath.

- We don't come into this world, we come out of it, as leaves come out of a tree.
- People who connect to spirit are strong and brave, and their efforts harmonise with the totality of life.
- Mystery cannot be named, but praying can help.

Epilogue

(For Brenda)

As I was writing this final chapter, I had to take an unexpected trip 3,000 kilometres to Western Australia. One of my favourite aunts, now 76, is dying from a combination of diabetes and Parkinson's brain disease. She is immobile, all the life in her condensed and shining from her moist, bright eyes. She is still sharp as a tack, but trapped in a failing body. Soon she will be gone.

I am glad to have gone to see her and say, 'Thank you for being in my life.' She was the first to escape the bleak Yorkshire town where I was born. She would return from time to time radiating femininity and quiet glamour, and the very air around her whispered of a larger world. As a school teacher she loved to inspire and teach others, and was always interested in even the dorkiest little boy.

That generation is thinning out; mine is the front line now. Sitting here at my desk, back at home again, I feel steady enough, but somehow blocked up, numb and stuck. Instinct drives me towards music: I log onto YouTube and come across Aretha Franklin singing 'Bridge Over Troubled Water' like you've never heard it sung before.

The contained energy, the groundedness of her big, strong body, the assuredness of the other musicians, her percussive hammering of the piano, driving spiritual energy into every word, sweating and quaking with transformation – I can feel my own body melting and shifting, too, re-arranging thoughts and emotions into the sheer intensity of being alive, and yet so soon gone.

Words in a book can only take you so far. Forest and mountain, surf and sky, dance and song, warm skin and tingling nerves, drumming and story, myth and magic – all came long before language tried to net down the divine energies of our lives.

This book is a signpost. Don't climb it, *go where it points.* There is a universe waiting.

Author's notes

'As Robert Bly said at the start of his famous book, Iron John...': Bly, R., *Iron John,* Addison Wesley, NY, 1990.

'Facing the facts' box: Australian Bureau of Statistics 3303.0 – Causes of Death, Australia, 18/03/2009; Australian Bureau of Statistics 4102.0 – Australian Social Trends, 2007 Lifetime Marriage and Divorce Trends; Australian Bureau of Statistics 4128.0 – Personal Safety Survey 2006a; Tyre, P. *The Trouble With Boys: A Surprising Report Card on Our Sons, Their Problems at School and What Parents and Educators Must Do,* Crown, NY, 2008; *Suicide leading cause of death in Australia,* Lifeline Press Release, 28 Oct 2009, sourced from ABS Causes of Death 2008.

'...some studies report a trebling of father-child time...': Bianchi, S.M., Robinson J.P. & Milkie, M.A. (Eds.) *Changing Rhythms of American Family*

Life, Russell Sage Foundation, NY, 2006.

'Scientists have found that trauma that has not been shared or properly processed...': Shin, L.M., Rauch, S.L., & Pitman, R.K., 'Amygdala, Medial Prefrontal Cortex, and Hippocampal Function in PTSD', *Annals of the New York Academy of Sciences,* Volume 1071, Issue: Psychobiology of Traumatic Stress Disorder, a Decade of Progress, pp.67–79, 26 July 2006.

'Robert Bly tells the story of a man phoning his father, long distance.': *A Gathering of Men,* PBS Television 1990. Robert Bly and Bill Moyers in interview. This program is viewable online on Google video; search under 'Bly and A Gathering of Men'.

'Robert Bly writes in Iron John, "Many men go to their graves convinced..."': Bly, R. *Iron John,* Addison Wesley, NY, 1990.

'In a Christian book on men's development, Healing the Masculine

Soul, Gordon Dalbey tells this story...': Dalbey, G., *Healing the Masculine Soul,* Thomas Nelson, NY, 2003.

'The poem ends with a trenchant line: "He's finding out what it means to be a man..."': Nowlan, A., 'The Rites of Manhood' in Biddulph, S., *Stories of Manhood,* Finch Publishing, Sydney, 2009.

'Neuroscientists believe that the hardest thing for the human mind...': Blakemore, S-J., 'Brain development during adolescence' in *Educational Theories, Cultures and Learning: A critical perspective.* Series edited by Daniels, H., Lauder, H., Porter, J.; Routledge, 2009.

Blakemore, S-J. 'Action and consciousness: neurological issues' in Wilken, P., Bayne, T., Cleeremans, A. (eds.) *Oxford Companion to Consciousness,* OUP, Oxford, 2009.

'Gordon Dalbey tells of a woman who phoned him after he had

counselled her husband.': Dalbey, G., *Healing the Masculine Soul,* Thomas Nelson, NY, 2003.

'John Lee, in his book At My Father's Wedding, wrote about confronting a wife's drinking and abusive behaviour.': Lee, J., *At My Father's Wedding: Reclaiming our true masculinity,* Piatkus Books, 1992.

'Jungian analyst Marie-Louise von Franz tells a story about a woman friend...': Franz, M., *Puer Aeturnus,* Sigo Press, Boston, 1981.

'Ending domestic violence' box: For more information about Stuart Anderson's work, see www.menandfamily.org.au/about.htm. For more information about anger management, see Dutton, D.G. & Corvo, K., 'The Duluth model: A dataimpervious paradigm and a failed strategy', *Aggression and Violent Behaviour,* 12(6), Nov 2007, pp.658–667; Donovan, F., *Dealing with Anger,* Finch Publishing, Sydney, 1999; and Alan Jenkins, *Invitations to Responsibility,* available from the Dulwich Centre, Adelaide.

'The science of happy couples' box: Gottman, J., *Ten Lessons to Transform Your Marriage,* Crown Publishers, 2006; Gottman, J., *And Baby Makes Three,* Crown Publishers, 2007.

A good summary of Gottman's ideas is at http://psychpage.com/family/library/gottman.html

The story of Drew and Claudine's interview is paraphrased from Gladwell, M., *Blink: The Power of Thinking Without Thinking,* Back Bay Books, 2007, and also online at www.enotalone.com/article/3937.html.

'In Gore Vidal's words, we went from a sexual revolution to a sexual circus.': Gore Vidal interviewed by Ramona Koval on ABC Radio National Books and Writing, 20/01/2002.

'In his book Intimacy and Desire, Schnarch describes how every

relationship passes through three stages.': Schnarch, D., *Intimacy and Desire*, Penguin Australia, 2010.

'Columnist Michael Ventura put it this way': Ventura, M., 'Shadowdancing', in *Wingspan*, Harding, M. (ed.), St Martin's Press, NY, 1992.

'John O'Hara, in Appointment in Samarra, has one of his characters express it this way': O'Hara, J., *Appointment in Samarra*, 1934.

'Paul Olson, in Wingspan, comments on this passage...': Harding, M., *Wingspan*, St Martin's Press, NY, 1992.

'When the first brave researchers began to document human sexual behaviour in the 1940s, they discovered that...': Kinsey, A., *Sexual Behaviour in the Human Female*, 1953.

'In Noa's own words...': Noa, J., 'The Cripple and the Man' in Baumli, F. (ed.), *Men Freeing Men*, New Atlantis Press, 1985.

'Preventing rape' box: See Renard, A., *Real men don't rape,* an action research project for the International Boys' Schools Coalition, St Andrew's College Grahamstown, June, 2009; Thamm, M. and Alison, *I Have Life,* Penguin Group, Cape Town, 2002. See also Ward, C.A., *Attitudes Toward Rape: Feminist and social psychological perspectives,* Sage, London, 1995.

'The so-called Playboy philosophy...': Dalbey, G., *Healing the Masculine Soul,* Thomas Nelson, NY, 2003.

'No one arouses us. We arouse ourselves...': Masters, R., 'Ditching the Bewitching Myth' in Thompson, K., (ed.) *To Be a Man,* Jeremy Tarcher, LA, 1991.

'Men say their penises have minds of their own...': Rhodes, R., *Making Love: an erotic odyssey,* Simon and Schuster, NY, 1992.

'Gordon Dalbey tells a striking tale about this.': Dalbey, *ibid.*

'**Andrew was well aware of the research that showed today's young people to be the most troubled...**': Eckersley, R., *Never better – or getting worse? The health and wellbeing of young Australians,* Australia 21, Canberra, 2009.

'**...the research indicates that programs for changing kids have little effect unless...**': Lines, A., 'Growing adolescents into adults', in *Independence,* 34(1), April 2009, published by AHISA (Association of Heads of Independent Schools of Australia), pp.30–34.+++

'**...the seven steps of "the hero's journey"**': Campbell, J., *The Hero With a Thousand Faces,* New World Library, 2008. Read everything you can of this man's ideas. He has the map.

'**Boys and cars**' box: For more information about Big hART and the Drive project, see www.bigheart.org and www.drive.org.au.

'As Richard Rohr describes it...': Rohr, R., *Adam's Return: The Five Promises of Male Initiation,* Crossroad, NY, 2004.

'Rohr points out that for all hunter-gatherer peoples...': Rohr, R., *Adam's Return,* Crossroad, NY, 2004.

'Richard Rohr puts it like this...': Rohr, R., *Adam's Return,* Crossroad, NY, 2004.

'Kahlil Gibran says, "The deeper that sorrow carves..."': Gibran, K., *The Prophet,* Alfred Knopf, USA, 1939.

'Australian agents ... were aware of, possibly even involved in the voyage. In late 2009 I met with Senator John Faulkner on behalf of the SIEVX Memorial Committee. At the time Senator Faulkner was Special Minister of State, five weeks later to become Minister of Defence. At the time of the SIEVX sinking, Senator Faulkner had been in opposition, and chaired a Senate enquiry into "A Certain Maritime

Incident" which he was able to broaden to also include the SIEVX tragedy. At our meeting Senator Faulkner stated his belief, which arose from information he had received but was not able to cite as evidence in the enquiry, that SIEVX had carried a satellite tracking device, and that the progress of the doomed vessel had been tracked by the Australian government. He was of the view that only a judicial inquiry would be able to require testimony adequate to make known the facts surrounding the deaths of such a large number of people in such inexplicable circumstances.

The closest that Senator Faulkner came to detailing his beliefs came in his carefully worded speech on SIEVX to the Senate on 25 September 2002:

'I intend to keep asking questions until I find out. And, Mr Acting Deputy President, I intend to keep pressing for an independent judicial inquiry into these very serious matters. At no stage do I want to break, nor will I break, the protocols in relation to operational matters involving ASIS or the AFP. But those protocols were not meant *as a direct or an indirect licence to kill.*' Speech available on www.sievx.com or in Hansard.

'**...there is pain in the world, but I will be here.**' This story in a similar form first appeared in *Raising a Happy Child,* Steve and Shaaron Biddulph, Penguin 2007.

'**Lately, though, we have begun to challenge this idea: research is finding that active fathers...**': Australian Fatherhood Research Network, Family Action Centre, University of Newcastle, initiated by Richard Fletcher and team, carry out the best research on, and also active encouragement of, good fathering in Australia.

'**Here are his [John Embling's] thoughts on fathers**': Embling, J., *Fragmented Lives,* Penguin, Victoria, 1986.

'The research picture is stunningly clear.': Burgess, A., *Fatherhood Reclaimed,* Vermilion, 1998; Blankenhorn, D., *Fatherless America,* Simon and Schuster, 1996. These two books blew the whistle on the fatherhood crisis in the UK and US, respectively (note the dates). Both books give meticulous and comprehensive surveys of the research, which in the years since has only strengthened – on the importance of involved, safe and caring dads to kids' life chances and the wellbeing of mothers.

'In his book At My Father's Wedding, John Lee describes four kinds of defective father...': Lee, J., *At My Father's Wedding,* Piatkus Books, London, 1992.

'Family therapists have discovered something important...': Biddulph, S., Practitioner Training Notes, Collinsvale Centre, 1994.

'Abraham Reichenberg, an assistant professor of psychiatry at the

Mount Sinai School of Medicine in New York': Reichenberg, A., et al, 'Advancing Paternal Age and Autism', *Arch Gen Psychiatry,* 2006(63), pp.1026–1032. See also BBC World News, 'Infertility link to autism risk', 26 October 2006.

'Professor Mary Croughan, of the University of California, studied 4,000 women and their children...': Sample, I., 'Children born after IVF treatment face higher health risks', *The Guardian,* 26 October 2006.

'The newest discovery in fatherhood research is the remarkable effect that dads have on daughters.': Meeker, M., *Strong Fathers, Strong Daughters,* Ballantine, 2006. Despite a slight sense of moral panic, this woman doctor gives a gritty and moving account of her work with hundreds of teenage girls, and the ways that they are vulnerable to unhappy sexual experiences. She greatly encourages active fathering, and gives specific and straightforward suggestions how to go about it.

'Far more girls are anxious and unhappy now than has ever been the case in the past.': Eckersley, R., *Never better – or getting worse?*, Australia 21, Canberra, 2009.

'The number of girls who have multiple sexual partners before the age of leaving school has doubled in the last six years': Smith, A., Agius, P., Mitchell, A., Barrett, C., Pitts, M.2009. *Secondary Students and Sexual Health 2008,* Monograph Series No.70, Australian Research Centre in Sex, Health & Society, La Trobe University, Melbourne. The increase referred to here was from about 8 to 15 percent. In another sobering statistic, the proportion of (sexually active) girls experiencing unwelcome or unwanted sex in the previous year, usually while affected by alcohol, was 38 percent. Along with Richard Eckersley's report on adolescent mental health, this study paints a picture of rapid and marked increase in vulnerability, not for all teens but for a significant and growing subgroup who are not being adequately cared for.

'As mentoring expert Joseph Palmour puts it...': Palmour, J., in Harding, C. (ed), *ibid.*

'As author Terry Pratchett puts it...': Pratchett, T., 'I'd rather be a climbing ape than a falling angel', Interview in *The Herald,* 4 October, 2004.

'A child of twelve could identify 100 plants useful to her...': Cruz García, G.S., 'The mother–child nexus. Knowledge and valuation of wild food plants in Wayanad', Western Ghats, India, *J Ethnobiol Ethnomed,* 2(39), 2006; Setalaphruk, C., Price, L.L., 'Children's traditional ecological knowledge of wild food resources: a case study in a rural village in Northeast Thailand', *J Ethnobiol Ethnomed,* 2007 Oct 15;3:33. 'Useful', of course, includes eating, wearing, using, healing and for shelter or ritual. Plants are our friends.

'Yunus told a television interviewer...': *Elders with Andrew Denton,* ABC1, 7/12/2009.

'Everyone agreed that condoms were a great idea...': Adapted from a story in *Whole Earth Review,* 1972.

'Marvin Allen says it beautifully...': Allen, M., in *Wild Man Weekend,* SBS TV, screened 1992.

'Research shows that a man who has a network of friends...': Eckersley, R., 'The politics of happiness' in *Living Now,* March 2007, issue 93, pp.6–7.

'Storyteller Michael Meade says that just as men's voices have a different tone...': Meade, M., 'Renewing of the Flesh', in Harding, *ibid.*

'The four levels of human communication' diagram: Biddulph, S., Lifeline Telephone Counsellor Training Handbook, 1974.

'Kate Grenville, in her beautiful novel about colonial Sydney...': Grenville, K., *The Secret River,* Text Publishing, Melbourne, 2005; and also the more positive Grenville., K., *The Lieutenant,* Text Publishing, 2008.

'This was a time that, for all its cultural sterility, still ranks highest in all the surveys of happiness and contentment.': Eckersley, R., 'Is modern Western culture a health hazard?', *International Journal of Epidemiology,* 2006 35(2): pp.252–258. You may by now have noticed that I am a great fan of Richard Eckersley's work. He consistently asks – and answers – the big questions about health and happiness and our society's directions. He is clear that our consumer society and our economy are going in directions which actually harm health and happiness, and that this can be objectively measured. The assumptions of government, and of individuals, as to what makes for a good life are in fact wrong. Read enough of his research, and you will be ready to walk away from supermarkets and suburbia.

'In a powerful book called Willing Slaves, journalist Madeleine Bunting

investigated...': Bunting, M., *Willing Slaves: How overwork culture is ruling our lives,* HarperCollins, London, 2004.

'Viktor Frankl, who wrote the classic Man's Search For Meaning, drew his observations...': Frankl, V. *Man's Search for Meaning,* Rider & Co., 2004. With nine million copies sold, this book was originally written in 1945 from his experiences as a psychiatrist inmate in a Nazi concentration camp, who worked to help his fellow prisoners survive. Frankl's thinking is a forward step in human civilisation. 'He who has a "why" to live for can endure almost any "how".'

'Primo Levi, another powerfully articulate survivor of the Holocaust, observed...': Levi, P., *Moments of Reprieve,* Abacus, 1988.

'Robert Bly, speculating on the modern workplace of today, asked whether the reason...': Bly, R., *Iron John,* Addison Wesley, NY, 1990.

'Many experts, especially in resource fields like oil, water and agriculture, feel this was just the foreshock of a larger collapse.': Thousands of studies now support this view, but a good overview was by Ross Gittins, 'Headlong to growth overload', *The Age,* 8 February, 2006.

'Robert Bly tells this story in Iron John.': Bly, R., *Iron John,* Addison Wesley, NY, 1990.

'Carl Jung is said to have taken misfortune in an interesting way.': cited in Bly, R., *Iron John,* Addison Wesley, NY, 1990.

'Erikson set out a map of life...': Erikson, E., *Childhood and Society,* Penguin, UK, 1950. A Wikipedia contributor explained the heart of Erikson's life stages very eloquently: Erikson's research suggests that we must learn how to hold both extremes of each specific life-stage challenge in tension with one another, not rejecting one end of the tension or the other. Only when both extremes in a life-stage challenge are understood and accepted as both required and useful can the optimal virtue for that stage surface. Thus 'trust' and 'mis-trust' must both be understood and accepted, in order for realistic 'hope' to emerge as a viable solution at the first stage. Similarly, 'integrity' and 'despair' must both be understood and embraced, in order for actionable 'wisdom' to emerge as a viable solution at the last stage.

'US writer Alan Watts very accurately summed up the physical truth of this…': Watts, A., *The Book on the Taboo Against Knowing Who You Are,* Abacus, 1973.

'That we are "the eyes with which the universe looks at itself", as one writer put it.': Watts, A., *The Book on the Taboo Against Knowing Who You Are,* Abacus, 1973.

'"When despair grows in me…"': Berry, W., 'The Peace of Wild Things'.

'"Do you mean," he wrote, "that lamp posts and kerbstones are

more real, more important, than heroism, sacrifice, striving together with friends?"' Tolkien, J.R.R., 'On Fairy Tales' in *Tree and Leaf,* Allen and Unwin, London, 1964.

Acknowledgements

I never wrote a book with as much intensity and purpose as this, so getting the words together was like harnessing wild horses. Lots of people had to help! I especially want to thank my wife Shaaron for her wisdom and groundedness, and the courage with which she goes through life. I've had fine teachers, but she has taught me the most. I thank and admire my son for his caring and professionalism in all he does. And I love learning from my daughter, who is a fine writer and researcher in her own right. The Johnstone tribe, which I married into 30 years ago, buoys me up every single day; beautiful sisters-in-law and good-hearted men.

Everyone needs elders and mentors to lean into, and Alan Dutton has been this for many years. He put great time and care into the manuscript to help make it a better and truer read. Sean Doyle of Lynk Manuscript Assessment Services helped enormously both as an editor and as a man interested in men's development whose views I respected. The SIEVX Memorial crew were there all along, and have been the best experience of teamwork in my lifetime. Samantha Miles managed the book's production tenaciously, but with sensitivity and understanding.

Rex Finch and his team have published my books for 26 years, with idealism and enormous hard work. They really do publish 'books which change lives'.

And to the Universe that gives us life. Thank you.

Contacts

School programs

The Rite Journey is now being introduced in schools across the country and overseas. For details, visit www.theritejourney.com.au.

Rock and Water: For more information, visit www.newcastle.edu.au/research-centre/fac/workshops/rock-and-water or Google 'Family Action Centre Rock and Water'.

Pathways to Manhood: For more information go to www.pathwaysfoundation.com.au

NITOR – Catholic Regional College – North Keilor

For more information contact Brian Horan, Nitor teacher at bhoran@crcnorthkeilor.vic.edu.au

Johh Coshan, Deputy Principal, jcoshan@crcnorthkeilor.vic.edu.au

Permissions

The photos Image 4, Image 17, Image 22 (from *The Herald* and *Weekly Times* Photographic Collection) and Image 29 (from *The Launceston Examiner* Photo Library) are courtesy of Steve Biddulph.

The photos Image 3, Image 11, Image 14, Image 20, Image 21, Image 24, Image 26, Image 31, Image 32 and Image 29 are reproduced with permission from Paul Hoelen of Paul Hoelen Photography.

The photos Image 5, Image 19, Image 23, Image 28, Image 30, Image 35 and Image 36 are reproduced with permission from Dave Hancock from David Hancock Photography.

The photos Image 6, Image 7, Image 8, Image 9, Image 10, Image 12, Image 13, Image 15, Image 16, Image 18, Image 27, Image 34 and Image 37 are reproduced with permission from iStock.com

The poem, 'The Peace of Wild Things' is copyright© 1998 by Wendell Berry from *The Selected Poems of*

Wendell Berry, reprinted by permission of Counterpoint, USA.

Index

A

A Million Miles in a Thousand Years (book), *300*
Aboriginal men, *355*
　domestic violence, *102*
　health, approach to, *433*
Abraham (Bible), *214*
addiction, *9*
　pornography, *158*
affection, *13, 16, 20, 29, 44, 111, 118, 203, 242, 290, 328, 333, 355, 365*
aid programs, *230, 363, 422*
alcohol ix, *16, 40, 129, 181, 249, 262, 263, 285, 326, 335, 355, 412, 431*
Allen, Marvin, *344*
American Civil War, *411*
Anderson, Stuart, *102, 106, 108*
anger, *25, 27, 35, 42, 97, 104, 127, 161, 183, 250, 254, 256, 258, 333, 351*
apartheid (South Africa), *373*
Appointment in Samarra (book), *149*
approval, *54, 56, 58*
Archer, Robyn, *195*
arguments, *38, 86, 88, 91, 93, 95, 102, 245, 361*
　arguing well, *88, 91, 93, 119*
arousal (sexual), *164, 165*
Arthur (King), *409*
ASDA (UK supermarket chain), *381*
Ashoka (King), *443*
At My Father's Wedding (book), *98, 250*
Attenborough, David, *209*

Aung San Suu Kyi, *209, 445*
Australopithecus afarensis, *314*
autism, *267, 269*
Aztec Empire, *443*

B

behaviour problems (school), *11*
Berry, Wendell, *448*
beyondblue (anti-depression organisation), *422*
Big Brother (tv series), *381*
Big hART (arts organisation), *195, 197, 199*
'big life' and 'little lives' (Mongol concept), *400, 443*
Billy Elliot (film), *337*
bipolar disorder, *269*
Black Knight, *409, 411, 412, 435*
blogs, *400*
Blue Like Jazz (book), *296*
Blues Brothers (film), *237*
Bly, Robert, *2, 9, 45, 51, 172, 174, 384, 411*
Bonanza (tv series), *368*
Bond, James (book/film character), *226*
Bonhoeffer, Dietrich, *445*
Book of Ecclesiastes, *222*
Bosporus Strait (Turkey), *379*
boyhood to manhood,
    boy vs man thinking, *211, 213*
    car accidents, *195, 197, 199*
    'In a Nutshell', *199*
    initiation, *131, 143, 203, 205, 208, 209, 211, 213, 214, 227, 229, 238, 239*
    mothers, relationship with, *227, 229*

'NITOR' program, *186, 188, 190, 192, 199*
prehistory, *174, 205*
'Rock and Water' program, *185, 186, 192, 199*
school as community, *174, 176, 199, 205*
stages of growing up, *285, 287*
'The Rite Journey' program, *176, 178, 180, 181, 183, 185, 188, 192, 199*
brain, emotional trauma and, *25*
breaking free, coming back, *38, 40, 42, 69*
British Empire, *443, 445*
Brogden, John, *420, 422*
Brothers Grimm, *407*
Buckley, Eamonn, *188*
Buddha, *214, 373*
Buddhism, *441*
Buffet, Warren, *318*
bullying, *186, 199, 330, 331*
Bunting, Madeleine, *381, 395*
Bush, George *xi*
bushwalking, *426*

C

cancer, *269, 406*
car accidents, *9*
   boys, and, *195, 197, 199*
   statistics, *11, 195*
career,
   see work,
Carr, Bob, *420, 422*
Carter, Jimmy, *445*
Catholic Church, *213*
Catholic Regional College (Melbourne), *186*
cerebral palsy, *269*
child sexual abuse, *9, 40, 129, 154, 158*
Chittagong (Bangladesh), *318*
Christianity, *180, 214, 309, 441, 443, 454*

see also spirit,
Cleese, John, *273*
climate change, *318, 398, 411, 447*
commit, deciding to, *75, 77, 119*
common myths, *86, 88, 91, 93, 95*
communities, *18, 24, 192, 197, 203, 235, 239, 287, 333, 360, 381, 382, 387, 392, 395, 400, 440, 456*
   school as, *174, 176, 199, 205*
compassion, *203, 411, 412, 416, 424, 430, 433, 443*
compatibility, *88, 93, 95*
   loving incompatibility, *108, 109, 120*
competition (male), *339, 340, 342, 344, 346*
   Bali, in, *339*
   beyond competition, *342, 344, 346*
   compulsive, *27, 29*
   Ireland, in, *339*

computers, *154, 318, 450, 454*
concentration camps (WWII), *384*
condoms, *340*
consumer culture, *125, 145, 216, 371, 379, 382*
Contact (film), *450, 452*
contempt, *116*
contraceptive pill, *129*
Cooney, Barry, *365*
Corneau, Guy, *360*
Costello, Tim, *209*
criticism, *60, 116, 280, 351*
Croome, Rodney, *333, 335*
Croughan, Professor Mary, *269*
Crowe, Russell, *58*
crying, *24, 25, 44, 420*
Cundall, Peter, *209*

D
Dads in Distress (organisation), *430*
Dalai Lama, *16*

Dalbey, Gordon, *54, 56, 167*
'database' of partner's world, *118, 119*
daughters and fathers, *274, 276, 278, 293*
  absent fathers, *16, 247, 249*
Deane, Sir William, *209, 235*
death, facing, *216, 218, 219*
death rates, *11*
  self-inflicted death, *11*
  young men, *11, 195*
defensiveness, *49, 116*
Delaney, Martine, *335*
dementia, *406*
denial, *22, 24, 42, 412*
depression, *9, 273, 280, 311, 326, 357, 381, 420, 422, 426*
desire (sexual), *136, 138, 142, 164, 167, 169*
  responsibility for, *164, 165, 167, 169*

despair, *7, 53, 156, 199, 226, 247, 412, 426, 448*
  integrity vs, *426*
  sexual, *125*
disappointment, *180, 223*
disease, *318*
divorce, *9, 247, 292, 293*
  see also marriage breakdown, statistics, *11*
domestic violence, *9, 16, 40, 158*
  ending, *102, 104, 106, 108*
Down syndrome, *267*
Dreams of my Father (book), *44*
drugs, *125, 181, 249, 263, 335, 355, 412*
Duluth program, *102*
duty, *35*

E

earthquake in Haiti (2010), *223*
ejaculation, *147, 169*
Ellyard, Peter, *183*
Email, *400*

Embling, John, *247*
equality, *38, 93, 95, 98, 108, 158, 227, 282, 287, 443*
erectile dysfunction, *430*
Erikson, Erik, *424*
Eve (Bible), *314*
exceptional people, *208, 209, 239*
exercise, *80, 276, 426, 431*
expectations and hopes, *27, 58, 86, 180, 203, 357*

F
façades,
  see masks,
facts about men,
  see statistics about men today,
failure, *7, 42, 156, 188, 192, 222, 237, 273, 293*
  allowances for, *404, 412, 415, 435*
fairy tales, *407*
Families and How to Survive Them (book), *273*
famine, *318*

fascism, *318*
  see also Nazi Germany,
'father-hunger',
  see underfathered boys,
fathers,
  absent, *252, 254, 293*
  career, and, *260, 262, 263, 293*
  children without, *247, 249*
  competitive feelings, *273, 274*
  critics, as, *250, 252*
  daughters, and, *274, 276, 278, 293*
  delaying parenthood, *267, 269, 271*
  divorce see divorce family mood, creating a, *256, 258, 260, 293*
  'In a Nutshell', *293*
  kings, as, *250*
  old roles, dropping, *249, 250, 252, 254, 293*

older generation, see older generation
fathers,
  passive, *252*
  peer groups, *263, 265, 267*
  sons, and, see sons and fathers,
  starting out, *271, 273, 274*
  suicide of, *42*
  underfathering, see underfathered boys,
  what is fatherhood ?, *243, 245*
fear, *24, 51, 60, 104, 127, 237, 258, 260, 342, 349, 351, 384, 448*
  homosexuality, *331, 333, 337*
Feldenkrais Method, *426*
Finch, Atticus (book character), *254*
Fisch, Harry, *271*

5 truths of manhood, *213, 214, 216, 218, 219, 222, 223, 226, 227, 229, 230, 233, 235, 237, 238, 239*
  control the outcome, inability to, *230, 233, 235, 237, 238*
  death, facing, *216, 218, 219*
  hard times and good times, accepting, *219, 222, 223, 226*
  'In a Nutshell', *239*
  non-importance of self, *226, 227, 229, 230*
  self-centredness, transition out of, *226, 227, 229, 230, 239*
forgiveness, *40, 66, 68, 127, 252, 309, 411*
Foster, David, *337, 339*
Fragmented Lives (book), *247*
Frankl, Viktor, *384*
Franz, Marie-Louise von, *100*
Fraser, Malcolm, *422*

friendships (male), *18, 25, 324, 326, 328, 330, 331, 333, 335, 337, 339, 340, 342, 344, 346, 348, 349, 351, 353, 355, 357, 358, 360, 361, 363, 365*
- see also men's groups,
- Anglo-Saxon heritage, and, *326, 328*
- beyond school, *20*
- building, *2*
- communication, levels of, *346, 348*
- competition, see competition (male),
- fathers, examples of, *25*
- fun, and, *355, 357, 358*
- how emotions work, *349, 351, 353, 355*
- 'In a Nutshell', *365*
- proving you're a man, *328, 330, 331, 344*
- proving you're not gay, *331, 333*
- today's generation, *328*

G

Galilee (Bible), *445*
Gallasch, Graham, *180, 181*
- see also 'The Rite Journey' program,
Gandhi, *373, 445*
gangs and gang culture, *205, 249, 262, 263, 331*
gaol populations, *11, 263*
gardening, *426*
Gates, Bill, *318, 321*
Gates, Melinda, *318*
gay men,
- see homosexuality,
Genghis Khan, *409*
Gibran, Kahlil, *223, 368*
girlhood, *13, 18, 174*
- fathers and daughters, *274, 276, 278, 293*
- absent fathers, *16, 247, 249*
- influences, *18*
- Keeping Kool,

see Keeping Kool program,
'Rock and Water', see 'Rock and Water' program,
sexual intercourse, *276*
sexualisation of girls, *129, 131, 142, 145, 274, 276, 278, 283, 285*
'The Rite Journey', see 'The Rite Journey' program,
global economy, *398, 400, 401*
global warming, see climate change,
Gobi Desert (Mongolia), *400*
God, *218, 219, 223, 237, 440, 443, 447*
    concepts of, *452, 454, 456, 457*
Gottman, John, *114, 116, 118*
grandfathers, see mentors (male),
Great Depression, *24, 72*
Grenville, Kate, *369*
grief, *30, 309, 326, 412, 435*
    admission of, *22, 24, 25, 27*
    brain, effect on, *25*
    Maori custom, *24*
guilt, *127, 153, 156, 309, 424*

H

happiness, *36, 69, 82, 84, 88, 140, 156, 230, 262, 318, 351, 379, 381*
Happiness Conference (Sydney), *422*
happy couples, *88, 114, 116, 118, 119*
hard times and good times, accepting, *219, 222, 223, 226*
hazing, *205*
Healing the Masculine Soul (book), *54*

health, *7, 11, 27, 69, 226, 318, 337, 344, 361, 379, 395, 430, 431, 433*
   mental health, *7, 11, 197, 363*
heart and backbone, *201, 203*
Hesse, Herman, *409*
Holocaust (WWII), *384*
homeless, *11, 335*
homophobia, *335, 337*
homosexuality, *58, 129, 441*
   fear, *331, 333, 337*
   growing up gay, *333, 335, 337, 339*
   proving you're not gay, *331, 333*
Horan, Brian, *188*
hormones, *38, 125, 145, 273, 390, 409*
Howard, John, *237*
Hunter-gatherer culture,
   see prehistory,
Huon River (Tasmania), *357*

Hussein, Saddam, *233*

I

I Have Life (book), *161, 163*
Indigenous cultures,
   initiation, *205, 287*
indigenous cultures, *16, 214, 229, 342*
Industrial Revolution, effect of, *16, 30, 377, 456*
infertility, *267, 269*
   treatments, *269*
initiation, *131, 143, 203, 205, 208, 209, 211, 213, 214, 227, 229, 233, 238, 239*
   Indigenous cultures, *205, 287*
insecurity, *54, 84, 104, 131, 138, 142, 333, 340, 342, 381*
integrity, *226, 426*
interdependence, *77, 79*
International Boys' Schools Coalition, *159*

Internet, *276, 400*
Intimacy and Desire (book), *136*
IQ, *269*
Iraq war, *440*
Iron John (book), *9, 51, 411*
isolation, *27, 29, 30, 125, 335, 424, 433*
   compulsive competition, *27, 29*
   emotional timidity, *27, 29, 30*
   loneliness, and, *27, 29, 77, 84, 125, 273*

J
jealousy, *351*
Jesus (Bible), *214, 373, 443*
Jiang Rong, *398*
job,
   see work,
jogging, *426*
Judge Judy (tv series), *77*
Jung, Carl, *420*

K
Keeping Kool program, *104*
King, Martin Luther, *209*
knifings,
   see stabbings,
Kornbluth, Jesse, *122*
Krishna, *214*

L
Laetoli (Africa), *314*
Lakota people, *227*
Lao Tsu, *214*
Lascaux cave paintings, *456*
learning problems (school), *11*
Lee, Harper, *254*
Lee, John, *98, 250*
Lennon, John, *44, 108*
lesbian women, *333*
Leunig, Michael, *438, 440*
Levi, Primo, *384*
life expectancy, *11*
Lifeline (counselling service), *422*

life's journey, *404, 406, 407, 409, 411, 412, 415, 416, 418, 420, 422, 424, 426, 430, 431, 433, 434, 435*
   Black Knight, *409, 411, 412, 435*
   8 stages, *424, 426*
   health,
   see health,
   'In a Nutshell', *435*
   map of journey, *424, 426*
   'mid-life crisis', *125, 406*
   Red Knight, *409, 411, 435*
   retirement, *35, 406, 431, 433, 434, 435*
   suffering,
   see suffering,
   Time of Ashes, *412, 415, 416, 418, 420, 422, 424, 435*
   White Knight, *409, 411, 435*
Lincoln, President, *411, 435*
Lines, Andrew, *180, 181*
   see also 'The Rite Journey' program,
loneliness, *27, 29, 77, 84, 125, 273*
Lord of the Flies (book), *330*
loss, *24, 30, 223, 247, 411, 412*
Lutheranism, *180*

M

Male Health Policy (Australia), *433*
male mentors,
   see mentors (male),
male needs, importance of, *80, 82*
Male Reproductive Center (Columbia University), *271*
Mandela, Nelson, *16, 209, 296, 373*
manhood,
   backbone and heart, *201, 203*
   boyhood to,
   see boyhood to manhood,

5 truths of,
see 5 truths of manhood, teaching, *13, 36*
see also initiation,
Manhood (book), *326, 416*
manic depressive disorder,
see bipolar disorder,
Man's Search For Meaning (book), *384*
marriage breakdown, *11, 247, 361, 381*
see also divorce,
Martin, Steve, *75*
masks, *2, 4, 18, 30, 335, 365*
  cool dude, *2*
  cracks in, *5, 7, 9*
  good bloke, *2*
  hard worker, *2*
  'sensitive New Age man', *4, 20, 203*
  tough guy, *4, 20*
Maslen, Robin, *172*
masturbation, *129, 153, 154*
mates,
see friendships (male),
McDonald, Professor John, *430*
Meade, Michael, *348*
meaningful lives, *296, 298, 300, 302, 303, 306, 307, 309, 311, 313, 314, 317, 318, 321*
  big picture, *313, 314, 317, 318*
  circle of life, *311, 313*
  finding the plot, *302, 303*
  goals, *300, 302*
  'In a Nutshell', *321*
  living for others, *318*
  what is 'meaning'?, *303, 306, 307, 309, 311*
  work,
  see work,
Medecins Sans Frontiers (organisation), *230*
meditation, *426, 448*

men's groups, *360, 361, 363, 365*
mental health, *7, 11, 197, 363*
mental retardation, *269*
mentors (male), *13, 18, 38, 40, 106, 174, 199, 262, 287, 288, 290, 293*
   see also men's groups; 'NITOR' program; 'Rock and Water' program; 'The Rite Journey' program,
Mesopotamian Empire, *443*
'mid-life crisis', *125, 406*
migrations, *16, 333*
Miller, Donald, *296, 303*
mitochondrial DNA, *313*
Mohammed, *214, 443*
Monty Python (comedy group), *300*
Morrison, Jim, *172*
mortality,
   see death rates,
mothers,
   breastfeeding, *273*
   discipline, *282, 283, 285, 293*
   divorce,
   see divorce,
   older, *267, 269*
   single, *290, 292, 293*
   sons, relationship with, *227, 229*
   women as, *226, 227*
Mount Sinai School of Medicine (US), *267*
Mowaljarlai, David, *201*
Mystery Creek Cave (Tasmania), *306*
mythologies, *407*

N

Narcissus (Greek god), *203*
Narihara (Zen poet), *404*
Nazi Germany, *382, 384, 445*

New York Stock Exchange, *443*
'NITOR' program, *186, 188, 190, 192, 199*
Noa, Jai, *154, 156*
Nobel Peace Prize, *318*
non-British/Australian culture, *16, 56*
non-importance of self, *226, 227, 229, 230*
nostalgia, *351*
Nowlan, Alden, *72, 74, 77*
nuclear war, *318*
nurture and care, ability to, *77, 79, 80, 119*

O

Obama, Barack, *44, 209, 412*
O'Hara, John, *149*
Ojibwa (people), *440*
Old Testament, *454*
older cultures, *15, 24, 205, 211, 213, 404, 406, 407*
  see also pre-industrial world; prehistory, concepts of God, *452*
  spirit, *443, 445*
  Time of Ashes, *412, 415, 416, 418, 420, 422, 424, 435*
older generation fathers, *13, 15, 16, 18, 20, 22, 201, 337, 361*
  Industrial Revolution, effect of, *16, 30*
  male friends, *324, 326*
Olson, Paul, *149*
orgasm, *143, 150, 169*
  female, *129*
other father figures, see mentors (male),
oxytocin (hormone), *145, 273*

P

Packer dynasty, *29*
paedophile, see child sexual abuse,
Palmour, Joseph, *288*

Pathways to Manhood (foundation), *211*
Payne, Kim, *242*
Peck, Gregory, *254*
peer groups, *263, 265, 267*
Playboy philosophy, *164, 165*
pornography, *140, 154, 158, 456*
post-Vietnam era, *203*
Pratchett, Terry, *311*
pre-industrial world, *16, 211, 213*
prehistory, *174, 205, 211, 213, 214, 314, 317, 369*
prejudices and biases (sons), *53, 54*
pride, *36, 134, 199, 229, 249, 293, 303*
problems, identifying, *63, 66*
  admission of grief, *22, 24, 25, 27*
  'In a Nutshell', *30*
  isolation, see isolation,
  masks, see masks,
  underfathering, see underfathered boys,
prostate, *430*
Purvis, Bronwyn, *197*

R

racism, *181, 306, 422*
Raising Boys (book), *185*
Rankin, Scott, *195, 197, 199*
rape, *15, 131, 140, 145, 158, 249*
  preventing, *159, 161, 163, 164*
recessions, *16*
Red Cross (organisation), *230*
Red Knight, *409, 411, 435*
Reformation, the, *180*
refugees, *412, 422*
  detention centres, *233*

Reichenberg, Abraham, *267, 269*
relationships with women, *72, 74, 75, 77, 79, 80, 82, 84, 86, 88, 91, 93, 95, 97, 98, 100, 102, 104, 106, 108, 109, 111, 114, 116, 118, 119, 120*
- arguments, see arguments,
- commit, deciding to, *75, 77, 119*
- common myths, *86, 88, 91, 93, 95*
- compatibility, *88, 93, 95*
- 'database' of partner's world, *118, 119*
- equality, *93, 95*
- happy couples, *88, 114, 116, 118, 119*
- 'In a Nutshell', *119, 120*
- loving incompatibility, *108, 109, 120*
- male needs, importance of, *80, 82*
- nurture and care, ability to, *77, 79, 80, 119*
- shared values, *109, 111, 120*
- standing together, alone, *82, 84, 86, 119*
- 'Warrior, the' utilising, see 'Warrior, the',

religion, *127, 213, 440, 441, 443, 445, 447*
- see also Buddhism; Christianity; spirit,

Renard, Andrew, *159, 161, 163*
resistance training, *426*
respect, *4, 5, 7, 9, 11, 13, 47, 49, 53, 54, 97, 98, 102, 108, 116, 163, 256*
- see also self-respect,

responsibilities of sons and daughters, *51*

'Rites of Manhood' (poem), *74, 77*
road deaths,
  see car accidents,
Roberts, Ian, *335*
Robinson, Mary, *209*
'Rock and Water' program, *185, 186, 192, 199*
Rodwell, Telen, *197*
role models,
  see mentors (male); underfathered boys,
Roman Empire, *443*
Roy, Arundhati, *209*
Rubenstein, Arne, *211*
Rudd, Kevin, *411, 435*

S
Sagan, Carl, *450*
same-sex couples, *337, 339*
samurai (Japan), *409*
schizophrenia, *267*
Schnarch, Dr David, *136*
school, *249*
  behaviour problems, *11*
  community, as, *174, 176, 199, 205*
  learning problems, *11*
'Rock and Water',
  see 'Rock and Water' program,
'The Rite Journey',
  see 'The Rite Journey' program,
seizures, *269*
self-awareness, *186, 254*
self-centredness, transition out of, *226, 227, 229, 230*
self-esteem, *156, 431*
  children and youths, *49, 197, 249, 330, 387*
self-respect, *82, 199, 387*
'sensitive New Age man', *4, 20, 203*
serial killer, *9, 158*

sex, *82, 108, 122, 123, 125, 127, 129, 131, 132, 134, 136, 138, 140, 142, 143, 145, 147, 149, 150, 153, 154, 156, 158, 159, 161, 163, 164, 165, 167, 169, 258, 263, 276, 282, 361, 447*
- 'creepification' of men's sexuality, *154, 156, 158, 159, 169*
- desire, *136, 138, 142*
  - responsibility for, *164, 165, 167, 169*
- despair, *125*
- differing appetites, *134, 136, 169*
- getting it right, *140, 142, 143*
- growing older, and, *138, 140*
- 'heart connection', *169*
- 'In a Nutshell', *169*
- junk sex and real sex, *131, 132, 169*
- male sexual climax, *147, 149, 150, 169*

masturbation, *129, 153, 154*

sexual revolution (60s and 70s), *127, 129, 131, 143*

splitting sex from love, *125, 127*

3 stages of love, *136, 138, 140*

'whole-person sex' rediscovering, *145, 147*

sexism, *181*

sexual abuse, *97, 145, 249*

sexual revolution (60s and 70s), *127, 129, 131, 143*

sexualisation of girls, *129, 131, 142, 274, 276, 278, 283*

shame, *127, 199, 415, 416, 422, 424, 435*

shootings, *411*
- gang culture, *205*
- school shootings, *9*

Siddhartha (character in book), *409*
SIEVX Memorial, *233, 235, 237, 238*
Simplicity Parenting (book), *243*
Simpson, Homer (from tv series), *252*
Skinner, Robyn, *273*
smoking, *431*
social determinants of male health, *430, 431, 433*
sons and fathers, *33, 35, 36, 38, 40, 42, 44, 45, 47, 49, 51, 53, 54, 56, 58, 60, 62, 63, 66, 68, 69*
   absent fathers, *16, 247, 249*
   approval, cravings for (sons), *54, 56, 58*
   breaking free, coming back (sons), *38, 40, 42, 69*
   discipline, *282, 283, 285, 293, 361*
   expectations and hopes (fathers), *58, 357*
   finding peace, *68, 69*
   gay fathers, *58*
   gay sons, *58*
   healing wounds (sons), *42, 44, 45, 47, 69*
   'In a Nutshell', *69*
   other father figures, see mentors (male),
   play, patterns of, *280, 282*
   powers of sons, *49, 51*
   relationships between, *33, 35, 36, 38, 69*
      fixing it, *60, 62, 63, 66, 68, 69*
   respect for fathers, *47, 49, 53, 54*
   rifts between, *22, 38, 40, 58*
   stages of growing up, *285, 287*

underfathering, see underfathered boys,
wrestling and physical strength, *278, 280, 293*
Sorkin, Aaron, *324*
sorrow, *223, 227, 331, 351*
Spate, Alastair, *280*
sperm, *147, 153, 269*
   donor, *243, 292*
spirit, *438, 440, 441, 443, 445, 447, 448, 450, 452, 454, 456, 457*
   big brain, big vision, *447, 448*
   concepts of God, *452, 454, 456, 457*
   history, in, *443, 445*
   how spirit works, *450, 452*
   'In a Nutshell', *457*
   sacredness of life, *445, 447*
St Andrew's College (South Africa), *159*
stabbings, *205*
standing together, alone, *82, 84, 86, 119*

Stanford Binet Intelligence Scale, *269*
statistics about men today, *11*
   behaviour problems (school), *11*
   death rates, *11*
     self-inflicted death, *11*
     young men, *11*
   divorce and marriage breakdown, *11*
   fathers in the home, *11*
   gaol populations, *11*
   homeless, *11*
   learning problems (school), *11*
   life expectancy, *11*
   violence, acts of, *11*
stealing, *205*
Steiner, Rudolph, *180*
stonewalling, *116*

stress, *25, 201, 233, 430*
stroke, *406*
Sudanese community (Australia), *303*
suffering, *4, 54, 66, 102, 153, 156, 159, 208, 213, 222, 223, 239, 318, 321, 335, 361, 406, 411, 412, 416, 435*
    exceptional people, *209*
    gay men, *335*
suicide, *7, 9, 195, 335, 384, 430, 433*
    father, of, *42*
    statistics, *11*
swimming, *426*

T

tai chi, *426*
Tao Te Ching (book), *368*
Taoist monks, *445*
teachers (male), see mentors (male),
teaching manhood, *13, 36*
    programs, see teaching programs,
teaching programs,
    'NITOR', *186, 188, 190, 192, 199*
    'Rock and Water', *185, 186, 192, 199*
    'The Rite Journey', *176, 178, 180, 181, 183, 185, 188, 192, 199*
television, *260, 276, 278, 339*
Tengger (Mongol sky god), *398*
testosterone, *38, 271*
Thamm, Marianne, *161*
'The Four Horsemen of the Apocalypse', *116*
'The Heart Family' (dolls), *260*
The Hobart Mercury (newspaper), *307*
The Jerk (film), *75*
'The Peace of Wild Things' (poem), *448*

The Rifleman (tv series), *368*
'The Rite Journey' program, *176, 178, 180, 181, 183, 185, 188, 192, 199*
The Secret River (book), *369*
The Sum of Us (film), *58*
The West Wing (tv series), *324*
Theresa of Avila, *140*
Thompson, Jack, *58*
Time of Ashes, *412, 415, 416, 418, 420, 422, 424, 435*
To Kill a Mockingbird (book), *254*
Tolkien, JRR, *456*
Tom: A child's life regained (book), *247*
Topp Twins, *58*
Torres Strait Islander men,
  see Aboriginal men,
transgender people, *335, 339*

tsunami in Indian Ocean (2004), *223*
Tuesdays with Morrie (book), *226*

U

uncles,
  see mentors (male),
underfathered boys, *13, 15, 16, 18, 20, 22, 280, 282*
  affection, *13*
  example, *13, 36*
  grief as a result, *22, 24, 25, 27*
  teaching manhood, *13, 36*
University of California (US), *269*
University of Newcastle, *186*
University of Western Sydney, *430*
Untouchable Girls (documentary), *58*

V

values, shared, *109, 111, 120*

Vedic scriptures (India), *454*
Ventura, Michael, *72, 147*
Vidal, Gore, *129*
violence, *16, 254, 361, 398, 431*
  see also shootings; stabbings,
  boys, *181, 185, 186*
  school, at, *328, 330, 333*
  sexual assault and rape, see rape,
  spouses, against, see domestic,
  violence statistics, *11*
Waldorf education, *180*

W

war, *16*
  see also World War I; World War II,
  memories of, *62, 63*
  returned soldiers, *16*
'Warrior, the', *95, 97, 98, 100, 102, 104, 106, 108*
  safe fighting, *98, 100*
Watts, Alan, *445*
White Knight, *409, 411, 435*
Whittaker, Carl, *132*
Whyte, Paul, *330*
wife-beating, see domestic violence,
Willing Slaves (book), *381*
Wingspan (book), *149, 365*
Wolf Totem (book), *398, 400*
women, *211, 344, 355*
  'biological clock', *267*
  emancipation of, *447*
  enemies, and, *30*
  girls, see girlhood,
  lesbian, *333*
  men, and,

see relationships with women,
mothers, as, see mothers,
orgasm, *129*
sense of self, *5*
warrior, as, see 'Warrior, the',
women's liberation movement, *9, 27, 147, 430*
work, *7, 138, 252, 260, 262, 263, 293, 368, 369, 371, 373, 375, 377, 379, 381, 382, 384, 386, 387, 389, 390, 392, 393, 395, 398, 400, 401, 404, 409, 415, 430, 431*
   changing landscape of, *9, 377, 379, 381*
   choice, *393, 395*
   'economic rationalism', *379*
   finding your true work, *371, 373, 375, 377*
   global economy, *398, 400, 401*
   'In a Nutshell', *401*
   Industrial Revolution, effect of, *16, 30, 377*
   job, differentiated from, *373*
   meaningful work, *382, 384, 386, 401*
      checklist, *387, 389, 390, 392*
   rating your job, *386, 387, 389, 390, 392, 393*
   slavery, as, *381, 382, 401*
workaholics, *56*
World Health Organization, *430*
World War I, *411, 456*
   Battle of the Somme, *129*
World War II, *400*
   concentration camps, *384*
   Holocaust, *384*

X

Xervante people (Brazil), *342*

Y

YMCA Explorers, *363*

yoga, *426*
Yrkema, Freerk, *185, 186*
Yunus, Mohammed, *318*
'Zorba the Greek', *80*

www.ingramcontent.com/pod-product-compliance
Lightning Source LLC
Chambersburg PA
CBHW071219290426
44108CB00013B/1229